W9-DHH-620

ELDER OLSON

GARLAND BIBLIOGRAPHIES OF
MODERN CRITICS AND CRITICAL SCHOOLS
(General Editor: William Cain)
Vol. 5

GARLAND REFERENCE LIBRARY
OF THE HUMANITIES
(VOL. 349)

Garland Bibliographies of Modern Critics and Critical Schools

ELDER OLSON
An Annotated Bibliography

James L. Battersby

GARLAND PUBLISHING, INC. • NEW YORK & LONDON
1983

Library of Congress Cataloging in Publication Data

Battersby, James L.
Elder Olson : an annotated bibliography.

(Garland reference library of the humanities ; v. 349)
Includes indexes.
1. Olson, Elder, 1909– —Bibliography. I. Title.
II. Series.
Z8643.72.B37 1983 016.818′5209 82-48273
[PS3529.L66]
ISBN 0-8240-9254-6

Printed on acid-free, 250-year-life paper
Manufactured in the United States of America

GENERAL EDITOR'S INTRODUCTION

The Garland Bibliographies of Modern Critics and Critical Schools series is intended to provide bibliographic treatment of major critics and critical schools of the twentieth century. Each volume includes an introduction that surveys the critic's life, career, influence, and achievement, or, in the case of the volumes devoted to a critical school, presents an account of its central figures, origins, relation to other critical movements and trends, and the like.

Each volume is fully annotated and contains listings for both primary and secondary materials. The annotations are meant to be ample and detailed, in order to explain clearly, especially for a reader coming to a critic or critical school for the first time, the point and purpose of a book or essay. In this sense, the bibliographies are also designed to be critical guides. We hope that the volumes will inform and stimulate the reader even as they give basic information about what material exists and where it may be located.

We have tried to include as many of the most important critics and critical schools in this series as possible, but some have been omitted. Some critics and critical schools have already received (or are in the process of receiving) adequate treatment, and we see no need to duplicate the efforts of others.

William E. Cain
Wellesley College

CONTENTS

INTRODUCTION

I. Life and Career

Many readers of this series of bibliographies can quickly and conveniently locate Elder James Olson on the specimen board and abruptly and peremptorily fix him in a formulated phrase. He is a "Chicago critic," or a "Neo-Aristotelian," or, as one recent critic, looking back at the turbulent wake of twentieth-century criticism from the stern of a thoroughly modern ship designed and built by the master craftsmen of Europe, would have it, one of the principal actors in "the curious episode" of Chicago Aristotelianism. To yield so readily to "appositization," to be in reciprocal relation to an epithet—to be as Richard is to lionhearted, lionhearted to Richard—is not an entirely unmixed blessing, especially when the term or phrase of distinction serves chiefly, as it does in the case of Olson, to drive from active consideration all the strength of mind, all the analytical subtlety by which the designatee's achievement is characterized. Like mercurial children, such epithets, when they essentialize, can be very, very good, but when they do not, they are awful; they trivialize achievement in their efforts to recognize it.

One way to characterize Olson is to follow the lead of the biographical dictionary, which with pithy directness identifies him as "poet, playwright, and literary critic." Such terms at least allow the mind to expatiate or browse in open spaces, to contemplate large endeavors, and may even prompt an engagement with the guarantors of their legitimacy and appropriateness, the works themselves. Moreover, they imply the richness and variousness of activity that his accomplishments manifest and that the other terms deny or bury. And, of course, Olson's activities and accomplishments are various, rich, and many. Indeed, the recital of the significant facts of Olson's several careers would occupy more space than can be allowed here, but some facts, because of their importance or because convention demands them, simply cannot or will not stay in the cellarage.

Elder James Olson was born on March 9, 1909, in Chicago, Illinois, and he received his early education in the public schools of that city (at Wells Elementary, Tuley High, and Schurz High). From 1918 to 1926, he studied piano under Professor Wilhelm Martin, and from 1926 to 1935, under Cleveland Bohnet at the American Conservatory of Music. After graduating from high school, he entered the University of Chicago and remained there for two years, until 1929, when he interrupted his undergraduate studies (for four years) to work for Commonwealth Edison Company (first as a junior and later as a senior adjustment clerk) and then to travel and study piano in Europe. During this period he was persuaded by Thornton Wilder, who had been impressed with his early poetry, to return to the University of Chicago, where he completed his literary training, receiving his B.A. in 1934, his M.A. in 1935, and his Ph.D. in 1938.

While he was still in high school, he began what was to become a warm and lasting association with Harriet Monroe, the founder and the first editor of *Poetry: A Magazine of Verse*. In response to some effusions of his young genius that he had submitted for publication, she invited him to her office and, after making him justify this word and that image for an interminable few minutes, advised him "to go home and write some real poems," which advice not every metrist with a full heart, it is fair to say, could turn to good use. But between 1926, when, according to Olson, his first "serious" poem appeared (in *Tambour*, a magazine published in Paris) and 1934, when his first volume of verse, *Thing of Sorrow*, was issued, Olson won several awards for his poetry, including the Witter Bynner Award, the Young Poet's Prize, the Guarantor's Award (for "Essay on Deity"), and the John Billings Fiske Award. With the publication of *Thing of Sorrow*, Olson, though Melancholy may have "mark'd him for her own," was not to Fame unknown, for the collection received wide attention and was almost universally praised in both special journals and national magazines (*Time*, for example). For this collection he was honored with the Foundation of Literature award, and one reviewer (see 235) noted that "many people thought Olson should have won the Pulitzer Prize last year."

Over the years Olson has produced an extraordinary body of poetry, indeed perhaps some of the most distinguished verse of our century, a judgment that the reader of the reviews will not find peculiar or idiosyncratic but that still awaits demonstration in a full-length study, though the groundwork for such a study has been laid in Thomas E. Lucas's *Elder Olson.* Public validation of this estimate of his poetic talent has regularly come in the form of honors and prizes, such as the Eunice Tietjens Award, the Longview Foundation Award, and the Emily Clark Balch Award. And, of course, immediate confirmation is available to anyone who is willing to read at least the collections of verse that Olson has published, which I can only list here in order of publication: *Thing of Sorrow*, 1934; *The Cock of Heaven*, 1940; *The Scarecrow Christ and Other Poems*, 1954; *Plays and Poems, 1948–1958*, 1958; *Collected Poems*, 1963; and *Olson's Penny Arcade*, 1975 (for the last of which he received the Society of Midland Authors Award).

In addition, Olson has written and published seven plays and seen several of them through production, one, *The Carnival of Animals* (a radio play in verse), being given the joint award of The Academy of American Poets and the Columbia Broadcasting System. To rehearse the production history of the several plays would require a setting as large and as fitfully moonlit as the woods outside Athens on a mid-summer's night and a speaker as prolific in "translation" as Bottom (*Faust: A Masque*, for example, has taken to the boards as itself, with Paul Sills in the role of Faust, and, at the University of Southern Illinois, under the guidance of a succubus not given to visiting the author, as a ballet; and *The Sorcerer's Apprentice* may soon be transformed by Ronald Hearst into a short opera), conditions that, unfortunately, this introduction cannot realize. Here it can only be said that the plays deserve the serious critical examination that they have not as yet found (though the reader should consult Horst Oppel's "Elder Olson als Dramatiker").

Even though celebrity has many enchantments and graduate school few, Olson continued his studies at the University of Chicago following the appearance of his successful volume of poetry, and in the year in which he received his doctorate (1938), the University of Chicago Libraries published his first critical work, *General Prosody: Rhythmic, Metric, Harmonics*, a study which Olson, as poet, musician, and philosophically trained critic, was peculiarly fitted to write; such a study enabled him to draw on and bring together the apparently diverse skills that he had been developing and perfecting in the preceding years. And presumably, the poetic and musical knowledge that fed into his critical and scholarly work were also enriched by his criticism. But beyond speculation, what is clear from his analyses of individual works and writers is that Olson, though often falsely accused of promoting mere *Formalismus* and of being insensitive to the verbal and metrical texture of poems, brings to the task of interpretation a poet's sense of the costs involved in finding the "right" or "proper" word and a musician's sensitivity to the contributions that sound and rhythm make to poems. It is perhaps unfair to say that only a musician can scan verse accurately, but no one can read *General Prosody* without recognizing that a mere arithmetician, a syllable counter, is not suited for the job and that "reading verse" requires, at the very least, an alertness to complex proportional relations among sounds and silences. Moreover, in taking in the whole range of Olson's production as a critic, one is struck not only by his formidable theoretical arguments, but by the number of essays and passages in longer works in which his musical and poetic knowledge find a local habitation and function.

Since this bibliography will undoubtedly be consulted by those to whom Olson is not a complete stranger, and since all his critical essays and books are cited and annotated in the bibliography proper, it would be pointless supererogation to run through titles here, but there is no impropriety in noting now that for more than five decades Olson has been addressing the most difficult and challenging issues that confront the literary theorist and practical critic in works philosophically acute and as demanding as they are rewarding. Since the publication of *Critics and Criticism* in 1952, Olson has been recognized as one of the chief spokesmen for what is inappropriately but persistently called "Chicago criticism," and Olson has done more than any other "Chicago critic" to define and defend the philosophic and theoretical bases of the approach to criticism with which he is commonly associated, to refine those principles and to extend them into new areas of analysis (witness, for example, his *Tragedy and the Theory of Drama*, his *The Theory of Comedy*, and his *The Poetry of Dylan Thomas*, recipient of the Poetry Society of America Award as the year's best critical book on poetry).

The bare facts of Olson's academic career can be quickly related. Both during and immediately following his graduate work, Olson taught at the Armour Institute of Technology (later the Illinois Institute of Technology), first as an Instructor (1935–39) and then as an Assistant Professor (1939–42). In 1942, he was invited to return to the University of Chicago, where, except during periods when he was fulfilling the terms of visiting appointments at universities both in the United States and abroad, he served with distinction (as Assistant Professor, 1942–48; Associate Professor, 1948–54; Professor, 1954–71; Distinguished Service Professor, 1971–77), until 1977, when he retired as Distinguished Service Professor, Emeritus. In squeezing his visiting appointments into the interstices of the preceding sentence, I may inadvertently have given the impression that Olson was not often to be found beyond the Loop and its immediate environs. Not so. A partial itinerary of his professional peregrinations would include Puerto Rico (University of, 1952–53), Frankfort (Rockefeller Professor), Indiana University (Mahlon Powell Professor of Philosophy, 1954; Visiting Professor of Literary Criticism, 1958–59; Patten Lecturer, 1965), the Philippines (University of, Rockefeller Professor of English and Comparative Literature, 1966–67), Houston (University of, M.D. Anderson Professor of English, 1978–79), as well as stops at the University of Texas, Wayne State University, the University of Virginia, Cambridge University, the University of the Far East, and many other schools to which he was invited to give lectures.

Throughout his career he has admirably satisfied the teacher's principal duties, to read and think in private and to speak in public. Moreover, if as a teacher he was exposed to censure (it comes with the territory), he was not, unlike Johnson's lexicographer, without the hope (and substance) of praise, for his efforts have been publicly recognized. He was presented with the Quantrell Award for excellence in teaching by the University of Chicago.

The excellence, however, also has its personal record in the memorial testimonies of former students, none of whom seems to be capable of recalling his classes with indifference. "I remember that sonofabitch; he put me through hell," captures a not untypical response. What the remark on the page does not capture, however, is the tone of the utterance, which has more fondness than rancor in it. From the trenches, beyond the seminar rooms at the University of Chicago, and through the mist of recollection, Olson is virtually indistinguishable from that cruel, but fair Drill Instructor whom Hollywood, in cooperation with the Marine Corps, is so fond of; a rigorous, yes, sonofabitch, who made the brain, not the body, sweat to some good purpose (and "damned glad am I that he did," says the tone). On the other hand, there were more than forced marches over rough terrain in Olson's classes. One former student, Thomas E. Lucas, has given expression to the following remarks in print: "I still have vivid memories of a classroom technique that was in the best Platonic manner. We were often surprised to find, under Mr. Olson's skillful questioning, that we knew many things of which we hadn't been aware" (*Elder Olson*, "Preface"). In the classroom, Olson clearly filled minds as well as hours.

As we know, much is expected from him to whom much is given, and Olson, no single-talent man, has not only enriched poetry and criticism, but brought his skills to the service of his communities. He has served, for example, as a Rapporteur for *Unesco*, as a member of the National Book Award jury, as an editorial consultant for *Modern Philology*, *Critical Inquiry*, and other journals, as a board member of the William Vaughn Moody Foundation and The Friends of Literature, and as the chairman of The Harriet Monroe Memorial Award and the Eudy Award.

Such, then, are the mostly bare facts that signalize distinctive achievement in Olson's several careers, the inert details that undoubtedly conceal as much as they reveal, the suits and trappings that invest with dignity as they hide the man, the father (of four children, Ann, Elder, Olivia, and Shelley), the husband (of Jerri Hays, the painter), and the friend (of many and "well tried through many a varying year").

II. Influence and Reputation

Olson's inclusion in this series of bibliographies certainly provides one clear and unequivocal indication of his reputation, if not necessarily of his influence, as a critic. And the custodians and chroniclers, who superintend local, regional, national, and international merit, have not thrown their credibility into doubt by neglecting to find room for Olson in their folios. The reader does not look in vain for Olson, Elder (James) in *Who's Who in America*, *Who's Who in the World*, as well as in, among many others, *Contemporary Poets of the English Language*, the *International Who's Who in Poetry*, *Contemporary Authors: A . . . Guide to Current Authors and their Works*, *The Writer's Directory*, *American Authors and Books: 1640 to the Present Day*, *Contemporary Literary Critics*, and so on, or for references to Olson in various handbooks to poetry and criticism. In general, of course, these notices give us our man preserved in amber; at most, they testify to achievement and imply significance and influence. To get a clear sense of how Olson walks abroad impinging on and actively affecting critical opinions and attitudes demands instruments of both observation and speculation. (Parenthetically, I should note that, given the nature of this book, in what follows I shall be concerned exclusively with Olson the critic, not Olson the poet. Although many of his poems continue to appear in anthologies, and although he continues to produce and publish strikingly powerful and masterfully wrought original poetry, I must wonder, with James Dickey and others, why he is not better known and hope that the reviewer of *Olson's Penny Arcade* in the *Virginia Quarterly Review* (see 331) is wrong when he supposes that Olson will apparently be obliged to "labor on . . . in conspicuous and unmerited isolation," unless he is awarded a Pulitzer Prize or a National Book Award, both unlikely possibilities, given his "aloofness from literary politics" or until he is brought back into prominence, reflexively, by the appearance of a serious, book-length study of his work.)

Some measure of a critic's importance can be taken by considering whether, by whom, for how long, with what degree of seriousness, etc., what he has committed to print has been noticed. By these standards, Olson is a critic of considerable importance. He has not suffered the worst fate of the writer; he has been besieged rather than starved. From the mid-forties to the present day, his essays and books have excited response—sometimes friendly (in the case, say, of Kenneth Burke) but usually in the form of strong, often truculent, opposition—from virtually all the modern candidates for theoretical honors, including W.K. Wimsatt, Eliseo Vivas, Murray Krieger, Monroe Beardsley, Northrop Frye, and so on.

Nothing that Olson has written has glided smoothly into print and immediately out of mind, but in reviewing the whole range of reaction to his work, one notices that three essays stick in the minds (not to mention the craws) of his antagonists, namely, "'Sailing to Byzantium': Prolegomena to a Poetics of the Lyric," "An Outline of Poetic Theory," and "William Empson, Contemporary Criticism, and Poetic Diction." These are the essays that provide his opponents with the openings, so they assume, for their knockout punches to the whole "Chicago" school of criticism, for it is in these pieces that Olson insists, among other things, on discriminating between mimetic and didactic forms, on defining four types of action considered independently of emotional effect, and on maintaining that words are the least important element in the poem. About the value of Olson's peccant remarks I shall have more to say later. For the moment, though the strictest construction of the principles of justice will not allow me to say that no adversary ever laid a glove on Olson's arguments, I can safely claim what can be independently confirmed by every impartial reader, i.e., that after going the distance, those arguments remain unscarred.

But if his theoretical essays have been subjected to sustained scrutiny over the years, his efforts in practical criticism have also elicited a fair share of notice, especially his "Rhetoric and the Appreciation of Pope" and *The Poetry of Dylan Thomas*, the first prompting nothing but praise, the second, praise muffled by loud roars of disapproval. In fact, in terms of sheer weight of commentary, nothing written by Olson has instigated more resistance from readers than his book on Thomas, and nothing in that book has provoked more comment than that aspect of his analysis of the "Altarwise by owl-light" sonnets based on the correlation between the progress of the sequence and the movements of the Hercules constellation. Olson's was the first serious book to be written on Thomas (an account of Thomas's poetry in which kind concern and judicial assessment compete for ascendancy), and in the heyday of *explication de texte*, those with a special interest in modern poetry and in Thomas's in particular were perhaps justifiably concerned about the preemptive potentiality of such a modest book. At any rate, Olson was regularly chastised for adjusting Thomas's text to the exigencies of an *a priori*, extra-poetic hypothesis (this, in spite of his eloquent caveats addressed to precisely this problem and habit of interpretation in the Thomas book itself). In general, however, unlike the critics who sought to discredit Olson's theoretical position, these critics paid him the courtesy of mining from within; that is, again in general, they took his arguments seriously and attempted to show from both internal and external evidence that his conception of the principle of unity in the sonnets was fatally flawed. For the most part, after granting with Olson the coherence of the whole, they attempted to show that only if this or that alternative hypothesis were true, could we account for the work in all its particularity, or that such and such a line or passage could not be accommodated by Olson's hypothesis. In short much of the controversy was conducted within the boundaries delimited by the basic canons of demonstration and proof.

Thus, it is clear that according to conventional criteria—is his work paid attention to, must his arguments be reckoned with, and so on—Olson is a critic of significance and importance and, hence, a critic whose reputation, being durable, seems secure. The question of how he shall persist is a matter of speculation and must be temporarily deferred.

Where there is significance and importance, there is likely to be, on the positive side, influence, and Olson's work has, indeed, been influential, has provided the impetus or the theoretical backdrop for a substantial number of studies. The reader of the last section of this bibliography will be struck by the number and variety of works which betray an indebtedness to Olson, both directly, when the works develop arguments from principles established by Olson, and indirectly, when they begin an independent line of inquiry from a clue dropped by Olson. To call the roll of those critics and scholars on whom Olson has exerted beneficial pressure is to bring to mind no unimpressive battalion of hardened veterans and young aces, who have distinguished themselves in several theaters and campaigns. In varying degrees, Olson has influenced the work of, for example, Wayne Booth, Sheldon Sacks (especially in large sections of *Fiction and the Shape of Belief*), Ralph Rader (who perhaps more than any critic writing today is carrying on and extending Olson's—and Crane's—efforts to provide special poetics for a wide range of forms, especially the various forms of lyric poetry and the novel), Norman Friedman,

James Phelan, Robert Denham, Irvin Ehrenpreis, and many others, not counting those critics whose books and essays honor Olson by working from his principal assumptions or by attempting to "correct" his extrapolations, such as John Reichert and James Kinneavy.

Less apparent, but no less real, is Olson's extensive but incalculable influence on the day-to-day business of instruction in the classroom. Successive generations of students trained by Olson are productively at work in our colleges and universities, formulating and raising questions that have their foundation in principles and methods of critical reasoning defined and exemplified by Olson. And to say as much is not to bow to any implicit, obligatory duty to heap upon the subject of a book such as this whatever merit the reader can tolerantly accept without gagging. The fact is that in the course of daily teaching, few instructors give students access to the theoretical bases of interpretive differences and the methods by which distinct problems can be identified and resolved. Olson is one of those few.

Nevertheless, reflection on Olson's reputation and influence causes as much dismay as elation, for it is sadly the case that to the multitudes he is the memory of some figure in a wax museum with a scarlet "A" (for "Aristotle," need I say) branded on his forehead. Ask virtually any aspirant to theoretical distinction (i.e., anyone, since to be a student of literature today without such aspirations is tantamount to being a Frenchman without a theory or a bartender without a philosophy) about Olson (or "Chicago criticism" generally), as he waits expectantly on the docks for the latest word from France, or at the gate at Penn Station for the mainliner to New Haven, and perhaps he might say, if he has an historical bent, "Oh yes, Olson; had a row with Empson, I think; was interested in Aristotle, plot stuff, genres, that sort of antedeluvian thing." And candor extorts from mind the recognition that Olson is largely neglected by most of the "phenoms" of contemporary criticism who dominate our journals and issue book after book in such rapid succession that from the moving toyshop of the intellect, theories theories drive. Olson is not *au courant.* If, to Olson, interpretation, as an enterprise involving the elucidation of the principles governing the construction of texts, is one of the necessary tasks of criticism, then that's just too bad for him, because (without going through the rigors of analysis) we are already "beyond interpretation." Even by critics who have found time for reading, as well as writing, Olson's arguments, if they are not neglected, are dismissed rather than confronted.

This state of affairs is particularly dismaying because Olson has a great deal to say to anyone interested in pursuing such knowledge of art as is appropriate to the subject, in learning something useful about how, as he says, "to discover a problem and formulate it precisely, to examine it on all sides, and to solve it on sound evidence." And unlike so many contemporary critics, Olson not only exhibits but confers powers, instructing in sound critical method as he displays it and, hence, contributing to, as he fits the reader for, an undertaking that can be advanced toward perfection only by the cooperative efforts of a succession of workers. Moreover, large books remain to be written on topics that he has raised and on distinctions that he has made, on, for example, the psychological bases of artistic effects; the differentiating characteristics of the enormously diverse texts that are grouped together under such broad classes as the novel, the lyric, the sonnet, etc.; the descriptive bases of sound value judgments in the various forms; the multiple functions that diction and meter serve in the achievement of artistic wholes; the distinctive powers of the various modes of disclosing information and, hence, of controlling the reader's expectations and inferences; the extra-poetic ends of art, and so on. That the paths cleared by Olson will be broadened in the immediate future seems unlikely, however desirable, though it is certain that throughout his career Olson has consistently taken up the issues worth thinking about and that his thought (to revise slightly a remark in "The Lyric") has always been worthy of what he has taken up.

To most critics today Olson has the wrong answers to the wrong questions, and he assumes what today cannot be granted, that, for example, the "basis of language is . . . determination"; its "elements function determinately," since language in use is selective or abstractive, since the terms we use function in this way and not that. No sooner has Olson (or, say, Crane) begun to answer a question about a stick—noting, for instance, that it is a wooden object with two ends and that, further, there are really many kinds of sticks of various lengths serving a variety of functions—than he is shouted down by the *one endians* or *no endians* or those who, with more than a hint of condescension, proclaim, "Well, yes, but all that is nothing to the point, for a stick is really a male talisman, a phallic symbol; or a sign of tribal or feudal authority; or a club; or *the* club which the primitive son applied with malice aforethought to the head of the primitive papa when he heard the primitive bedsprings squeaking at the primal scene; or, since a stick is nothing but inert and incidental matter considered independently of "sticker" or "stickee," a sign either of stickwielder or stick-feeler; or, to carry the matter beyond logocentrism, merely a cultural sign having only relational or differential value within an underlying *system* of relations or differences." To all these critics, and perhaps especially to those who are convinced that words (i.e., systems of language) speak people, Olson, it is true can only offer a discouraging word.

Olson never forgets that works of art are the embodied acts of men. And he does not suppose that an account of systems of relations, however rich in its paradigmatic and syntagmatic features, can supply us with anything more useful than a large stock of terms capable of entering into a multiplicity of substitutional or combinatorial relations, for just as the system of rules governing the relations in which chess pieces may enter do not and cannot determine the strategy of any particular game (as Michael Polanyi observes), so the conditions of language, considered as a relational system of possible combinations and substitutions, cannot determine the nature of any particular literary work. Although it would be a mistake to assume that people are not played by systems—in the sense that we are all creatures of the terms available to or forced upon us and, as such, all limited to working out what falls within the semantic and logical range of those terms—it would be a greater mistake to fail to realize that the boundary conditions for the operation of the relational systems cannot be supplied by the systems themselves.

Well, there you have it, I suppose. Olson is trapped in logocentrism. But once we have experienced the heady excitement of saying the word "chair" over and over again, until the object on which our backside rests falls in all its arbitrariness into the black hole of insignificance, what are we to do then? Is it permissible to wonder whether the pleasing terror we have experienced might slip without a *trace* from mind and not make a *différance*, and whether the projects that Olson has directed us to might be taken up again? There is, I think, at least this comfort: that however unjustly Olson may be displayed by some as a costume piece out of the fifties, and however slight his influence on the most popular critics of today may be, he has produced and is continuing to produce a large body of criticism, notable for its philosophic sophistication and intellectual acuity, that more than a few good readers are putting to good use. Whatever else may be said of Olson, he has defined and employed a philosophically sound critical method, and since it is a "worthy method," it is "not one which produces merely passive results, but one though which [any reader] may actively inquire, prove, and know." In sum, reputation owes his achievements a larger share than they have been given, and influence owes him its promissory note.

III. Major Critical Concerns

In an impressive series of articles and books, which began to appear in the nineteen thirties, Elder Olson has been persistently addressing the fundamental questions of hermeneutics, critical theory, and what we are inclined today to call "metacriticism," has been seriously and thoughtfully concerned with the basic issues relating to the construction, interpretation, and judgment of literature. Perhaps more than anything else, he has contributed to the demonstration that criticism is a special branch of scientific knowledge and that knowledge in criticism, like knowledge in the sciences, can progress (to paraphrase him) vertically, with many significant consequences springing from few approaches, rather than horizontally, as it seems to be doing with a vengeance at the moment, with very few significant consequences emerging from a great many approaches. And it is fair to say that, with the possible exception of R.S. Crane, none of the so-called "Chicago" critics has written more extensively on the theoretical foundations of critical systems, on the principled bases of practical criticism, and on particular literary works than Elder Olson.

On the other hand, it is perhaps equally fair to say that the views of no modern critic have been subjected to more misrepresentation, distortion, and oversimplification at the hands of commentators than those of Olson (and other "Chicago" critics as well), despite the fact that few critics have done more than he to articulate his views clearly, precisely, and fully, to define the philosophic or theoretical bases of his positions, and to delineate carefully what aspects of the subject matter under discussion legitimately fall within the range of his concern and the competence of his special modes of discourse. The fruits of misprision can be quickly illustrated by looking at the three aspects of his criticism that have provoked the most response and that were referred to in the preceding section.

To get at fatal weaknesses, the commentator typically isolates a doctrine or statement from its context and from the principles and assumptions only in relation to which it has determinate meaning and then delivers a blistering attack against it. For example, in going through Olson's "An Outline of Poetic Theory," critic after critic has fastened onto his remark that "words are the least important element in the poem" and treated it as though it were a species of blasphemy. Restored to its context, Olson's comment presents no real threat to sacred institutions or values. His point is not that words are unimportant, but that they are less important than other elements *in* the poem, as, of course, they clearly are. They are certainly less important than their functions, less important, that is, than that for the sake of which they are present at all. As Olson says, "the words must be explained in terms of something else, not the poem in terms of the words, and further, a principle must be a principle of something other than itself; hence the words cannot be a principle of their own arrangements." The words cannot subsume what they subserve. The relation is a one-way, lower to higher relation. It is the principle or function that endows the words with determinate meaning or power.

Another controversial element in Olson's theory is his broad division of works into mimetic and didactic categories, one that places *King Lear* in the former and *The Divine Comedy* in the latter class. By suggesting, say, that *The Divine Comedy* is a didactic work, Olson earns a circle for himself, and his opponents abandon all hope for him. He seems to be establishing an equivalence between Dante and Pope, *The Divine Comedy* and some sermon, to be coming dangerously close to saying that Dante's work is not a poem or, alternatively, that there are no ideas (or, more likely, no recurrent themes) in *King Lear*. (Some critics consider this division as simply a peculiarly virulent strain of a "Chicago" disease that manifests itself symptomatically in a desire to adjust all works to the dimensions of a severely restricted number of genres and then to determine the value of works on the basis of their conformity to the preestablished genre definitions.) Such rumors persist, in spite of Olson's eloquent and repeated denials. When Olson focusses on this division, he is not suggesting that there are no ideas, that there is no "thought," in mimetic works, or that there is no "poetry," "action," "character," or "emotion" in didactic works; he is merely making a broad distinction according to kinds and degrees of emphasis in the principal parts of works, the sort of distinction that if kept in mind by many critics rushing to judgment would have prevented them from treating *Gulliver's Travels* as in any way a *Bildungsroman* (from tracing the progress of Gulliver's development) or from bothering about what happens to the pilgrims at the end of *Rasselas* (as though they were characters in a novel). Properly understood, the distinction can help the reader to formulate useful, though basic questions. And the reader who would make neither too little nor too much of one of Olson's most useful and least understood distinctions should not trust to the reports of scandal but go directly to what he has to say of it in the "Empson" essay, in "An Outline of Poetic Theory," and in "A Dialogue on Symbolism."

Space permits the consideration of only one further instance of Olson's "narrowmindedness," his view (as expressed in "An Outline of Poetic Theory," *Tragedy and the Theory of Drama, The Theory of Comedy,* "The Lyric," and elsewhere) that we can distinguish four kinds of actions considered independently of emotional effect, from the most basic ("a single character acting in a single closed situation," i.e., any verbal activity that is presented without being complicated by the appearance or activity of any other agency) to the maximal forms of action, such as we find, for example, in the grand plots of tragedy, comedy, and epic. It is essential to realize, as many of his critics do not, that Olson is not defining "forms" of literature or attempting to establish principles of construction with these distinctions; he is merely charting, in a propaedeutic way, the range of activities that are possible to and achieved by imitative forms. That is, he is considering possible variations within the object of imitation, but they are such variations as must be noted by anyone who is interested in developing a special poetics for any particular kind of literature which imitates human action. When these distinctions are returned to their contexts, it becomes clear that Olson is not compelling all works of literature to adapt to his categories; rather, he is exploring one line of differentiation in certain kinds of works. Full definitions of species would require similar analyses of the means, manners, and ends of imitation in the various forms.

From the preceding examples, the reader should derive at least one homely injunction: before you assume you have Olson's number, make some effort to understand doctrine or statement within its context and context within the body of principles and assumptions, within the theoretical framework, that governs the posing and resolution of his problems. There can be no dishonor in reading before writing, understanding before speaking.

Because Olson is a philosophic critic, because he thinks distinctly and speaks with exactness, his prose can, at times, make the head ache, but what he says of Marianne Moore's poetry applies with equal validity to his own writing: Olson is a difficult writer, but not an obscure one; on the contrary, he is extremely clear, and our difficulty comes primarily from his insistence that we think and think well at every point in his essays and books. Moreover, even though Olson deals with an enormous number of important issues and works, and even though each of his productions is sufficient unto itself and entirely commensurate in analysis or exposition with the subject under discussion, his work, taken as a whole, exhibits a unified and coherent system of entailments. His various works, written over a long span of time and addressed to a variety of discrete problems, both imply and are implied by a unified system of principles. And Olson's philosophic system, like that embodied in Reynolds's *Discourses* (as Olson points out), "derives its unity, not from the time of its utterance, but from the compendency of its parts." Additionally, the reader should recognize that, except when he is engaged in the tasks of practical analysis, Olson is throughout concerned as much with what critics think *with* as with what they think *about*; i.e., he is interested not only in the critic's subject matter, but in his mode of reasoning about that subject matter. Only when we bear these matters in mind can we approach the job of understanding Olson's contributions to critical theory and practice.

Notwithstanding the efforts of his commentators to place him by the shores of Lake Michigan or by the side of the Stagirite, Olson is not a "Chicago" critic or a "Neo-Aristotelian"; he is a Pluralist (as distinct from a dogmatist, a sceptic, or a syncretist). But since "pluralist" is what a great many with whom Olson has virtually nothing in common also claim to be today, it is important that we do not confuse his "pluralism" with whatever else may have decided to march under that banner. Underlying Olson's pluralism is a conception of the legitimacy and validity of many different critical principles and methods. And his most cogent, incisive, analytic, and detailed discussion of his kind of pluralism is found in "The Dialectical Foundations of Critical Pluralism," an essay which, to my knowledge, no critic has succeeded in dismantling by any acceptable intellectual means. As Olson explains in that essay, pluralism maintains that

> any philosophic problem must be relative to its formulation; and since any solution to a problem is also relative to the problem, the solution must also be relative to that formulation. But that formulation [because of the selective and restrictive nature of language in use] . . . must be finite. It follows that there can be no single philosophic system embracing all truth; and by the same token, no method which is the only right method. . . . [Philosophic variation] is a function of two things: first, the fundamental dialectic of the system; second, the subject matter on which the dialectic is exerted.

In "An Outline of Poetic Theory," Olson distinguishes between dialectic and subject matter as grounds of variation in the following way:

> It is impossible within the scope of this essay to discuss all the factors in the foundations of philosophies and criticisms; but perhaps a rough and partial statement may serve for illustration. I propose that the number of possible critical positions

> is relative to the number of possible philosophic positions and that the latter is determined by two principal considerations: (1) the number of aspects of a subject which can be brought into discussion, as constituting its *subject matter*; (2) the kinds of basic dialectic which may be exerted upon that subject matter. I draw this distinction between the subject and the subject matter: the subject is what is talked about; the subject matter is that subject in so far as it is represented or implied in the discussion. Philosophers do not discuss *subjects themselves*; they can discuss only so much as the terms or materials of the discussion permit; and that is the subject matter. We cannot discuss what we cannot first of all mention, or what we cannot bring to mind. In other words, any discussion of a "subject" is relative to its formulation. But, further, any discursive reasoning must employ some method of reasoning or inference; and, since there are various possible systems of inference, we may say that a given discussion is a function of its subject matter and of the dialectic, i.e., system of inference, exerted upon that subject matter.

A proper understanding of Olson's analysis of the causes of variation in critical discourse enables us to recognize that much of what appears to be conflict or contradiction in critical essays is really *difference* brought about by the systematic operations of different assumptions and methods on different problems.

The consequences attendant upon Olson's pluralism are everywhere apparent in his work. By examining critical documents in the light of the peculiar problems, assumptions, and principles of reasoning determining their natures, Olson avoids (and teaches us to avoid) the all-too-common tendency either to associate or to distinguish critical systems simply on the basis of some ostensible (or real) similarity or disparity in the nature of the particular statements or doctrines expressed in those systems. A striking illustration of this tendency is presented in a discussion of Longinus and Reynolds, in which Olson, after isolating a number of doctrinal correspondences between *On the Sublime* and the *Discourses,* trenchantly demonstrates that, while both critics concentrate on qualities rather than species of art and share an interest in the faculties of the artist and the emotional effects of art, they are as critics "not only dissimilar, but quite unrelated to each other. They do not deal with the same critical problem; they make different assumptions; and they pursue different methods of argument. Longinus views the products of several arts in terms of a single effect [the sublime]; Reynolds views all the effects of a single art [painting]."

The analysis and recovery of the principles underlying and informing various critical systems lead Olson, not to eclecticism or scepticism, but to a healthy respect for the explanatory powers of diverse critical approaches and a finely tuned, earned awareness of the limitations correlative to and necessarily implicated in the strengths of those systems:

> Recognition of the methodological differences between systems of criticism, and of their consequent respective powers and limitations quickly establishes the fact that twenty-five centuries of inquiry have not been spent in vain. On the contrary, the partial systems supplement one another, the comprehensive intertranslate, to form a vast body of poetic knowledge; and contemporary theorists, instead of constantly seeking new bases for criticism, would do better to examine the bases of such criticism as we have and so avail themselves of that knowledge. Many a modern theory of criticism would have died a-borning, had its author done a little more reading as he thought, or thinking as he read. ("An Outline")

What Olson looks forward to is vertical progress in literary study, and if there is to be such progress, critics must take advantage of the available valid approaches, extending sound methods into new areas of investigation and applying established principles to materials and problems not previously examined. It is to this program that Olson is fully committed, as is evidenced, to cite two obvious instances, by his application of the Aristotelian method to the analysis of comedy and the lyric. As a pluralist, Olson has actively and persistently encouraged "the development of every valid approach" ("Art and Science"). Indeed, every reader should recognize that he himself worked extensively not only with Aristotelian and Platonic methods of reasoning, but with various other dialectics as well, especially the Humean and the Longinian. (*Tragedy and the Theory of Drama* is thoroughly Humean, for example; it is concerned, not with the *reasoning* part of poetics, but with the *making* part, and it begins, after all, with a distinction between impressions and ideas. And *The Poetry of Dylan Thomas* is Longinian, as the chapter headings by themselves clearly indicate.)

Nevertheless, of the many valid approaches susceptible to extension and refinement, Olson concentrates on two comprehensive systems, the Aristotelian and the Platonic, and Olson—and this point should be stressed—is no more fully dedicated to the development of an Aristotelian method of art than to the development of a Platonic one, as a close reading of his work clearly evinces. Olson, of course, sharply discriminates between the Aristotelian (a differential) and the Platonic (an integral) dialectic, and in several of his essays he discloses the efficacy of the two approaches. For example, the Platonic dialectic is displayed in full power and act in a "Dialogue on Symbolism" and "A Dialogue on the Function of Art in Society," two essays constituting part of a projected series of twelve dialogues which, when completed, will make up a comprehensive theory of art in the Platonic mode.

Of course, the practical utility of the Aristotelian dialectic is more fully represented in Olson's works than the Platonic. And although Olson is appropriately considered as a writer who has extended and refined the Aristotelian method, the reader should remember that when he works as an Aristotelian, he is engaging in only one of many useful critical ventures and using the method to deal with those problems, and only those problems, which it is inherently capable of resolving. To the "Aristotelian" aspect of his criticism we must now turn.

Olson knows that, as a productive science (as distinct from a theoretical or practical science) focussing on the artistic product—a discrete, complete composite of parts functioning to achieve a peculiar effect—"Aristotelian poetics" cannot deal directly with, say, the artistic faculties or processes, or the nature of audiences, or the political or social functions of art. As he points out in "The Poetic Method of Aristotle," an Aristotelian poetics takes

> for its starting point, or principle, the artistic whole which is to be produced and [proceeds] through the various parts of the various kinds to be assembled. The reasoning is hypothetical because it is based upon hypotheses: If such and such a work, which is a whole, is to be produced, then such and such parts must be assembled in such and such a way; and if

> the work is to have excellence as a whole, then the parts must be of such and such a kind and quality. The reasoning is regressive because it works backward from the whole, which is to exist, to the parts which must have existence previous to that of the whole. Since the reasoning is based upon a definition of a certain whole as its principle and since that definition must be arrived at in some fashion, any productive science must consist of two main parts: inductive reasoning toward its principle, and deductive reasoning from its principle. One part must make possible the formulation of the whole; the other must determine the parts according to that formulation.

Now, to understand what working with Aristotelian principles means to Olson in practical terms, we can turn for a convenient example to " 'Sailing to Byzantium': Prolegomena to a Poetics of the Lyric," where, before examining Yeats's poem in detail, he observes that the primary task of the critic is

> to discover some principle in the work which is the principle of its unity and order—a principle which, it goes without saying, will have to be a purely poetic principle, i.e., a formal principle of the poem, and not something extrinsic to it such as the differentiation either of authors, audiences, subject matters, or orders of diction would afford. Since in a formal consideration the form is the end, and since the end renders everything else intelligible, a mark of the discovery of the formal principle would be that everything else in the poem would be found to be explicable in terms of it.

As an Aristotelian critic (and only as an Aristotelian critic), then, Olson is concerned with synthesizing principles of form, with those formal principles of works which govern the functions of discernible and differentiable parts and in relation to which the parts have their functions. Whether he is dealing with Dylan Thomas's sonnets, lyric poems, comedies, tragedies, with mimetic or didactic works, Olson is interested in discovering the intrinsic causes of their artistic integrity and in appreciating them for the "unique literary structure in which they are constituted."

That Olson is not interested in issuing edicts to works and authors should be apparent to any attentive reader. But to those who accuse him (and other "Chicago" critics) of constructing prescriptive definitions of artistic forms and, then, of judging works well or ill on the basis of the extent to which they correspond, point for point, to the generic ideal or paradigm, he can only say again what he has said again and again: the critic does not and cannot legislate to that artist, and the artist "is properly bound by no law but the dictates of the individual work" ("The Poetry of Dylan Thomas"). From Olson's point of view, each work is a unique particular, a concrete whole, a unique synthesis of parts, the structure and effect of which are consequences of a unique principle of form. On the issue of the particular and the species, Olson sharply discriminates between natural and artificial objects (though some critics have accused him of conflating biology and poetics) as follows: natural things (horses, trees, bananas, etc.) have (to paraphrase Olson) such and such characteristics because they belong to a class, whereas artificial things (sonnets, tragedies, paintings, etc.) belong to a class (a *constructed* class) because they have such and such characteristics. In other words, the materials of nature are, as Olson says, "programmed," in a manner of speaking, to be what they are (they obey the instructions of their genetic code), whereas the materials of art (wood, stone, words, etc.) are not naturally disposed to assume any particular form. Once a particular work has been formed, as a result of an artist's imposing some form upon some material in some manner for some purpose, however, the realized or achieved form can be discussed in relation to other works which are similarly formed by similar means for similar purposes and, hence, formally associated with those works or *construed* as a representative of a distinguishable class of works. Moreover, from a close formal analysis of a single work, one can discover the principles that would necessarily obtain in any work that elected to use similar means in similar ways for similar purposes. And all this can be done without affecting the unique particularity of the work. Indeed, the definition of classes depends upon the existence of individuals. Only when the works exist can a theory of forms be developed which provides a complete causal account of the possibilities of formal achievement in the various kinds. Whatever misrepresentation may have suggested and idleness credited, the fact is that Olson is no Procrustes busy at the task of adjusting literary works to prefabricated frames. Before critics place him in the ranks of those supporting narrow or broad theories of artistic species, they should at least come to terms with what Olson has contributed, tentatively and partially, to the theory of forms in his several works, especially the "The Lyric," *Tragedy and the Theory of Drama,* and *The Theory of Comedy.*

In presenting this brief summary of Olson's major concerns as a critic, I have been obliged to force a large and capacious mind into an uncomfortably small space and to neglect the extraordinary range of topics and issues that he has addressed. Among other things, he has dealt over the years with the grounds of criticism in the arts, the nature of definitions and hypotheses, the bases of emotional responses to art, the theory of forms, the relation between art and morality, the establishment and validation of value judgments, and so on, and with the works of a great many writers, including Aristophanes, Shakespeare, Marianne Moore, Wallace Stevens, Alexander Pope, Eugene O'Neill, Harold Pinter, Molière, etc., in a variety of tones and styles (from the easily familiar in "A Letter on Teaching Drama" to the occasionally playful in the Platonic dialogues to the philosophically precise in "The Dialectical Foundations of Critical Pluralism"). Of Olson, in fact, it is entirely appropriate to say what Walter Jackson Bate says of Samuel Johnson: regardless of the direction in which you set out, you always meet Olson on his way back.

More important, in treating Olson's views in summary fashion, I may have inadvertently contributed to the misrepresentation and oversimplification that I intended to thwart. On the other hand, there is some partial consolation in the knowledge that no brief account of his work could sufficiently satisfy the demands of justice, for the fact is that Olson's thought can no more be adequately represented by summary treatment than the stateliness of a house can be represented by its unassembled bricks. Only the works themselves can adequately display the range of his activity and the strength of those arguments that are capable of overwhelming resistance and forcing assent (at least in those who can be persuaded to yield by reason and cogent argument; Olson, of course, can supply readers with reasons, not understanding).

Throughout I have written unashamedly as a partisan supporter. But I am convinced that those readers who are nothing if not critical will be overmatched by Olson, if they read him carefully, and that even those few who are animated by nothing more exalted than the retrograde ambition to shine by means of excoriation will turn out to be in the end, to alter Goldsmith slightly, as fools who came to scoff, but remained to learn. At any rate, this book will have satisfied its author if it contributes in any way to a renewed interest in the works of Elder James Olson, poet, critic, teacher, scholar, humanist.

IV. The Text

This bibliography is designed to provide a comprehensive review of materials written by and about Elder Olson; in arrangement, books precede essays and reviews, and Olson's works precede those of his commentators. Like any reference source, this one will be valuable to the extent that, as Johnson said of lexicons, it clears "obstructions from the paths through which Learning and Genius press forward." This work is directed primarily to the serious student of modern criticism, and it should enable him to gain quick and convenient access to information relating not only to the existence, but to the substance of documents produced by and relevant to Olson. Moreover, any reader interested in Olson as a poet and dramatist, in "Chicago" criticism, in the history of critical thought, in those issues that distinguish humanistic inquiry, should find much in this work that is useful.

Although the bibliography is comprehensive, it is not exhaustive. In every section there are lacunae that neither determination nor diligence could fill. In some instances, I have listed without annotation an item that I could not find (in such cases, my sources usually sent me where the thing was not, and where it was I could not discover by deliberate searches). Where suspicion, not testimony, pointed to an item, I listened, hunted, and, then, let "mum" be the word. To preclude being charged with neglecting what I could not find and to facilitate the inquiries of future researchers, I call the reader's attention to the following "problems":

1. Early poems. Many of Olson's very early poems appeared

in magazines and journals now extinct and unavailable for scrutiny. My knowledge of their existence derives from Olson himself. (For example, his first "serious" poem appeared in 1926 or 1927 in *Tambour,* a magazine published in Paris and not now to be located; also, several other early poems appeared in *The Chicagoan,* gone without a trace, it seems, and in *Voices,* a volume edited by Harold Vinal but no longer accessible.)

2. Reviews by Olson. He wrote a handful of reviews for the *Chicago Tribune* and the *Chicago Daily News* that have escaped detection.
3. Reviews of Olson's work. Olson recalls a few that I have been unable to find (for example, a review of *Thing of Sorrow* in the English periodical *Life and Letters Today*). Also, although I located a large number of newpaper reviews of his work, I have certainly missed many that were published in local papers around the country.
4. Poems published in anthologies. Once I had exhausted my sources and Olson's recollections, I could only count on random searches and the aid of fortune, who smiled upon me infrequently. Nevertheless, the anthology terrain is not entirely barren.
5. Reprints of articles. Several may have escaped my notice. Having found many by accident (in textbooks, for example), I suspect the existence of more.
6. Translations. Olson has imperfect records of many that I have not located.
7. Lectures. In general, Olson did not keep copies. Those not subsequently published have disappeared, with the exception of the two cited and annotated in the bibliography.
8. Tapes of readings and productions of his plays. A mine in which I did not dig.
9. References to Olson in essays and books. Certainly there are more than I have found. To seek is not always to find, and chance does not always cooperate with assiduity. Nevertheless, I have cited everything that I found in my ramblings through the stacks of three major libraries.

The principal sources consulted in the preparation of this bibliography are:

Abstracts of English Studies. Vols. 1–22. Boulder, Colorado: National Council of Teachers of English.

Annual Bibliography of English Language and Literature. London: Modern Humanities Research Association.

Arts and Humanities Citation Index. 1977–80. Philadelphia: Institute for Scientific Information.

Book Review Index. Detroit: Gale Research Company, 1965–80.

Chicago Tribune Index. Wooster, Ohio: Newspaper Indexing Center, Micro Photo Division, Bell and Howell Company.

Comprehensive Dissertation Index. Ann Arbor, Michigan: Xerox University Microfilms, 1973–78.

Congdon, Kirby. *Contemporary Poets in American Anthologies,* 1960–1979. Metuchen, New Jersey: The Scarecrow Press, 1978.

Contemporary Poets of the English Language. Ed. Rosalie Murphy. Chicago: St. James Press, 1970.

Current Book Review Citations. Vols. 1–5. Ed. Paula de Vaux. New York: The H.W. Wilson Co., 1977–81.

Dissertation Abstracts International. Ann Arbor, Michigan: University Microfilms International.

Elton, William. *A Guide to the New Criticism.* Revised edition. Chicago: Modern Poetry Association, 1951.

Essay and General Literature Index, 1900–1979. Vols. 1–9. New York: The H.W. Wilson Co., 1934–80.

Granger's Index to Poetry. Morningside Heights, N.Y.: Columbia University Press, 1953, 1962. Supplements 1957, 1967.

Humanities Index. Vols. 1–7. *Social Sciences and Humanities Index.* Vols. 19–27. *International Index.* Vols. 5–18. New York: The H.W. Wilson Company.

Index to American Little Magazines, 1920–1939. Compiled by Stephen H. Goode. Troy, N.Y.: Whitston Publishing Company, 1969.

Index to American Periodical Verse, 1971–77. Metuchen, New Jersey: The Scarecrow Press, 1973–79.

Index to Book Reviews in the Humanities. Williamston, Michigan: Phillip Thomson, 1961–81.

Index to Little Magazines. Denver: Alan Swallow, 1943–67.

Index to Plays and Periodicals. Ed. Dean H. Keller. Metuchen, N.J.: The Scarecrow Press, 1979.

McNamee, Lawrence F. *Dissertations in English and American Literature: Theses Accepted by American, British, and German Universities, 1865–1964.* New York: R.R. Bowker Co., 1968. *Supplement One, 1964–68* (New York, 1969); *Supplement Two, 1969–73* (New York, 1974).

MLA International Bibliography of Books and Articles on the Modern Languages and Literatures. New York: Modern Language Association of America.
New York Times Book Review Index, 1896–1970. 5 vols. New York: Arno Press, 1973.
New York Times Index. New York: New York Times, 1913–.
Reader's Guide to Periodical Literature. Vols. 7–81. New York: The H.W. Wilson Company, 1925–81.

With regard to the annotations, the reader should know that length has been determined, for the most part, by the complexity and importance of the work under discussion. Throughout the writing of this book, I have had not only in my mind but before my eyes Olson's implicit admonishment to any abridger: "if he is like most authors, he [Robert Penn Warren, in this case] must feel that his best summary is his own work" ("A Symbolic Reading of 'The Ancient Mariner' "). The Olson entries sit tall, not only because he is the subject of this work, but also because it is impossible to do justice to his arguments without indicating the dependencies upon which they are based and the careful stages through which they pass. In general, I have avoided evaluative commentary, except when to be silent was to be a party to a felony. Usually, I have scrupulously attempted to let reviewers and critics be their own advocates or enemies, trusting to the reader to recognize when intellectual acuity made its appearance or when bile or inanity suffocated itself in its own too much.

As modest as this book is, it would not have found its way into print without the abiding concern and generous assistance of many. I am especially grateful to Patricia Morrison and Dennis Shanahan, who performed much of the basic research required by a bibliographic project and without whose industry and intelligence I could not have completed my work. I am also grateful to the chairman of my department, Julian Markels, the dean of my college, Diether H. Haenicke, and the Trustees of The Ohio State University for supporting my work and providing me with one quarter of released time to finish my writing. For crucial and timely assistance, I owe thanks to Kim Gainer and to librarians at The Ohio State University, Yale University, and the University of Chicago. Also, I am grateful to the editors of the *Chicago Review* for allowing me to use material from my article, "Elder Olson: Critic, Pluralist, and Humanist," in this introduction. To Rolf Soellner and Lisa Kiser, my colleagues, I owe special thanks; both came to my aid as translators when my small Latin and less Greek had been exhausted, when I desperately needed to understand in English what authors had taken the liberty of saying in German, Italian, Spanish, and Rumanian. No acknowledgement of indebtedness to two people, however rich in expressions of gratitude, could be equal to the benefits that they have conferred upon me, for in addition to supplying me with materials essential to this work, they brought social comfort to hope's delusive mine. Elder Olson and Lisa Kiser not only contributed in substantial ways to this bibliography, but also extended human gifts to me that, through my actions, I shall study to deserve and recompense.

LIST OF ABBREVIATIONS

MP	*Modern Philology*
NLH	*New Literary History*
UTQ	*University of Toronto Quarterly*
SEL	*Studies in English Literature*
JAAC	*Journal of Aesthetics and Art Criticism*
ECent	*The Eighteenth Century: Theory and Interpretation*
TSLL	*Texas Studies in Language and Literature*

I
PRIMARY MATERIALS

A. BOOKS AND COLLECTIONS OF ESSAYS

1. *General Prosody: Rhythmic, Metric, Harmonics*. Chicago: The University of Chicago Libraries, 1938.

Contents:

I. The Nature of the Problem

II. The Element and its Characteristics

III. The Constitution of Emphasis

IV. Elementary Proportions: Primitive Rhythm

V. Post-Primary Structures: The Hierarchy of Rhythm

VI. Non-Positional Entitative Structures: Harmony

Appendices

I. Specimen of Analysis

II. Material Constitution

III. Glossary

Bibliography

Defines the bases of a general science of prosody, as distinct from special sciences--the designation of special prosodic principles for each language--and develops an argument for such a science by employing a differential method of analysis, a method concerned with the enumeration of the parts of prosodic synthesis and with the ways in which such parts (speech-sounds) may be combined to enhance or embellish diction, the perspicuity and appropriateness of which is in turn determined by the formal ends of whole works.

After outlining the problems confronting anyone interested in ascertaining the principles of a general theory of prosody and distinguishing his method from that of his predecessors, the synoptic method, which, in general, operates by analogy (considering the subject matter of prosody in relation to music, grammar, physiology, and any number of other "sciences"), Olson argues that all rhythm depends upon the juxtaposition of speech-sounds, and he takes proportional relation among speech-sounds as his guiding prosodic principle. The material basis of rhythm is the syllable, and relations among speech-sounds in rhythmic intervals are governed by such characteristics of pronunciation as position, duration (or quantity), intensity (or accent), pitch, and timbre (or phonetic entity). In every primary rhythm, the measurable unit is compounded of an emphatic (thesis) and a non-emphatic (arsis) element, with emphasis being determined by duration, intensity, etc. From the two possible relations of the formal components of rhythm (arsis before thesis, arsis after thesis), Olson derives all the possible formal relations (i.e., all the podal possibilities, iamb, trochee, dactyl, etc.). Beyond primary rhythm, there is post-primary rhythm, i.e., aspects of rhythm in which measurable units are matters, not of emphatic relations, but of successions of sound as demarcated by devices either intrinsic (divisions based on number of feet, number of syllables) or extrinsic (divisions based, for example, on acrostics, abcedarianism, etc.). All such units are called caesural divisions by Olson.

To complete his discussion of general prosody, Olson considers speech-sounds in their harmonic relations, i.e., those involving the consonance or dissonance of adjacent entities (vowel and consonant combinations) and the repetition or conjunction of such entities, harmonics thus being a consideration of speech-sounds apart from their emphatic value or position.

Added to the study are three appendices: the first, an application of the theory to a variety of poems (in several languages); the second, a brief essay explaining why prosodic structure must be based on formal, not material components, and the third, a useful glossary of prosodic terms.

2. (With R. S. Crane, W. R. Keast, Richard McKeon, Norman Maclean, Bernard Weinberg) Critics and Criticism: Ancient and Modern. Ed. with an introduction by R. S. Crane. Chicago and London: The University of Chicago Press, 1952.

Contents

Introduction (R. S. Crane)

I.

I.A. Richards on the Art of Interpretation (R. S. Crane)

William Empson, Contemporary Criticism, and Poetic Diction (Elder Olson) See 29

The Critical Monism of Cleanth Brooks (R.S. Crane)

The "New Criticism" and King Lear (W.R. Keast)

A Symbolic Reading of the Ancient Mariner (Elder Olson) See 27.

II.

Literary Criticism and the Concept of Imitation in Antiquity (Richard McKeon)

Aristotle's Conception of Language and the Arts of Language (Richard McKeon)

The Argument of Longinus' On the Sublime (Elder Olson) See 22

Rhetoric in the Middle Ages (Richard McKeon)

Poetry and Philosophy in the Twelfth

Century: The Renaissance of Rhetoric (Richard McKeon)
Robortello on the *Poetics* (Bernard Weinberg)
Castelvetro's Theory of Poetics (Bernard Weinberg)
English Neoclassical Criticism: An Outline Sketch (R.S. Crane)
The Theoretical Foundations of Johnson's Criticism (W.R. Keast)
From Action to Image: Theories of the Lyric in the Eighteenth Century (Norman Maclean)

III.
The Philosophic Bases of Art and Criticism (Richard McKeon)
An Outline of Poetic Theory (Elder Olson) See 28
A Dialogue on Symbolism (Elder Olson) See 31
Episode, Scene, Speech, and Word: The Madness of Lear (Norman Maclean)
The Concept of Plot and the Plot of *Tom Jones* (R.S. Crane)

Contains twenty essays, six of which appeared for the first time in this collection, including Olson's "A Dialogue on Symbolism," by a group of critics who have come to be known as the "Chicago critics" or the "Chicago Neo-Aristotelians." The collection is divided into three sections which examine respectively 1) doctrines, assumptions, principles, and critical methods of representative modern critics, 2) significant critics and "episodes in the history of criticism from the Greeks through the eighteenth century," and 3) broad theoretical issues relating to the criticism of criticism and the definition of poetic forms. Taken together, the essays both define and exhibit the critical philosophy that distinguishes their collective enterprise, i.e., pluralism, which for these critics, involves the recognition of the strict relativity of critical statements to the terms and distinctions of their formulation and the understanding that no subject can be completely formulated. Hence, to these critics, there are many valid criticisms, each with its own inherent powers and limitations and each capable of advancing our understanding of the nature and determinants of art. The essays in practical criticism exemplify the ways in which one historical system of criticism--the Aristotelian--can be developed and refined to account for the peculiar power and integrity of literary forms that have emerged in the course of literary history.

3. (With R.S. Crane, W. R. Keast, Richard McKeon, Norman Maclean, Bernard Weinberg) Critics and Criticism. Abridged edition. Edited and with a new introduction by R.S. Crane. Chicago: The University of Chicago Press, 1957.

Contents

Brings together eight of the essays that appeared in the collection above (2). These essays are to be considered representative of a general program to look at criticism from a "critical point of view," to examine the conditions determining the nature of critical statements and "the appropriateness or workability" or critical methods.

4. The Poetry of Dylan Thomas. [With a Bibliography by William H. Huff.] Chicago: The University of Chicago Press, 1954.

Table of Contents

Based in part on lectures given at the University of Frankfurt am Main (while Olson was serving there as Rockefeller Exchange Professor) and at the University of Chicago, this short book (judged the best book of poetry criticism in 1954 by the Poetry Society of America) focusses on the intellectual problems, lyric activities, and poetic devices that characterize Thomas's poetry and differentiate his achievement from that of other poets. Olson's study, an exercise in Longinian dialectic, moves steadily from the nature of Thomas's poetry and the quality of his exemplified poetic character broadly conceived to the kinds of activities he represents and the distinctive means by which he brings his poems to formal completion, the whole book coming to culmination in a detailed analysis of the "Altarwise by owl-light" sonnets, "surely among the greatest poems of our century."

To Olson, Thomas's poetry achieves importance, not because of its subject matter (birth, sex, death, etc.), but because of the intensity and complexity with which such universal subjects are treated. And Thomas's poetry is difficult to read, in large part, because his imagination finds congenial expression in a symbolism that is both traditional and unique.

The early poetry, taken at large, tells us that "to a serious and sensitive individual, life in the absence of a sustaining faith is a nightmare." Thomas's vivid, nightmarish world, however, has nothing of the Grand Guignol about it; his poetry is not melodramatic, but tragic: his symbols have tragic power because "they have reference to the serious suffering of a man of some nobility."

Olson discerns three phases in Thomas's poetry: 1) a dark period centering on personal problems; 2) a middle period exhibiting powerful and poignant feeling for others, and 3) a late period expressing exultant faith and love. Each period is marked by peculiarities of diction and syntax, the general movement being from terseness to verbosity.

In his work Thomas assumes a single character. He is a poet only of the "most exalted emotions," and his character is a "lofty, heroic one." As a lyric poet of the "lofty kind," he either achieves the sublime or fails. When the conception underlying his poetry is powerful and elevated, Thomas is "magnificent"; otherwise, he is trivial, sometimes bathetic. ("When Thomas is not master of his tricks, his tricks master him.")

In his discussion of poetics proper, Olson gives a chapter each to 1) the kinds of activities in which the poetic character engages, 2) the extra-linguistic devices through which the character is shown to be engaged in such activities, and 3) the ways in which Thomas's handling of language serves his artistic purposes. Essentially, Thomas is a poet "of the internal moral workings of the soul, and he deals, not with moments, but with processes." In terms of his devices of representation, two stand out prominently: pseudo- drama (either the use of dialogue to suggest that the action represents interplay between persons when in fact the "persons" of the dialogue are not distinct, or the use of monologue in which a "supposed character--who is really, however, only the object of thought of someone thinking--utters the thoughts of the person thinking of him") and pseudo-narrative (poems in which the characters referred to are "symbolic masks of the underlying lyric character"). The poetics section is completed when Olson discusses what is most likely to provide the first obstruction to the reader's pleasure, Thomas's handling of language. This useful chapter supplies "a list of things that Thomas is likely to do with language," so that the reader will know what to look for and "how to deal with it when he finds it."

Olson's last chapter provides a detailed analysis of Thomas's sonnets, which present "a meditation on a problem of great seriousness by a character in serious suffering because of that problem." The strange legend of the sonnets is a device for representing the real processes of his hero's mind, as it works its way from the mortality of nature to the prospect of immortality. Thus, the sonnets, their peculiarities of style and imaginative conception notwithstanding, make up a poem of the "same sort as," for example, Lycidas or "Ode to a Nightingale."

Consistent with his efforts to facilitate access to Thomas's poetry and his desire, not to preempt, but to occasion discovery and understanding, Olson adds two useful appendices to his book: one, prose paraphrases of five poems and two, a glossary of difficult terms. Assessing Thomas's production as a whole, Olson says that it is inconceivable that his best poems should "perish, except through mischance," for "in his struggle from darkness to light, he uncovered darknesses in us that we should otherwise not have known, and brought us to a light we should not otherwise have seen."

5. The Poetry of Dylan Thomas. Chicago: The University of Chicago Press, 1961.

A reprint, in paper, of the above (4) without the Bibliography prepared by William H. Huff.

6. Tragedy and the Theory of Drama. Detroit: Wayne State University Press, 1961. (Reissued in 1966. Ed. Barbara Woodward)

Contents

Growing primarily out of lectures delivered at Wayne State University in 1958, this book deals with an extraordinary range of complex issues in a style at once familiar and precise. Throughout Olson writes from the point of view of the "working dramatist," and thus he focusses on "the problems of the dramatist, the technical means for their solution, and the principles governing the different methods of solution."

His method of analysis is problematic (based on actual problems of construction), matter of fact (addressed to discernible traits in plays), and conditional (concerned with the conditions necessary to particular effects and consequences).

Chapter one explores the implications of the fact that a dramatic action is one which is set before us most effectively "through the visible and audible behavior of the characters." Since the dramatist affects his audience chiefly through sensation and only secondarily through imagination, dramatic action depends for its effectiveness upon 1) physical action (which can be represented directly) and 2) signs (which make possible the representation of inner conditions). Signs, moreover, are either _natural_ (tears, faltering voice, etc.; they are always "the effects that manifest a given internal condition as cause") or _artificial_ (e.g., a conventional gesture; these always depend upon "some convention or agreement that must be known").

From these basic observations, Olson turns to an examination of the principal elements of drama, beginning with the most important, plot, which he defines as a "system of actions of determinate moral quality" governed by a "unifying principle" of form. Olson sharply distinguishes this conception of plot from others (plot as myth, legend, story, intrigue, conflict, etc.) and plot from the representation (the scenario). "Representation is what represents; plot is what is represented." Nevertheless, plots can differ from one another in terms of magnitude (the range stretches from the action of a single character in a closed situation to the maximal forms of action found in the grand plots of tragedy, comedy, and epic), lines of action (single and multiple), simplicity and complexity, kinds of complication and probability, and unifying principles. With regard to principles of unity, Olson observes, by way of illustration, that plots can be unified by consequential action (_Macbeth_), description (_Our Town_), pattern (Schnitzler's _Reigen_), and thesis (_Ghosts_). What all plots have in common, however, is "some end in view," by reference to which they achieve completeness.

Moving next to incident and character, Olson argues that both are determined by their dramatic function. He identifies four general functions of incidents, two relating to plot, two to representation. An incident of the plot is either essential or factorial (i.e., providing necessary conditions for the occurrence of the essential); incidents of representation, on the other hand, "either make the plot or representation more probable...or they are ornamental purely." If in life character governs action, in drama plot (action) governs character, since the dramatic character must act in a way "useful to the plot." Thus, the functions of character correspond to those of incidents; they are essential, factorial, representational, or ornamental.

In the next chapter, the last on the elements of drama (chapter IV), Olson discusses the subordination of representation and dialogue to plot, noting that the representation determines what the audience is to know at any given time and, hence, what the audience is to feel, and that dialogue determines what is to be said in what order and, hence, what the "quality and power" of the plot is to be. To Olson, language and verse have significance and power to the extent that they put action and character before us "vividly and convincingly." Since the greatness of, say, *Macbeth* survives translation, its excellence cannot be attributed to its language or verse, but to what is translatable, i.e., the "whole dramatic conception which underlies language and verse."

Chapters five and six take up large issues and develop complex distinctions. In five, Olson demonstrates that the principal mechanism in the production of impressions and emotions is inference (the basis of opinions, on which our emotions are, in turn, based) and that the only differences between our reactions to fiction and reality are grounded in the "additional reflection" that the real events are real, "since it constitutes the sole difference between the fictional and the real which can affect thought or belief." Five leads naturally into six, a discussion of the relationship between art and morality. Olson argues that our emotional responses are functions of a system of values and "are regulated by that system," and that no work can have a value beyond the "dignity of its underlying conception." Thus, assuming perfect craftsmanship, we still evaluate works according to the ends to which the craftsmanship is subservient, according to the value of the experience we get from works.

In the last four chapters, the principles established in the preceding six find immediate vindication and exemplification as Olson examines the formal integrity and moral power of works by Aeschylus (_Agamemnon_), Shakespeare (_King Lear_), and Racine (_Phèdre_). The last of the four (and of the book) looks closely at O'Neill's _Mourning Becomes Electra_ and Eliot's _Murder in the Cathedral_ (and at several other works in passing) in an effort to determine whether we are still producing tragedies. From his analyses of these works, Olson is obliged to conclude that we are not now producing tragedies. Nevertheless, that great tragedies still affect us as powerfully as they do attests at once to their enduring value and our unextinguished capacity for tragic pleasure. At the end, Olson informs, as he reminds, us that we are not lacking subjects, but strong conceptions.

7. _Tragedia_. _La teoria del drama_. Trad. Salvador Oliva Llinai. Barcelona: Seix Barral, 1974.

   Spanish translation of _Tragedy and the Theory of Drama_

8. _The Theory of Comedy_. Bloomington: Indiana University Press, 1968.

Books and Collections of Essays

Contents

Based primarily on lectures given at Indiana University in 1965, when Olson was "Visiting Professor for the Patten Foundation," this book develops an Aristotelian theory of comedy from an examination of artistic practice and from an analysis of the principles of the comic. As the chapter headings indicate, Olson moves from large theoretical issues to the exemplification of his formal distinctions in the works of particular playwrights, a procedure that allows him to show, incidentally but deliberately, how forms persist, change, and extend themselves through time in response to the exploitation of the potentialities of the chief parts and conventions of comedy by artists busy at the task of making particular works maximally effective.

In chapter one, after reviewing the inadequacies of the best-known theories of the comic, Olson defines the "laughter-emotion" (our response to the comic) as a "relaxation or katastasis of concern due to a manifest absurdity of the grounds of concern." The comic, thus, is the contrary to the serious, and any act contrary to the serious in any of its circumstances (i.e., the agent, the person attacked, the instrument used, the place, time, result, etc.) is comic. Sharply distinguishing between the ridiculous (a comic act resulting from the character of the agent) and the ludicrous (a comic act depending upon chance or an agent's ignorance of circumstances) and between the witty and humorous (both functions of the quality of the act), Olson examines the nature of each and then suggests that the comic includes all four, since, in spite of their differences, they all contribute to the minimization of the claim of any particular thing to be taken seriously, "either by reducing the claim to absurdity or by reducing it merely to the negligible in such a way as to produce pleasure by that very minimization."

From an analysis of the comic (a quality found in drama and much else besides), Olson moves in chapters two and three to a _poetics_ of comedy (a certain form of drama). Since comedy, like tragedy (and other constructed things as well), is an artificial and composite thing, it has its nature as a result of some _form_ being imposed upon some _matter_ by some _means_ for some _purpose_ and its definition in the specification of the causes of its production. Having discussed each of its causes, Olson presents his definition of the form (modelled on Aristotle's definition of tragedy): "Comedy is the imitation of a worthless action, complete and of a certain magnitude, in language with pleasing accessories differing from part to part, enacted, not narrated, effecting a _katastasis_ of concern through the absurd." By "worthless action," Olson simply means one "which comes to nothing, so that, in hindsight at least, it would seem foolish to be concerned about it." Once he has defined the complete whole, he goes on to treat each of the parts in an effort to discover the dramatic possibilities of each, taking up, in addition to _katastasis_ (the comic equivalent to tragic _katharsis_), plot, character, thought, spectacle, music, and diction.

In his discussion of plot, Olson identifies four basic kinds: plots of folly (the ridiculous) with well- or ill-intentioned fools, and plots of cleverness (the ludicrous) with well- or ill-intentioned wits. From these basic plot forms, all others are generated. Although critics have classified comedies according to various differentia--including comic quality, subject matter, kinds of probability, etc.--Olson argues that distinctions should be based on plot and on what gives the plot its effect, and in his subsequent chapters, in which theoretical issues are discussed in the context of practical analyses of particular works, he concentrates on subsumptive principles of form, i.e., those principles that imply and are implied by the details of the texts. By attending to unifying principles, he determines that Aristophanes does not fail to make consecutive plots; rather, he succeeds in using dramatic action "as an instrument of persuasion." He achieves unity of statement, not unity of action. Plautus and Terence, on the other hand, wrote plays unified by comic action, but "if we may observe a shrinkage in the comic from Aristophanes to the New Comedy ... we may observe a further shrinkage from Plautus to Terence."

In his extensive discussion of the refinements and complications of artistic form achieved by Shakespeare (only five of whose works traditionally labelled as comedies can be properly enrolled under his definition; the rest require separate poetic treatment) and Molière, Olson concludes that although Molière is a pure comedian, capable of handling the wicked, mean, and base as Shakespeare could not, Shakespeare's range is greater, his actions more extensive, his characters richer, and his diction more luxuriant.

Olson concludes the book proper with a discussion of various modern experiments with comic form, especially those of Wilde (who produced "not so much comedy as theatrical badinage"), Shaw (who sought to subvert specific forms, employing "suspension of form" as his chief device), and the Absurdists (who use every device of comedy in the service of a serious effect to produce what can be seen, finally, as an "off-shoot of the mock-heroic").

In the Appendix, presented originally as a paper before the National Council of Teachers of English in 1965, Olson argues that drama is not a form, but a manner or method of representation in a given form and that unless the critic discusses the principal parts of drama "as functioning within a whole," he is not discussing them as parts but merely as topics.

9. Teoria de la comedia. Trad. B. W. Wardropper. La comedia espanola del Siglo de Oro. Barcelona: Ariel, 1978.

Spanish translation of the Theory of Comedy, with an essay on Spanish comedy of the Golden Age by Bruce W. Wardropper based on Olson's theory. Reviewed in Bulletin of the Comediantes, 32 (Spring, 1980), 87-89. See 360.

10. On Value Judgments in the Arts and Other Essays. Chicago and London: The University of Chicago Press, 1976.

Contents

Conveniently assembles in one volume twenty-one of Olson's essays representing more than forty years of thoughtful concern with the principles of critical and philosophic reasoning and with the fundamental issues of the three primary branches of literary inquiry, poetics, hermeneutics, and criticism. With the exception of "Art and Science," all the essays were published separately, the earliest, "Rhetoric and the Appreciation of Pope," appearing in 1939 and the latest, "The Poetic Process," in 1975. Each essay is annotated below, in section D.

B. BOOKS--POETRY

11. Thing of Sorrow. New York: The Macmillan Co., 1934.

Contents

Prologue to His Book
The Tale
Wishes for His Poem
Dirge
Talisman of Words
Inscription for the Tomb of Man
To Man
Essay on Deity
Prelude to Despair
The Ghostly Spring
Madrigal
The Strange Summer
Arabesque
Spring Ghost
Children
Calendar
Ms. Unearthed at Delos
The Changeling
Reply to April
Elegy
Catechism at Midnight
Colloquy
Novel in Pictures

For this, his first book of poetry, Olson won the Friends of Literature award for 1935. Several of the lyrics in this collection had appeared earlier in Poetry: A Magazine of Verse, including "Talisman of Words" and "Essay on Deity," for the latter of which he received the Guarantor's Award.

Of the twenty-three poems in this volume, Olson reprinted thirteen in his Collected Poems.

12. The Cock of Heaven. New York: The Macmillan Co., 1940.

In "A Note on the Poem," Olson observes that The Cock of Heaven, a long poem in nine books (each divided into several sections), takes the form of a "commentary on a text." The text itself, a prose narrative preceding the poem proper, "might be called an epitome of human history; consequently, the commentary has the character of an historical summation" of the condition of sin-soaked man in a world so vile that even God "can but make it worthy to be destroyed." Olson reprints "The Tale" from his first volume of verse in Book IV, section vi, because he "needed such a poem and could see no reason for fashioning another like it."

13. The Scarecrow Christ and Other Poems. New York: Noonday Press, 1954.

Contents

Part I

The Tale
Protagoras
Essay on Deity
Wishes for His Poem
Madrigal
Catechism at Midnight

Part II

Liber de Causis
The Crusade
Anthropos
Gian Maria Concerning Death
Abailard Sleeps at His Book
The Angel of the Annunciation
Cry Before Birth

The Christmas Meditation
The Devil in Crystal
The Atonement
No. 10 Blucher Street
The Night Journey
The Shepherd and the Conqueror

Part III

Last Autumnal
The Rebellion
Ice-Age
Winter Nightfall
The Statue
Horror Story
The Midnight Meditation
On an Adagio by Beethoven
The Mirror Men
Childe Roland, Etc.
Poem
Ballad of the Scarecrow Christ
Plot Improbable, Character Unsympathetic
The Night There Was Dancing in the Streets
Elegy (In mem. Dr. P. F. S.)
Jack-in-the Box
The Son of the Enemy
The Pole
The Four Black Bogmen
Able, Baker, Charlie, Et Al.
Crucifix
First Death, Second Death, and Christ Crucified
The Fountain

In his remarks on this collection , Olson notes that the poems in Part I have been selected from _Thing of Sorrow_ and those in Part II from _The Cock of Heaven_. The poems in the third part represent a selection of Olson's work since 1939; several of them had appeared originally in journals and magazines.

14. _Plays and Poems, 1948-58_. Chicago: The University of Chicago Press, 1958.

Contents

Contains all the plays that Olson had written prior to 1958, eleven poems from _The Scarecrow Christ_, and nineteen new poems, though most of the "new" lyrics had appeared previously in magazines and journals. Full particulars on the plays and poems are given below.

15. Collected Poems. Chicago: The University of Chicago Press, 1963.

Contents

I

Prologue to His Book
The Tale
Wishes for His Poem
Dirge
To Man
Essay on Deity
Madrigal
Arabesque
Spring Ghost
Children
Catechism at Midnight
Colloquy
Novel in Pictures

II

Liber de Causis
Anthropos
Abailard Sleeps at His Book
The Night Journey
The Assumption
The Crusade
G. M. H. Asks the Question in the Fells
The Atonement
Byzantium
Sonnet
Imago Mortis
"Socrates mused a day and night"
Gian Maria concerning Death
Winter Marketplace
Voice Heard from the Third Planet
The Discourse on the Usual Matter
The Christmas Meditation
The Angel of the Annunciation

Late Encounter
The Devil in Crystal
Cry before Birth
The Cock of Heaven
No. 10 Blucher Street
The Wood of Vampires
Prometheus Speaks

III

Last Autumnal
The Rebellion
Ice-Age
Winter Nightfall
The Statue
Horror Story
The Midnight Meditation
On an Adagio by Beethoven
The Mirror Men
Childe Roland, Etc.
Poem
Ballad of the Scarecrow Christ
Plot Improbable, Character Unsympathetic
The Night There Was Dancing in the Streets
Elegy (In mem. Dr. P. F. S.)
Jack-in-the Box
The Son of the Enemy
The Pole
The Four Black Bogmen
Able, Baker, Charlie, Et Al.
Crucifix
First Death, Second Death, and Christ Crucified
The Fountain

IV

The Exegesis
Wild Horse
For a Friend Defeated
The Altar
The Cry
A Farewell
A Nocturnal for His Children
Entertainment for a Traveller
In Defense of Superficiality
The Cocks of Babylon

London Company
The Minstrels Rebuked
Punch and Judy Songs
Preview, Informal
For the Demolition of a Theater
A Valentine for Marianne Moore
Mobile by Calder
The Last Entries in the Journal

V

Ice-Skaters
Mirror
Taxco
The Green Christmas
A Dream for a Sad Lady
The Attack on the Jungle Train
At a Military Ceremony
Old Story New Hero
Chess-Game
Palindrome
Directions to the Armorer
The Side of the Bread
The Impersonation
Plaza Mexico
Conversation between a Mirror and the Sea
Exposition of the Quarrel of the Birds
The Argument about the Decoration of the Punch Table
Exhibition of Modern Art
A Toast
The Graveyard by the Sea
The Voice
Poet to Reader

Contains representative pieces from Olson's first four volumes of verse, as well as new poems, previously uncollected, all but a few of which, however, had appeared in magazines and journals. The poems in Part I are taken from _Thing of Sorrow_; in Part II, from _The Cock of Heaven_; in Part III, from _The Scarecrow Christ_; in Part IV, from _Plays and Poems_. Part V contains the new, previously uncollected pieces. In his "Author's Note," Olson tells us that for Part II he chose to "break up" his single long poem, The Cock of Heaven, into separate lyrics, "salvaging parts which still interested me." Full documentation on the individual poems is presented below. The Collected Poems was also published in a paperback format by the University of Chicago Press in 1963.

16. Olson's Penny Arcade: Poems by Elder Olson. Chicago and London: University of Chicago Press, 1975.

Contents

Prefatory Note

ONE

The Daguerreotype of Chopin
Souvenir of the Play
Munich: New Year's Eve, 1936
Nightfall
The Mad Priest of the Mountain
Directions for Building a House of Cards

TWO

Four Immensely Moral Tales
That We Have Some Delusions of Which it is not Wise to Divest Us
That Everything is a Matter of Circumstance
That Nothing is Evidence to Those to Whom it is not Evident
That if Clothes Make the Man it is Dangerous to Undress

Rabbinical Legend
Knight, with Umbrella
Abdication of the Clown

THREE

The Abstract Tragedy: A Comedy of Masks

FOUR

Olson's Penny Arcade

Re-reading H.M. Tomlinson's _The Sea and the Jungle_
A Restaurant in South-East Asia
Reflections on Mirrors
The Old Man in the Tropical Aviary
City
Puerto Vallarta

All the poems in this collection were written after the publication of _Collected Poems_, except "Munich: New Year's Eve, 1936," which was composed in the year of its title. Most of the poems were published separately in journals and magazines; the play originally appeared in _First Stage_. Although in appearance a "mere sequence," the title poem is a single work, employing, as Olson says, a technique similar to that used in the "Connect-A-Dot games that amuse children; the individual poems are the dots." Of the collection as a whole, Olson says: "if these poems range from jocosity to fury and near-suicidal despair, that is because they reflect the kind of person I happen to be and the world we happen to live in." The volume was also issued in a paperback format in 1975 by the University of Chicago Press.

C. BOOKS EDITED

17. Longinus, On the Sublime and Sir Joshua Reynolds, Discourses on Art. On the Sublime trans. Benedict Einarson. Introd. Elder Olson. Chicago: Packard and Co., 1945.

Contents

Introduction (see 24)

Longinus On the Sublime

Appendix to Longinus

Alexander On the Figures of Thought and of Diction

Excerpts from Dionysius of Halicarnassus

Discourses on Art

18. American Lyric Poems: From Colonial Times to the Present. New York: Appleton-Century-Crofts, 1964.

Includes in this anthology of lyric expression in American poetry the significant achievements of seventy-nine poets, from Bradstreet and Taylor to Robert Lowell and Richard Wilbur. For an account of Olson's introduction to this volume, see 42 below.

19. Aristotle's Poetics and English Literature: A Collection of Critical Essays. Chicago and London: The University of Chicago Press, 1965

Contents

Introduction (See 44)

I. James Harris: A Discourse on Music, Painting, and Poetry (1744)
II. Henry James Pye: From *A Commentary on the Poetic of Aristotle:* Notes to Chapter XV (1792)
III. Thomas Twining: On Poetry Considered as an Imitative Art (1789)
IV. Thomas Taylor: From the Introduction to his translations of the *Rhetoric*, *Poetic*, and *Nicomachean Ethics* (1811); Note on Catharsis (1811)
V. John Henry Cardinal Newman: Poetry, with Reference to Aristotle's *Poetics* (1829)
VI. Sir Arthur Quiller-Couch: A Note on the *Poetics* (1934)
VII. John Gassner: Catharsis and the Modern Theater (1937, 1946).
VIII. Maxwell Anderson: The Essence of Tragedy (1938)
IX. Kenneth Burke: The Problem of the Intrinsic (1945)
X. Francis Fergusson: On Certain Technical Concepts (1949)
XI. Reuben A. Brower: The Heresy of Plot (1952)
XII. Elder Olson: The Poetic Method of Aristotle: Its Powers and Limitations (1952) (See 30)
XIII. Bernard Weinberg: From Aristotle to Pseudo-Aristotle (1953)
XIV. Richard McKeon: Rhetoric and Poetic in the Philosophy of Aristotle (1965)

Assembles in this collection of fourteen essays works which are Aristotelian in the sense of displaying an interest in "concepts and problems of an Aristotelian order." Thus, the book is not a storehouse of references to Aristotle or an anthology of arguments incidently concerned with "Aristotelian" doctrine; rather, it focusses on essays exhibiting "some philosophical affinity with the *Poetics*."

Books Edited

20. Major Voices: 20 British and American Poets. New York: McGraw-Hill Book Company, 1973.

Contains a generous selection of poems by each of twenty distinguished poets, from Shakespeare, Donne, and Milton in the seventeenth century to Stevens and Eliot in the twentieth, as well as representative pieces from the works of thirty-two additional poets. Aimed chiefly at undergraduate students in introductory courses, the anthology gives emphasis to works written during the last four centuries which have stood the test of time or which (as with those of the modern period) stand in the front rank as probationers to lasting fame. It should be noted that between the text as it appears and the text as it was originally designed and prepared by Olson the resemblance is slight. The list of negative correspondences between the two texts is very copious. For an account of Olson's introduction to and his dissatisfaction with this text, see 52 below.

D. ESSAYS, INTRODUCTIONS, AND REVIEW ARTICLES

21. "Rhetoric and the Appreciation of Pope," MP, 37 (August, 1939), 13-35. Reprinted in 10.

Takes issue with the critical method employed by Tillotson and Root to reinstate Pope in the Pantheon of great poets and presents an example of an alternative method that could contribute to a secure respect for Pope's poetic genius. After summarizing their arguments, Olson demonstrates that both critics rely on an analogical method of reasoning that finds the predicates of strictly literary or critical terms in the character of the poet and that both consider Pope's poems as a whole, not as unique structures, locating in the poems some quality illustrative of his poetry in general and identifying each quality isolated with traits of the poet and man. Argumentation is founded on reciprocal relationship: a historical "guarantee of Pope's moral excellence affords a guarantee of excellence in the poem," and excellences in the poem argue for the moral excellence of the poet. As an alternative to extinsic approaches, Olson proposes an appreciation of the poetry based, not on any general values or qualities reflected in the poems, but on the "unique literary structures in which the poetry is constituted."

Taking the Epistle to Arbuthnot as an example of a common tendency in Pope to order his materials according to rhetorical rather than poetical principles, Olson shows how Pope excels in the three modes of persuasion possible to the spoken word and uses all the available means to his particular rhetorical purpose, i.e., to answer the accusations of his enemies in a manner appropriate to a man of good sense, good moral character, and good will. Olson also notes that Pope sharpens the satire as he gains increasing control over the reader. By approaching the poem in terms of its rhetorical end, Olson is able to account for all the particulars of the poem. Although his analysis is not offered as a "final explanation of the poem," it does exemplify a critical method that, by examining the poem as a structure governed by the aim to induce belief, allows us to comprehend why Pope "must be reckoned among the few first figures of English literature."

22. "The Argument of Longinus' <u>On the Sublime</u>." <u>MP</u>, 39 (February, 1942), 225-58. Reprinted in 2 and 10.

Argues that the lasting value of <u>Peri Hypsous</u> is attributable, not to its extraordinary insights, its enthusiasm, or its originality, as editors and commentators usually claim, but to its logical scheme or "reasoned structure." The work is a coherent critical document the power and authority of which derive from the deliberate working out of specific problems within a discrete critical framework. Working with a text that is fragmentary and incomplete, Olson--by attending to the questions that Longinus poses, the principles and assumptions guiding the discussion, and the end in view--is able to reconstruct the whole argument of the treatise, and the legitimacy and validity of the reconstruction are assured not only by the consonance between what Olson supplies and what is under discussion when the text breaks and begins again, but also by the logical and semantic demands of the intellectual framework itself.

In his analysis, Olson shows that since the work is a practical treatise the order of inquiry is from the effect to be produced to the means by which the author achieves it. Moreover, the sublime results from the faculties of the author, inasmuch as in order to realize it, the author must 1) conceive it, 2) determine whether the subject is excitative of passion, and 3) express it. Thus, the sources of the sublime effect are noble conception, strong passion, and the proper handling of figures of thought and language, diction, and harmony and rhythm. The basic problem with which Longinus began (the determination of the means necessary to the achievement of a certain quality of art) is resolved when he has demonstrated that the five sources identified complete the list of possible causes of the sublime and are conducive to the end aimed at.

Olson discusses the logical entailments of Longinus' assumptions and vocabulary in great detail and skilfully elucidates his method in operation, giving substantial attention to educing Longinus' conception of the passions from the scattered remarks in the extant treatise.

23. "'Sailing to Byzantium': Prolegomena to a Poetics of the Lyric." University [of Kansas City] Review, 8 (1942), 209-19. Reprinted in 10. Also reprinted in the following (and perhaps elsewhere): The Permanence of Yeats. Ed.J. Hall and M. Steinmann. New York: Macmillan, 1950, 286-300.; Reading Modern Poetry. Ed. Paul Engle and Warren Carrier. Chicago: Scott, Foresman and Co., 1955.; Five Approaches to Literary Criticism. Ed. Wilbur S. Scott. New York: Macmillan, 1962, 215-30.; Approaches to the Poem: Modern Essays in the Analysis and Interpretation of Poetry. Ed. John Oliver Perry. San Francisco: Chandler Publishing Co., 1965, 181-95.;

Master Poems of the English Language. Ed. Oscar Williams. New York: Trident Press, 1966, 833-38.

Through a detailed formal analysis of "Sailing to Byzantium," Olson proposes to show how a poetics of the lyric may eventually be framed. Olson's task is twofold: to show that his critical method can efficaciously determine poetic principles and then to define the kind of lyric realized by Yeats's poem. Olson argues that while an individual work is a unique composite of form and matter, the principles underlying its unity are poetic principles and, as such, determinants of kinds of poetic structure. Since the focus is on the parts of the work and the interrelations among them, the method seeks to discover "some principle in the work which is the principle of its unity and order" (an intrinsic principle, not an extrinsic one based on a system of differentiation emphasizing authors, audiences, subject matters, diction, etc.). Moreover, since to Olson the parts are functional relative to some end, "a mark of the discovery of the formal principle would be that everything else in the poem would be...explicable in terms of it."

Turning from the method to "Sailing to Byzantium," Olson demonstrates that it is a work in which a certain problem--finding "suitable compensation for the losses suffered in old age"--orders the whole, and in which argument, as that for the sake of which everything else is present, is, thus, the principle of the work. From this principle, he accounts for all the particular choices made by Yeats (including his ordering of events as "dialectically separable stages in the treatment of a problem" and his selection of diction) and, as a consequence, concludes that there "exists a kind of poem that has argument as its principle."

The reader should compare this essay with Olson's later comments on the poem in the penultimate section of "An Outline of Poetic Theory," in which what is called argument here is discussed in terms of an act "actualizing and instancing moral character." Olson alters his reading slightly, but, in the end, the two essays, founded on the same intellectual framework and method, are compatible.

24. "Longinus and Reynolds." Introduction to <u>Longinus, On the Sublime and Sir Joshua Reynolds, Discourses on Art</u>. Chicago: Packard and Co., 1945. See 17.

Argues that the general tendency among critics to emphasize doctrinal similarities in the works of different writers regularly obscures real differences in the questions, assumptions, and principles of reasoning underlying the critical documents. Longinus and Reynolds are two critics who have frequently been linked in critical histories on the basis of their ostensible doctrinal compatibility, Reynolds being cited often as one of the chief instances of Longinus' influence on eighteenth-century aesthetic thought. Olson brings the two together so that their real differences--which are "essential and fundamental" --not their similarities--which are "incidental and superficial"--may be considered.

After quickly reviewing the doctrinal commitments that they apparently share, Olson proceeds to outline the arguments of the critics, then to examine the principles and assumptions informing them with determinate meaning, and finally to identify their basic differences, the whole effort culminating in the recognition that the two critics address different problems (Longinus being concerned with the causes determining an effect found in many kinds of writing, and Reynolds with the education of the painter), work from different assumptions about art, genius, etc., and pursue different methods of argument (Longinus views the "products of several arts in terms of a single effect"; Reynolds views "all the effects of a single art"). Finally, when the writings of these critics are seen as the consequential products of fundamentally different critical frameworks, it becomes clear that they even mean different things by sublimity: "for one defines it ultimately in terms of human faculties [Longinus], the other in terms of abstract realty," i.e., external reality as constituted by the imagination in response to experience with the diversity of the natural world and by the representations of that world by other artists.

25. "Contemporary Poetry: Critique." Chicago Review, 2 (Spring, 1948), 156-59.

Finds that the complaints of readers against the avoidance of emotion in and the unintelligibility of contemporary poetry have more than a little justification and can be attributed to the tendency of poets to dehumanize poetry either by leaving men and women out of it altogether (giving us instead "objective" depictions of commonplace objects) or by failing to depict them in interesting and intelligible situations. When life is excluded from poetry, human passions are no longer evoked by it, and attention shifts to the medium and to technical devices.

When some twenty-five years ago poets such as Eliot and Pound supplemented the English with the French tradition and left more and more to inference, many young poets saw the "new" poetry, not as an alteration of conventions, but as a revolt against principles and form. Moreover, the critics cooperated with the misunderstanding and added to the confusion by treating poetry as "language" or "discourse" or as a branch of psychology, anthropology, sociology, history, etc., thus failing to supply the poet with propositions that were of use to him in the making of his poems.

To Olson, poetry is not words or subject matters; rather, it uses words as speech, and speech is either human action or a sign of character, thought, and passion. At any rate, humanity is "common to, and principal in, all the arts of poetry," and in order to build upon and extend what has been accomplished, it is essential that poets "set clearly and vividly before us men and women in interesting situations, speaking as they would in such circumstances." As far as the "reflection of our age" and any further ends of poetry are concerned (e.g., the influence of poetry on human action, individual, social, or political), they will be best achieved when the artist "has realized his artistic end." Because art enables us "to conceive vividly" and "apart from self-interest," it is "potent to avert" the causes of the misdirection of human action.

26. "Is Theory Possible?" _Poetry: A Magazine of Verse_, 71 (February, 1948), 257-59.

Establishes, in this brief and sympathetic response to Karl Shapiro's case against criticism ("A Farewell to Criticism," printed in a previous issue of _Poetry_), the ground rules for the conduct of critical inquiry and the development of theories of art commensurate with artistic practice. To Olson, the problems of the critic must be precisely those with which the poet deals in the making of his poems and which he resolves in the process of artistic construction. From this conception of the task, it follows that the method of poetic theory must be inductive and _a posteriori_. Moreover, its method must not be derived from other branches of inquiry. Although Shapiro's argument identifies real deficiencies in criticism as it is currently practiced, it finally points "rather to a task as yet unachieved than to one impossible."

27. "A Symbolic Reading of the Ancient Mariner." MP, 45 (May, 1948), 275-283. Reprinted in 2.

Argues that Robert Penn Warren's reading of Coleridge's poem is valuable, not as a commentary on the work, but as a practical illustration of the shortcomings of a particular critical method that proceeds by analogical reasoning. Assuming that the Ancient Mariner has symbolic meaning, Warren rejects the interpretations of Griggs and Lowes, because they fail to recognize that for Coleridge symbol combines idea and feeling and implies a complex body of ideas. According to Warren, the poem has two themes: 1) that of the "sacramental vision" (in killing the bird, the Mariner commits murder, which symbolizes the Fall) and 2) that of imagination (driven from the comfortable world by the wind, which symbolizes the creative urge and which, along with the moon and the bird, is associated with the imagination, the Mariner commits a crime against the imagination).

Turning from a review of Warren's reading to significant passages in the Biographia Literaria and the Literary Remains, Olson argues that Griggs and Lowes were correct in claiming that the poem is designed to afford pleasure rather than truth. Moreover, in making his case, Warren has neglected Coleridge's distinction between poem and poetry and his insistence on the cognitive nature of the image only in poetry. Warren transforms the poem into a species of what Coleridge would call allegory, "the employment of one set of agents and images to convey in disguise a moral meaning." In brief, Olson can find no warrant in Coleridge's criticism for Warren's sense of symbol. When we look closely at Warren's equations (for example, moon and imagination, sun and understanding) and his argumentative manipulations of them, we discover that interpretation is really a form of "uncontrolled analogy." Warren's approach--based on double themes, their fusions, and multivalent symbols--permits "anyone to make of the poem whatever he may choose."

28. "An Outline of Poetic Theory." In _Critiques and Essays in Criticism, 1920-1948_. Ed. Robert Wooster Stallman. New York: Ronald Press, 1949, pp. 264-88. Reprinted in 2, 3, and 10.

One of Olson's most important theoretical statements, this essay examines the bases of philosophic discussion, distinguishes the grounds of difference in theories of art, explores the functional value of the Aristotelian method as it applies to the general problems of art and to the definition of species that have emerged since Aristotle wrote, and concludes with a formal analysis of "Sailing to Byzantium" as a kind of lyric.

In opposition to the dogmatist, the syncretist, and the sceptic, Olson argues for a fourth position, pluralism, which, taking "both doctrine and method into account" allows the possibility of a "plurality of formulations of truth and of philosophic procedures." In criticism, as in philosophy, what can be said is determined by the subject-matter--those aspects of a subject implicated in one's formulation of it--and the kinds of dialectic--system of reasoning or inference--exerted on that subject matter. He then considers the diverse ways in which the subject matter of art has been construed (e.g., art as product, art as certain faculties of the artist, etc.), noting that, since there can only be contradiction within the same system of reference, these various approaches are different, not contradictory, and examines the two basic systems of reasoning, the integral (based on likenesses) and the differential (based on differences), bringing this whole section to conclusion with an examination of two comprehensive systems, the Platonic (integral) and the Aristotelian (differential).

Having established the bases of critical variance, Olson goes on to show why the Aristotelian method (one which views the product of art as a "differentiable synthesis of differentiable parts having the capacity to produce certain peculiar emotional effects" and which takes the composite whole produced by art as its starting point and then reasons back to the parts necessary to its realization) is peculiarly suited to the definition of forms.

In the final section of the essay, Olson brings the method to bear on Yeats' poem, but only after first discriminating among four kinds of action considered apart from their effects or moral quality (from the action of a single character in a closed situation to the maximal forms of action found in the grand plots of tragedy, comedy, and epic). To Olson, the poem is a species of lyric which imitates a serious action of the first order (i.e., a single character in a closed situation) and produces an effect of "noble joy or exultation." The speaker of the poem performs an act of choice "actualizing and instancing his moral character."

In his definition of the form of "Sailing to Byzantium," Olson exhibits at once his own analytic skill and the durable value and utility of the differential approach to criticism, which is but one approach among many, but one which, with its assumption that the poetic arts have "as their ends certain pleasures produced through the play on our emotions," is crucial to our understanding of the further ends and effects of poetry.

29. "William Empson, Contemporary Criticism, and Poetic Diction." MP, 47 (May, 1950), 222-52. Reprinted in 2, 3, and 10.

In this important and influential essay, Olson looks first at the shortcomings of Empson's criticism, then at his theoretical affinity with the practitioners of the two chief branches of contemporary criticism, and finally at some of the complex ways in which diction, as diction, may function in mimetic works.

To Empson, poetry "is simply an aspect or condition of language" and may, thus, be defined in terms of its medium, and "ambiguity" is the distinctive feature of poetic language. His method, then, is one of working out the "permutations and combinations of all the various meanings of the parts of a given discourse," with the OED serving as the major, if silent, partner in the enterprise of discovery. But once he admits that the range of meaning is constrained and justified by the peculiar "requirements of the situation," as he does, he inadvertently undermines his theoretical position by subordinating ambiguity to something else (ambiguity cannot be a principle of poetry if its propriety is determined by a "valuable situation"). In the end, by failing to distinguish between speech as meaning (lexis) and speech as action (praxis; speech as determinative of inferences), Empson can concentrate only on a single attribute of diction, one "neither peculiar to poetry nor universal" to all forms.

The weaknesses in Empson's approach have their allies and counterparts in the two major forms of contemporary criticism, both of which seek to differentiate poetry from other forms of discourse, either by insisting that poetry conveys unique truths by means of a special language or special use of language (the "New Critics") or by treating poetry as a special reflection of a more general subject matter (the myth, archetypal, psychoanalytic critics). Since, for Olson, poetic theory is a form of explanation that must account for all the causes combining to make a thing what it is, these modern theories are inadequate because they are based on one or another single cause (i.e., either style or subject matter) and because they fail to satisfy the condition of "reciprocal implication" required of all hypotheses (the facts must imply the hypothesis, and the hypothesis must imply the facts). Moreover, such qualitative approaches (emphasizing this or that quality) tend to obscure or neglect the variousness of artistic production and fail to provide any information relevant to the construction or judgment of "a poem of a given kind."

In the final section of the essay, Olson first distinguishes broadly between the ends of mimetic and didactic poetry and then examines how language serves the ends of mimetic form, emphasizing that while words are governed by everything else they are chiefly responsible for disclosing the poem to us. Olson concludes by considering the ways in which vagueness, obscurity, ambiguity, and so on (as evoked by images, metaphors, syntax, and sentence relations) contribute to the effectiveness of poems.

30. "The Poetic Method of Aristotle: Its Powers and Limitations." In _English Institute Essays, 1951_. Ed. Alan S. Downer. New York: Columbia University Press, 1952, pp. 70-94. Reprinted in 10 and 19. Also reprinted in _Twentieth- Century Criticism:_

The Major Statements. Ed. William J. Handy and Max Westbrook. New York: The Free Press (Macmillan), 1974, pp. 134-45.

Demonstrates that as a philosopher Aristotle was interested in scientific knowledge (i.e., knowledge of causes "as appropriate to or commensurate with the inherence of attributes in a subject," necessarily, not accidentally), and that he divided the sciences into three branches: 1) the theoretical (e.g., math and physics), which have knowledge as their end and are concerned with necessary propositions; 2) the practical (e.g., ethics and politics), in which knowledge is subordinate to action; and 3) the productive (the arts, practical or fine), which have as their end neither knowledge nor action, but a product to be produced. The Poetics, then, is a treatise of productive science, concerned with the reasoning involved in poetic making.

With these distinctions established, Olson then outlines Aristotle's methodological procedure, which involves inductive reasoning toward the principle informing the whole to be constructed (the first five chapters lead to the definition of tragedy in chapter six) and deductive reasoning from the principle (chapters six through twenty-two resolve tragedy into its proper parts: plot, character, thought, diction, melody and spectacle). In his subsequent exposition of the detailed working out of the method in the Poetics, Olson shows how it provides a full causal account of the nature and structure of concrete wholes.

That Aristotle was, from our perspective, familiar with very few forms cannot be considered a significant limitation of his treatise, since the method it employs, when it is properly understood, can be applied successfully to later, emergent forms. The real limitations of the Poetics are the ineluctable consequences of its powers; like any method, it can deal with some things and not others. The *Poetics* cannot deal with all questions relevant to poetic art--questions, for example, peculiar to individual works, questions relating to the artistic process, to the psychology of audiences, to the social and political functions of art--but only with those questions relevant to the synthesis of concrete wholes. (Aristotle can deal with such other questions, of course, but not under *poetic* science.) Concerned with the nature of the "forms at which the artist must aim and the causes of success and failure," Aristotle has nevertheless developed "not only a permanently true but also an indefinitely operable poetic method."

31. "A Dialogue on Symbolism." In *Critics and Criticism: Ancient and Modern*. Ed. with an Introduction by R.S. Crane. Chicago: The University of Chicago Press, 1952, pp. 567-94. Reprinted in 10.

In this delightfully witty, but thoroughly serious essay, Olson uses the Platonic dialogue to bring the reader by successive stages to progressively more complex states of awareness. At the outset, Socrates-Olson has great good fun with the ostensibly sensible but demonstrably naive suggestions of his alternately temerious and timid questioner (*homme moyen rationale*-Olson), quickly dispatching with his confused notions of how to represent one thing by another by dividing the cases into samples, examples, copies, imitations, and so on, and by asserting that the key issue in symbolism is not likeness, convention, or association.

As the colloquy develops, *homme de paille*-Olson learns that in symbolism one idea or concept is represented through the medium of another, and that symbolism has to do, not with things, as in metaphor and simile (where a ground of resemblance--merely verbal--is established between two things, our concepts of which remain distinct), but with a mode of conception (the symbol can stand directly for the symbolized because the concepts of the two are identified). Moreover, the symbol, unlike the metaphor or simile, which has its basis in resemblance only, can be based on a variety of relations to the symbolized, for example, shape, agency, instrumentality, purpose, or even accident (by an accident of history, the Liberty Bell can symbolize democracy).

In the final section of the dialogue, after elucidating the means by which symbols can be developed and perfected, Socrates-Olson discusses symbolic poetry. Here he examines how didactic and mimetic poems are made symbolic and notes that while any differentiable part of a complete whole can be symbolic, the true symbolic poet makes the principal part symbolic (i.e., action in mimetic works, argument in didactic). The dialogue is concluded when Socrates distinguishes symbolic poetry from allegory and myth and reminds his interlocutor, in true pluralistic fashion, that there are "many approaches to the temple of truth where the light of Reality shines."

32. "Criticism." Encyclopedia Britannica. Chicago: Encyclopedia Britannica, 1952 (and later editions).

Presents a brief history of criticism from the comprehensive approaches of Plato and Aristotle to the diversity of partial views in the twentieth century. Appended to the essay is a brief list of surveys, histories, and bibliographies of criticism.

After distinguishing the method of Plato from that of Aristotle and delineating how each critic used the term "imitation," Olson observes that in the Alexandrian age (300-146 B.C.) poetics and rhetoric, having split away from philosophy, were treated either as autonomous studies or as branches of grammar, and that with the disappearance of Aristotle's texts in 287 B.C., the distinction between mimetic and didactic poetry was lost. Concomitant with the shift of learning from Alexandria to Rome, following the conquest of Greece in 146 B.C., rhetoric became the master science, to which other branches of inquiry were subordinated.

Olson quickly reviews the achievements of such writers as Cicero, Quintilian, Demetrius, and "Longinus," and then indicates how through the efforts of the early Church poetry became primarily didactic allegory and how discussion came to center on tropes and figures (as in the works of such writers as Macrobius, Servius, Matthew of Vendome, Geoffrey de Vinsauf, John of Garland, and even Dante). With the recovery of works by Cicero and Quintilian, the translation of the Poetics by Valla (1498), and the emergence of new forms (e.g., chivalric romance, novella, etc.), new ranges of method opened up, the various productions of Vida, Scaliger, Castelvetro, et al. coming to culmination in a neoclassicism based on Roman rhetoricians, Horace, and Aristotle (as interpreted by Italians in the sixteenth century and by Dutch and Germans in the seventeenth) and codified in such works as Boileau's Art Poetique. These works eventually provoked the attacks against fixed species and "rules" by, for example, Hume, Johnson, and Schiller.

With technical criticism discredited, emphasis shifted to such qualitative matters as taste, genius, and imagination and away from kinds. Criticism became more general in the nineteenth century (Saint-Beuve, Arnold) and "eventuated" in impressionism (A. France) or intuitionism (Croce). Olson quickly glances at developments in the twentieth century, highlighting the search for new bases of art in psychology, anthropology, semantics, and political theory and the consequent preoccupation with the medium or subject matter of poetry. In conclusion, Olson notes that, even though criticism exhibits an absence of steady progress, each age generally solved the problems it posed, and that the hindrances to critical progress are not attributable to the inexactness of the subject matter of the arts, but to the human tendencies to frame or reject theories prematurely.

33. "Verse." Encyclopedia Britannica. Chicago: Encyclopedia Britannica, 1952 (and later editions).

Presents an extremely useful introduction to verse and the principles of prosody, which begins with a discussion of the hierarchical structure of metrical language (explaining how a group of syllables, completely expressing a rhythmical relation, the foot, enters into combinations to form a unit completely expressing a given metrical line, and so on through stanza and complete verse forms), continues with a brief history of prosodic theory and poetic practice, and concludes with a succinct but detailed analysis of the nature and components of rhythm. A short bibliography of works on prosody, on the transition to modern poetry, and on Classical, Teutonic, English, French, Italian, and Spanish verse is appended to the essay.

The longest and perhaps most important section is that on rhythm, defined simply "as a numerical proportion, perceptible to sense, occurring in different intervals of time." Olson notes that rhythms can be distinguished in terms of form and matter, form being the numerical proportion constituting the rhythmic ratio and matter the sounds or movements belonging to that ratio. Olson then goes on to consider the formal and material differences in rhythmic units, emphasizing how the same rhythms, the equal or proportional intervals, can appear in different rhythmical figurations as a consequence of the principle that in rhythmic, "as in other proportions," equals are substituted for equals. After further distinguishing rhythm based on sound or movement from that based on multitude only (e.g., number of alliterated or accented syllables; demarcative rhythm), Olson ends the essay with some brief remarks on tempo and scansion.

34. "Education and the Humanities." <u>Pedagogia</u>, 1 (1953), 85-95.

Addresses two major questions--can art be a field of scientific inquiry and, if scientific knowledge of art is possible, how can we account for the failure of theory in art, unlike theory in science, to develop additively--the answers to which lead to the specification of the desiderata of an aesthetic curriculum.

After examining the sciences and the humanities as departments of knowledge, to the clear disadvantage of the humanities, Olson argues that, since propositions relevant to essential aspects of two or more works can be made (we are not restricted to particulars), and since every art employs a medium with distinguishable powers and limitations, knowledge in the arts is possible, and necessary propositions can be obtained by reasoning from a whole to be produced in a particular art to the nature, number, and arrangement of the parts necessary to its realization; i.e., if such and such a form is to be produced, then such and such parts will have to be put together in such and such a fashion in cooperation with the powers of the medium.

That theory in art has not progressed proportionately to theory in science can be attributed to many causes (for example, the evolution of art forms and the consequent failure of theory to expand with its subject), but especially to the tendency to interpret the diversity of critical assumptions and methods as signs of theoretical contradiction and the unwillingness to recognize the possibility of many valid philosophies, each capable of dealing with only so much of its subject as falls within the logical and semantic range of the terms by which its problems are formulated. Genuine knowledge appropriate to the arts is certainly possible, but Olson concludes that "humanistic studies will regain their ancient prestige as the body of studies primarily responsible for what we call culture in man" only when students are "equally skilled in the perception of art and in the theoretic disciplines," only when "logic, dialectic, and the study of philosophic and scientific method" are integrated with the study of the arts themselves.

35. "The Poetry of Dylan Thomas." *Poetry: A Magazine of Verse*, 83 (January, 1954), 213-20. Reprinted in 10. Also reprinted in *Dylan Thomas, The Legend and the Poet: A Collection of Biographical and Critical Essays*. Ed. E. W. Tedlock. London: Heineman, 1960, pp. 229-35.

Written when Thomas was still alive, this essay identifies and discusses the distinctive characteristics of Thomas's poetry. (The reader should note that this essay, like Olson's book on Thomas, is "Longinian," concerned, that is, with problems of a Longinian order.)

To Olson, Thomas is a poet of the "most exalted states of mind," and he causes the reader trouble because his powerful conceptions are mediated through complex symbols and through a language that is at times ambiguous and that often obscures who is saying what to whom under what circumstances. Nevertheless, when the conception underlying and informing his poetry is sufficiently grand, the manner of presentation and the unusual linguistic devices have their justification in their necessity and appropriateness. Moreover, since the poet always appears as a single character and always relies on the same devices, his works succeed or fail in direct proportion to the value of the energy and feeling with which what he addresses is conceived. When Thomas's conception is at its height, "something like sublimity results," but when his conception is merely odd or fanciful or when his devices obscure or distort it, he is trivial. In Thomas's best poems, the reader recognizes and is himself exalted by conceptions possible "only to a man of great imagination and feeling," whereas when the lofty conception is lacking, "energy becomes violence or plain noisiness; ecstasy, hysteria; high style, obscure bombast; tragic passion, morbid melodrama." To facilitate the reading of Thomas's poetry, Olson provides the reader with a series of illustrations of the linguistic devices found in the poems.

Taking stock of Thomas's realized achievements and looking ahead to the future, Olson, in remarks that Thomas's premature death make poignant, says: "It is difficult to say how he may develop; we must be grateful for the genius already manifest, and for the rest, have faith in the poet, a faith by no means without firm foundation."

36. "Louise Bogan and Léonie Adams." Chicago Review, 8 (Fall, 1954), 70-77. Reprinted in 10.

Occasioned by the publication in 1954 of Bogan's Collected Poems: 1923-53 and Adams's Poems: A Selection, this essay displays not only acute insight into the principal features of the poetry of the two poets, but the affection that the craftsman feels for others who are similarly engaged in the process of enlisting words into the service of forms of genuine significance and power.

According to Olson, in terms of subject, lyric character, style, imagery, and diction, the two poets are virtually the opposites of one another. Bogan is "a poet of violent emotions; she depicts with severe economy...and by implication; her images are objective, and her language is plain and natural." Adams, on the other hand, is a poet of the "calm and gentle emotions"; her poetry is private, in that her poetic character is moved "not so much by what happens as by what her subtle and exquisite mind makes of it"; she depicts "not with economy and implication, but by aggregation and suggestion"; her imagery is "seldom objective," and her language and thought exhibit "deliberate archaism." Moreover, whereas in Bogan's poetry the effect depends upon our considering the poetic character "as distinct from ourselves," in Adams's identification with the character is demanded. As he makes his qualitative distinctions between the works of the two writers, Olson also manages, in the process, to discriminate among terms that are often used interchangeably by critics (image, description, metaphor, and symbol) and to differentiate the function of ideas in science or philosophy (valuable relative to their adequacy or truth) from their function in poetry (valuable relative to their effect on imagination or emotion).

Although not generally considered to be startling innovators, Bogan and Adams have made significant advances in versification. By highlighting the larger aspects of their poetry, Olson hopes to demonstrate that their achievement is greater and richer than the anthologies suggest.

37. "The Poetry of Wallace Stevens." *College English*, 16 (April, 1955), 395-402. Also in *English Journal*, 44 (April, 1955), 191-98. Reprinted in 10.

Counters the tendency among critics to consider Stevens as a poet of ideas and his poems as forms of philosophic statement with the view that he is quintessentially a poet of images. Looked at philosophically, Stevens's poetry betrays a preoccupation with relatively few ideas relating to some of the "most hackneyed" epistemological and metaphysical problems, and if his doctrines are familiar, his arguments, as arguments, are unconvincing. Also, the ideas in his poetry are not logically or philosophically presented; they are presented through images that achieve their emotional power through psychological relation. For Stevens, the image does not exist for the sake of the idea; rather, the idea exists for the sake of the image.

To illustrate his conception of Stevens's poetry, Olson looks closely at several poems (especially "Life is Motion," "The Emperor of Ice-Cream," and "Sunday Morning"), noting that they emphasize image and insight and that they depict characters who function, not as characters proper would in poems involving, say, an interesting or "exciting external situation" or a "drama of moral choice," but as "objects of someone's thought," probably Stevens's. Although that "someone" takes on or assumes various persons, he is, at bottom, a constant character, the aloof spectator of what is going on, even of his own emotions. "Sunday Morning," for example, is not about what a woman thinks, "but about what someone thinks and feels about what she thinks." In Stevens's poetry, we have, finally, not philosophic poetry, but a kind of "dialectic of the imagination playing on the diverse relations of ideas, images, and emotions." What moves Stevens more than anything else is the breakdown of belief in our time, his response to which is his conception of poetry as the supreme fiction and "of the imagination as the architect of that fiction." His creation of imaginary objects of emotion is designed "to replace the older objects no longer capable of sustaining belief." If he is not a profound philosopher, he is, nevertheless, a very good poet, and "he should be read, for he has one of the most exquisitely fastidious minds of our age."

38. "The Poetry of Marianne Moore." _Chicago Review_, 11 (Spring, 1957), 100-04. Reprinted in 10.

Defines in a few pages the characteristic subtlety and power of Marianne Moore's art. Distinguishing her work from that of other contemporary poets, Olson, while acknowledging its modernity, places it in a tradition that begins with the _Satires_ and _Epistles_ of Horace, one that presents sensation (undistorted by emotion or imagination) by means of objective and accurate images and a diction "so close to ordinary discourse that its artifices can hardly be detected." It is the poetry of "personal discussion" dealing with "ordinary matters and normal mental conditions." Although her poems are all of a "certain kind," they are marvelously various within that kind, the similarity being achieved by the persistence of the speaker (honest, just, urbane, witty, prudent) and the variety by the abundance of objects upon which she deliberates.

To illustrate her capacity to deal with "the hardest of all things to imagine, the fact perfectly known (or apparently so)," Olson quotes substantial passages from several poems. She gives us access, it seems, to what our immediate consent tells us we always knew but what we could never have claimed as ours without the intercession of her mind. The structure of her poems depends, not upon deductive logic, but upon a series of insights gathering to a final, compelling insight. "Marianne Moore is a difficult poet, but not an obscure one; on the contrary, she is extremely clear, and our difficulty comes from her insistence that we think and think well at every point in her poems."

This essay, both personal and toughminded, allows Olson at once to demonstrate how qualitative criticism can illuminate characteristic excellence and to suggest what gives him "particular joy in her work. In the words of another and quite different poet, it is 'the fine delight that fathers thought.'"

39. "A Letter on Teaching Drama." <u>Chicago Review</u>, 11 (Summer, 1957), 80-91. Reprinted in 10.

Cast in the form of a letter to "Fred," a device enabling Olson to be precise in a familiar style, this essay moves from a consideration of what students need to know about drama and dramatic action prior to reading texts to a consideration of what they need to do to develop and test the conjectures and judgments they make while reading.

He begins by reminding his "correspondent" that a play is a work which is "acted out" and that, consequently, dramatic action achieves its most "appropriate and powerful effects through external signs, through vivid impressions and sensations." After a few words on the pace of drama, Olson examines the principal part of the drama of "consequential action," the plot, first by distinguishing plot from the sorts of things with which it is often confused (i.e., argument, myth, legend, etc.) and then by proposing that it can be defined as a "morally determinate system of actions." Plot is 1) unified, in that all the parts are integrated into one system of relations; 2) complete, in that the "consequences of the initiating action have been exhausted"; and 3) morally determinate, in that a specific moral response in the audience is determined by the moral character of the agents of the drama. The discussion of plot is completed when Olson notes that plots vary in terms of magnitude, lines of action (single or multiple), types of incidents, and emotional effect.

He then enjoins his "correspondent" to have his students sketch out the "causal connections, as necessary or probable, of the basic incidents" and reason backwards from the "prime" incident to the conditions necessary to its accomplishment, thus inviting them to engage in a form of "invention after the fact" that leads to an immediate understanding of the artistic necessities of the realized work.

Finally, students are encouraged to consider such matters as the scale of representation, the degree and kind of emotion produced, the kinds of characters represented, the functions of speeches as signs of character and thought, and the ways in which figures of speech and forms of utterance direct inferences and responses. From first to last, students are invited to discover how dramatists have solved dramatic problems and how critical judgments are established and tested.

40. "The Nature of the Poet." In _A Casebook on Dylan Thomas_. Ed. John Malcolm Brinnin. New York: Thomas Y. Crowell, Co., 1960, pp. 72-79. Excerpted from 4.

A reprint of the entire second chapter of _The Poetry of Dylan Thomas_, this essay traces the general movement of Thomas's poetry from doubt and fear to faith and love and examines the peculiar features of his poetry in each of its three phases: the dark, early period concerned chiefly with personal problems; the middle stage charged with "powerful and poignant" feeling for others, and the late phase containing "exultant expressions of his faith and love." Accompanying the changes in Thomas's subject matter are changes in other aspects of his poetry as well, the progress proceeding in the direction of increasing complexity of sentence structure, with the early limited diction and terseness yielding to expanded diction and verbosity. Nevertheless, throughout his work, Thomas is a poet only of the most exalted emotions, and, however extensive the reach of his imagination, he speaks always as one character, himself. As a "lyric poet of the lofty kind," he either "aims at and achieves the sublime" or fails completely. To add substance to his general remarks, Olson looks closely at several poems, singling out "The Ballad of the Long-legged Bait," the "Altarwise by owl-light" sonnets, "Fern Hill," and "Poem in October" as examples of Thomas's poetic genius at its best and most sublime, and "Dawn Raid" as an example of the same genius thundering ineffectively.

41. "A Dialogue on the Function of Art in Society." _Chicago Review_, 16 (1964), 57-72. Originally published in Spanish, in _La Torre_, 1 (1953). (A copy of this issue of _La Torre_ could not be obtained.) Reprinted in 10.

Invokes the aid of the shade of Socrates to settle a dispute between a Humanist and a Mathematician concerning the primacy of humanistic or mathematical studies, with the ensuing exchanges moving inexorably to a conception of the role of art in society and of the duties of the humanist in fostering that role.

Steadily pinpricked by Socrates's naive but devastating questions, the Humanist's claims for the superior value of art (e.g., art is a virtue in itself, is a good beyond necessity or utility) explode one after another until, with the recognition that whatever is beautiful is so because it is "perfectly determined to its function," he is obliged to confess that such apparently self-contained beauty can confer no useful or necessary benefit upon either man or society. Exulting in the chagrin of his opponent, the Mathematician reaches for the palm of victory, secure in the knowledge that the necessity and utility of mathematics are immediately evident, only to discover slowly and reluctantly that mathematics (and the sciences founded on it) cannot be supreme, since it cannot have knowledge of the nature of things, "except in respect of quantity." Moreover, if the "goodness or badness of a thing is always in reference to its function," and if its function is determined by the nature of the thing, mathematics is incapable of judging its worth and, lacking a concept of the good, can offer no principle for directing the use of science to the good.

The argument that Socrates has been slowly developing requires for its completion a turn first to an examination of the good society and government, then to a discussion of the good citizen, and finally to a consideration of how the habit of good action can be acquired and refined. Reflection on these matters brings us to the function of art, for, to Socrates, it is the artist who is peculiarly capable of setting before our senses and imagination vivid images that cause us to form opinions and, hence, to love and fear and desire and hate in complete abstraction from our self-interest. In watching a play, for example, an audience--composed of individuals of mixed character--will react uniformly and throughout the performance favor the good and dislike the bad. Thus, although the dramatist seeks to write a good play, he must necessarily follow virtue to do so, and by reacting appropriately to art the individual forms habits based on proper inferences concerning the ethical nature of character, action, event, scene, etc. In pursuing "the Beautiful, the artist must necessarily advance the Good." And by satisfying his obligation to interpret and teach what the artist creates, the humanist will learn to improve his science; "his science will improve art, and art in turn will improve man and society."

42. "Introduction." American Lyric Poems: From Colonial Times to the Present. New York: Appleton-Century-Crofts, 1964, pp. 1-9. See 18.

Divides the "Introduction" to this collection of American lyrics into two sections, the first focussing on the characteristics that distinguish lyric forms from such larger forms as novel, drama, and epic, and the second on the development of the formal and technical resources of lyric poetry by a succession of American writers.

Chief among the features that differentiate lyric forms from the longer forms is the span of human behavior depicted, the most common forms of lyric presenting a single character acting determinately (perceiving, thinking, feeling, etc.) in a single situation. From the limitations on behavior and action, certain consequences follow, for example, economy of depiction, concision of expression, and immediacy of effect. If every art develops by exploiting and exploring the conditions that determine its nature, by expanding and complicating its medium, devices, subjects, and effects, then the quality of artistic production bears some relation to the state of the art, inasmuch as the range of artistic freedom increases relative to the availability of resources. (The relation between the condition of an art and the quality of artistic production is, of course, a potential, not a positive or absolute relation, since works of great quality can be produced when the resources of art are few.)

After quickly reviewing the American lyric in its early manifestations, Olson shows how the art "progresses" at the hands of Bryant (finding his own perceptions), Emerson (refining argument down to image and metaphor), Longfellow (exploiting European forms), Poe (developing the musical resources of poetry), Whitman (complicating poetic character), Dickinson (demonstrating the powers of condensation), and a large number of twentieth-century writers (extending the range of subjects and devices), all of whom, in addition to creating works of enduring value, added substantially to the technical resources available to the lyric poet.

43. "*Hamlet* and the Hermeneutics of Drama." *MP*, 56 (February, 1964), 225-37. Reprinted in *10*.

Aims to provide an outline of an interpretive instrument capable of delimiting the laws of evidence that must be adhered to in dealing with problems relevant to imaginative literature and of distinguishing sound from unsound interpretations. Since Olson is here concerned with principles of interpretation, not with interpreting a text, *Hamlet* is used primarily as a point of reference to illustrate the bases or grounds of propositions.

He begins by separating the problems of interpretation from those of textual and linguistic study (interpretation begins where these problems end and assumes the resolution of such problems) and from those of criticism (interpretation depends upon textual and linguistic study as criticism depends upon interpretation). Now, since interpretation "is in its essence hypothesis," and since the interpretation of extended works requires complex hypotheses involving subhypotheses that address the parts and their interrelations, the "correct" interpretation of a work will be based on component propositions of three distinct orders: basic, inferential, and evaluative propositions. Basic propositions (e.g., Horatio informed Hamlet of the ghost) are about facts and occurrences and do not depend upon other propositions. Inferential propositions (e.g., Hamlet was sent to England) are about facts and occurrences "*implied* by basic propositions, and evidence for them rests upon basic propositions." Finally, evaluative propositions (e.g., Hamlet is noble), a sub-class of the inferential, are characterized by having predicates that qualify an action or agent, such qualification always referring to a standard of some kind. A common tendency is to confuse an evaluative with a basic proposition, as in the case, say, of "Hamlet delays," which appears to be basic, but which in fact entails reference to a standard (how rapidly he should have acted). A perfect interpretation, then, is one "which is absolutely commensurate in its basic, inferential, and evaluative propositions with the data, the implications, and the values contained within the work;" in whole and in part, it would contain nothing not warranted by the text.

With these distinctions established, Olson, in the remainder of the essay, gives the general discussion immediacy by concentrating on drama, addressing directly the problems of how we can know what constitutes data and how we can know when inferences and evaluations are warranted. Olson's argument can barely be suggested in summary, but he does demonstrate that from the irreducible facts of _Hamlet_ we can derive, by correct methods of inference, the implications and evaluations demanded by them and, thus, define and interpret the effect that the work has upon us. In the end, he also convinces the reader that "if problems are to be solved and if interpretations are to be probably sound," some such instrument as the one that he has "adumbrated here" must be employed.

44. "Introduction." _Aristotle's Poetics and English Literature: A Collection of Critical Essays_. Chicago and London: The University of Chicago Press, 1965. See 19.

Provides a brief overview of the influence of the _Poetics_ on English criticism and a concise summary of the contents of the collection. As a scientific treatise based on the application of a particular philosophic method to a particular subject matter, the _Poetics_ has had remarkably little influence on critical thought and analysis (until the twentieth century), if by influence we mean the serious and deliberate adaptation of Aristotle's principles and method to new species of artistic production. We have no evidence that the _Poetics_ was widely known or highly regarded in antiquity, and the only period in which it achieved even token ascendancy was that roughly between the publication of Robortello's _Commentary_ (1548) and the mid-eighteenth century. And although Aristotelianism is generally associated with neoclassicism, the fact is that the *Poetics* survived in this period in the form of *disjecta membra*, discrete terms and doctrines that were filtered through prevailing rhetorical assumptions and blended with doctrines deriving from, for example, Plato, Cicero, Quintilian, Diomedes, Euanthius, Donatus, and especially Horace.

If as a treatise outlining the foundations of a given productive science, the *Poetics* were hardly influential at all, even in the period supposedly most Aristotelian, what influence can be attributed to the work? To Olson, the *Poetics* has been influential on three counts: its critical vocabulary has persisted; its doctrines, albeit isolated from their informing argument, have energized much critical debate, and its problems have continued to excite attention. Ironically, as the *Poetics* declined in authority in the late eighteenth century, it gained as a critical document as the result of the efforts of first-rate translators, notably Henry James Pye and Thomas Twining. This concern with what Aristotle actually said was an indispensable prerequisite to a concern with what he meant. In a real sense, serious philosophic inquiry into Aristotelian principles only becomes possible with the publication of good translations, and in his collection Olson has selected essays that reflect such inquiry. Although few of the critics represented could legitimately be called "Aristotelians," they all are concerned with investigating problems that "Aristotle would have found relevant to poetics." In the concluding section of the introduction, Olson briefly comments on each of the essays, identifying the problem or issue with which it deals and explaining why it was selected for inclusion in the volume.

45. "Modern Drama and Tragedy." In *Tragedy: Vision and Form*. Ed. Robert W. Corrigan.

San Francisco: Chandler, 1965, pp. 177-83. Excerpted from 6.

Reproduces approximately half of the tenth chapter of Tragedy and the Theory of Drama ("Modern Drama and Tragedy"), omitting Olson's comments on O'Neill's Mourning Becomes Electra and Eliot's Murder in the Cathedral.

According to Olson, to the question of whether we have tragedy in the modern theater, the answer, in general, must be "no." To the question of whether tragedy is possible in present times, the answer is "yes." Olson finds in modern drama a great deal of richness and variety, an expansion of subject matter, a fertile exploration of technique and method, but, at the same time, a concomitant commitment to a narrow realism, entailing a debasement of language and, consequently, a reduction in the range of expression. Because of the restricted range of modern drama, the more subtle and profound thoughts and emotions are curtailed or foregone. In short, for all its technical ingenuity, the modern theater has not, for the most part, given scope to a wide range of character, thought, and passion.

Nevertheless, there is nothing in the state of the language, in the modern world-view, in the conditions of modern life that precludes the production of tragic literature, which has power only in proportion to the quality of the artistic conception of action, character, thought, and passion. It is the moral quality of the action that produces tragic effect, not the rank of the characters, the elevation of the style, the employment of verse, etc.

Tragedy need not be written at any time, of course, but Olson supplies two reasons why it ought to be revived: "tragedy offers the dramatist greater scope for his genius; and it offers audiences a superior kind of pleasure, one which no other art can give."

46. "The Dialectical Foundations of Critical Pluralism." Texas Quarterly, 9 (May, 1966), 202-30. Reprinted in A Symposium on Formalist Criticism. Ed. William J. Handy. Introd. Mark Schorer. Austin, Texas: The Humanities Research Center, The University of Texas, 1965, pp. 26-54. Also reprinted in 10. (The essay was originally presented as a paper at "A Symposium on Formalist Criticism" on February 11, 1965, University of Texas, Austin, Texas.)

In this important essay, Olson presents his fullest and most philosophically rigorous defense of pluralism and analysis of the causes of variation in philosophical and critical theories. To Olson, although all systems of philosophy ultimately depend upon a theory of discourse, because the very formulation of a philosophy is impossible without it, certain properties of language are acknowledged by all, namely, that language is selective (its terms function determinately, since we cannot talk about what cannot be distinguished) and restrictive (once a meaning has been selected for a term, we can speak of no more than is implicated in that term under that meaning). Consequently, the nature of any problem is relative to its formulation, as is the solution, to the extent that it is a solution to the problem as formulated. Furthermore, where there are consecutive propositions, a dialectic or system of inference is necessarily involved.

From these bases, Olson goes on to consider philosophic variation in terms of 1) the dialectic employed, giving emphasis to the conditions on which inferences depend (i.e., significant expressions, their arrangement into propositions allowing for truth or falsity, and a principle of validation); 2) the concern of a given dialectic with likenesses, differences, or both; 3) the employment of significative or evocative terms, and 4) the way all dialectic turns on the interrelation or lack of interrelation of the triad of things, thoughts, and words.

By means of these investigations, Olson arrives at six basic kinds of criticism considered in terms of dialectical form alone: two concerned with likeness or difference exclusively (partial dialectics); two emphasizing some part of the triad (partial); and two stressing not only likeness and difference but also things, thoughts, and words in such interrelation as to allow cross inference. Whatever additional variety is possible must be based on the subject matters to which the dialectical forms are applied, and in the interests of brevity, Olson restricts his focus to the principal aspects of art on which criticism has centered, i.e., art as a product or object, as the activity or passivity of the artist, as the activity or passivity of the audience, or as the instrument to some end. Olson considers each approach to art from an integral (likeness) and differential (difference) dialectical perspective and then looks closely at how approaches to art as product may vary according to whether the causal analysis of the product stresses subject matter, medium, artist, or end. In sum, Olson aims to show how partial criticisms supplement one another and how the total criticisms (for example, those of Plato and Aristotle) intertranslate.

Olson's position, the pluralist position, is based on the recognition that there are many valid approaches to art, each with its own peculiar powers and limitations springing from a concern with different aspects of art and the utilization of different methods of investigation and reasoning. Olson is proposing, "not one question, but many," and he understands that "to answer these wholly, we shall have to find as many answers as we have [legitimate] questions."

47. "The Universe of the Early Poems." In _Dylan Thomas: A Collection of Critical Essays_. Ed. C. B. Cox. Englewood Cliffs, New Jersey: Prentice-Hall, 1966, pp. 45-59. Excerpted from 4.

Reprints in its entirety the first chapter of _The Poetry of Dylan Thomas_. Olson here concentrates attention on what in Thomas's early poetry caused interpreters the most difficulty, i.e., his symbolism, and he notes that because Thomas takes his symbols from a variety of sources, we cannot discover their values by appealing to any universal key or glossary (Freudian, Jungian, or whatever); rather, we must find their values in the poems themselves. Moreover, we must recognize that symbolism is merely a poetic device, valuable or not, as all devices are, only to the extent that it functions effectively in individual works. Nevertheless, since symbolism involves the representation of one idea through the medium of another and is, thus, always presented in the form of an image, it has the capacity to exhibit something to us as an actuality, unlike metaphor and simile, which, being based on verbal resemblance only, put before us what is so only "in a manner of speaking."

The universe evoked by the symbols of Thomas's early poems is a "nightmare universe." But for all its harshness and despair, Thomas's landscape of human suffering should not be aligned with that of melodrama or Grand Guignol theater. In the sensational forms of art, mere sensation is the end; horrors are cultivated for their own sake in these forms, and they exhaust their significance in their expression or exhibition. Thomas's poetry is not sensational or melodramatic, but tragic, for the horrors in his poems reach beyond themselves, informing us that "life in the absence of a sustaining faith is a nightmare." The images by which Thomas's scenes are conveyed transcend the sensational or morbid because they "have reference to the serious suffering of a man of some nobility."

48. "The Elements of Drama: Plot." In _Perspectives on Drama_. Ed. James L. Calderwood and Harold E. Toliver. New York: Oxford University Press, 1968, pp. 284-97. Excerpted from 6.

Reproduces all but the first four and a half pages of Chapter Two of _Tragedy and the Theory of Drama_. Olson here examines the shortcomings of the various ways in which critics have construed plot (as argument, myth, legend, historical sequence of events, intrigue, conflict, dramatic representation) and then suggests that plot is "a system of actions of determinate moral quality," rendered systematic by some unifying principle that both implies the nature, number, and order of the particulars of the drama and is implied by them. He goes on to consider plots in terms of their magnitude or extension of action (isolating four degrees of magnitude considered independently of emotional effect), their lines of action (linear or polylinear), their "laws of probability," and their unifying principles. In illustration of the possibilities of formal integrity, Olson examines four plays--_Macbeth_, _Our Town_, _Reigen_, and _Ghosts_--showing that each is unified by a distinct principle of form, respectively, consequential action, description, pattern, and thesis. Although each work is a unique synthesis of parts, evocative of a specific effect, each is representative of a different kind of unifying principle. As an indication of the additional formal differentiations possible within the broad classes of plot, Olson concludes this essay with an examination of simple and complex action in the "consequential action."

49. "The Lyric." In <u>Poetic Theory, Poetic Practice: Papers of the Midwest Modern Language Association</u>. Ed. Robert Scholes. Iowa City: Midwest Modern Language Association, 1969, pp. 59-66. Reprinted in 10.

Attempts in this essay to provide a "geography of the lyric," to determine, that is, its boundaries, so that we may know "where it begins and where it leaves off." In art, as in nature, there are structures of greater and lesser complexity, and by considering a progression from the most fundamental units of structure to the grand plots of epic and tragedy, Olson hopes to locate the lyric.

In a haiku by Issa he finds what must be one limit to expression, a poem conveying a single perception. Since perception is not merely a matter of sense, but a mental activity as well, it must be possible to construct poems of expression from other elementary activities, such as recollecting, imagining, inferring, expecting, and so on. Moreover, it is surely possible to use these irreducible and indivisible activities of mind as elements in a sequence of, say, perceptions, so long as the sequence has "unity and continuity." Additionally, the speakers of such poems can range from the universalized voice of Issa's poem to the particularized speaker of Browning's "Soliloquy of the Spanish Cloister." One form of lyric poetry, then, would be the poetry of <u>expression</u>.

In a poem like Marvell's "To His Coy Mistress," however, we have not merely an expression of the internal condition of a lover, but an act, a verbal act (of persuasion), but an act nonetheless. Since there are many verbal acts (commanding, informing, beseeching, etc.), and since such acts may be extended in sequence, it is possible to imagine a variety of poems of action and, thus, to isolate a second major stage beyond the poetry of expression, the poetry of address.

The supposition of a reply by Marvell's lady leads to a third stage, the poetry of colloquy, a kind exemplified in many poems, including "The Nut-Brown Maid." By further refining in this category on the basis of sequence and speaker, Olson reaches what he takes to be the limits of lyric, since beyond the continuity of exchange or interaction, we encounter works in which expression, address, and colloquy are subordinated to further ends, in which they are parts of more complex forms.

Looking back from the border, Olson can conclude that we can no longer speak of the lyric as a single form or seek to define the lyric, inasmuch as different things--expression, address, and colloquy--cannot be governed by a single principle and, further, that without a discussion of emotional effect full differentiation of the forms within the structures identified is impossible.

50. "'Mighty Opposites': Remarks on the Plot of Hamlet." In Studies in Theatre and Drama: Essays in Honor of Hubert C. Heffner. Ed. Oscar G. Brockett. The Hague: Mouton, 1972, pp. 48-63. Reprinted in 10.

Finds the extreme diversity of commentary on Hamlet a sign, not of the richness of the play, but of the "irresponsibility of commentators" and attributes the confusing proliferation of interpretations to two causes: 1) the failure of critics to separate "facts, inferences, and value judgments" and, hence, to distinguish between "warranted and unwarranted inferences and value judgments," and 2) the tendency among critics to reduce the play to Hamlet's actions only and then to treat him "as a real rather than a fictional person, in terms of natural rather than artistic considerations."

To counteract the first cause, Olson clarifies what happens in significant scenes (those creating interpretive difficulties and engendering various solutions), discussing first the verbal acts initiating action (the accusations that the ghost makes) and then the question responsible for subsequent action, i.e., whether the ghost's statements are true and his demands just (the justice of the demands depends, of course, upon the truth of the statements). From an analysis of the state of the court (where seeming and being have no relation to one another), Hamlet's character (he can act, but not without deliberation), and the problematic state of his knowledge, it becomes clear why of the two options open to Hamlet--direct and immediate action or action calculated and delayed--he chooses the latter and adopts insanity as his basic strategy. Working from such basic facts and warrantable inferences, Olson establishes the dramatic necessity behind the presentation of such scenes as the granting of Laertes's request, Hamlet's "to be or not to be" soliloquy, Claudius's opening speech, etc.

In the concluding section of the essay, Olson seeks to counteract the second cause of critical failure by looking at the plot as a whole and treating Hamlet and Claudius, not as static figures in a "static relation," but as "mighty opposites" engaged in a protracted duel, with the parries and counterthrusts changing in agent and purpose according to changes in their relative states of knowledge. "In a curious way, the situations of protagonist and antagonist parallel each other."

In dealing with the bases of warrantable inference in the scenes and with the movement of the plot as a whole, Olson seeks to lay the foundation for a full-scale, detailed analysis of _Hamlet_, one capable of meeting the tests of sound critical discussion.

Essays, Introductions, and Review Articles

51. "Drama and Dramatic Action." In *The Play and the Reader*. Alternate Edition. Ed. Stanley Johnson, Judah Bierman, and James Hart. Englewood Cliffs, New Jersey: Prentice-Hall, 1971, pp. 10-18. Reprinted in 6.

Reprints all but the first four pages of the first chapter of *Tragedy and the Theory of Drama*. In this essay, Olson deals with fundamental issues concerning the nature and conditions of dramatic representation. As a work designed to be acted out, a play depends, as other literary forms do not, upon the cooperative efforts of many persons for its realization. Moreover, a play, as essentially an imitation of an action involving the interrelations of characters to whom we respond in determinate emotional ways, proposes to affect an audience principally through sensation and only secondarily through imagination, since it is by means of the visible and audible behavior of characters that we are chiefly moved. Physical action can be represented directly, whereas the inner condition of characters can be known only by means of natural or artificial signs. The natural are universal effects reflecting a "given internal condition as cause" (e.g., tears, faltering voice, etc. as signs of grief); the artificial, on the other hand, are established by social or dramatic convention (e.g., funeral wreaths, black arm bands, etc. as signs of mourning). Olson's delineation of the rudiments of drama is completed when he notes, referring to works that imitate action, that the action of drama tends to be interpersonal, that action must be of a certain magnitude or extension, and that action is not incidental, but primary and comprehensive.

52. "Introduction." Major Voices: 20 British and American Poets. New York: McGraw-Hill Book Company, 1973. See 20.

As originally prepared, this anthology contained a long introduction (about seventy pages) dealing with the whole range of poetry, critical analyses of representative poems, and pragmatic illustrations of different critical methods. The text submitted was so drastically altered by the publisher in its scope and theoretical and practical utility that Olson will claim responsibility only for the considerably revised introduction (nine pages), which, as truncated, offers a useful, if propaedeutic, discussion of basic issues.

Putting aside the varieties of hypotheses about the general nature of poetry, Olson concentrates on how poems differ from one another in ways that can be "verified by observation and comparison." Olson notes that poems differ in what they present (single and simple actions, interactions, extended actions, arguments, etc.), in length (a function of extent and scale of action), in their effects (their emotional quality), in their methods of presentation, and in their style or diction. Olson briefly considers the implications of these distinctions, exemplifying his points with references to specific poems, and concludes by arguing that an understanding of poetic forms can only be acquired by studying a number of individual poems and then comparing them in terms of their likenesses and differences. To encourage discovery, Olson urges the student to ask each poem two basic questions: what effect does the work have upon him and how was it produced.

53. "On Value Judgments in the Arts." Critical Inquiry, 1 (September, 1974), 71-90. Reprinted in 10.

Addresses, in this important essay, one of the most complex issues in criticism, value judgments, and makes a compelling case for objective knowledge of value.

Although we speak of something as having value, a value is really a relation between a thing or a property of the thing and something further. For example, a building has a certain size and has this absolutely, but it is great or small only in relation to something further, even though it is still one or the other by virtue of its size.

Because standards of value change with and are determined by what we are evaluating (a work of art, for example, is neither poisonous nor nutritious), the "peculiar character of art" must be determined. To Olson, it is essential that we identify the principle of form governing the parts and their interrelation, since a "work of art is a structuring of sensory materials into some form perceptible to sense, and this perceptible form is the basis or material for the construction of...a mental or conceptual form," which has its origin in the artist's mind.

With the centrality of form established, Olson next considers the grounds (the propositions) upon which the probability of value judgments is based, a move made necessary by the fact that such propositions, having relative terms as predicates, are "correlative of something which justifies them" and, hence, require warranting correlatives which are found either in the judge or the judged. Our warranting correlatives can be identified by examining the five principal ways by which we distinguish value judgments. Such judgments 1) are subjective or objective; 2) are based on emotion or reason; 3) proceed from the expert or the inexpert; 4) are held by the few or the many, or 5) are the result of the application of some standard. Only the last of these (as the only kind of warrant that is not an appeal to the judge, to authority, or to a kind of argumentum ad verecundiam) "holds a possibility of being relevant to value."

Since by earlier determination values in art works have reference to and are contingent upon form, Olson can now outline the "ten conditions of sound value judgment," the first five relating to the concept of the work and the second five "to the establishment of the judgment as such." They are: 1) there must be a perceptible trait or characteristic; 2) it must be essential to the work; 3) the sensible form must be accurately perceived; 4) it must be correctly interpreted; 5) the suprasensible substructures must be understood as constituting the subsumptive whole which is the form of the work; 6) the standard must be an actual value; 7) it must be appropriate to the form; 8) it must be appropriate to the characteristic or trait; 9) the value syllogism must be a valid syllogism, and 10) it must be clearly and unequivocally expressed in words. In what follows, each of the conditions is fully explained and justified, and examples of how particular common criteria of value (e.g., high seriousness, intensity, nationalism, etc.) violate one or more of the conditions are given.

In the concluding sections of the essay, Olson distinguishes among kinds, degrees, quantities, and orders of value, shows how the descriptive leads to the evaluative (how the values inhere in the objects), and deals with the problem of whether criteria of value are prior or posterior to judgment, sensibly determining that the good of the work is prior, though our proof of its value, as the "conclusion of inference," is posterior.

54 "The Poetic Process." Critical Inquiry, 2 (Autumn, 1975), 69-74. Reprinted in 10.

Finds that the many discussions of poetic process fall into three classes: 1) those that analyze faculties or activities and then arrange them in such distinct stages as preparation, incubation, illumination, and verification; 2) those that describe the working habits of poets in terms of characteristic circumstances or conditions, and 3) those that give the "history of the composition of a poem." All three approaches are unsatisfactory, the first because it is too general, founded as it is on accidental features and a consideration of the activities in abstraction from the work produced, and the second and third because they are too particular, based on what is peculiar to the individual poet or poem. Moreover, each emphasizes what the poet does as a man, not what he does as a poet in making a product. To the extent that the process is mental, it can have "only one witness," and he is incompetent, because he is concentrating on the poem, not the process. Thus, we have the paradox that "in proportion as he is qualified, he is disqualified by his very qualification."

From the roundhouse there is a way out, however, if we assume that a poem is "a certain kind of whole composed of parts," for then the process is "nothing other than the process of supplying the constitutive parts and ordering them into a whole." And the order of this process is not determined by chronology, but by subordination, the order of the relation of the parts to the whole. From this conception, it follows that there can be no such thing as a single poetic process, inasmuch as the process varies according to the differences in the <u>kinds of products</u> produced.

To Olson, several clear advantages follow immediately from the adoption of his approach to the problem of poetic process. Hereafter, we shall be able to discuss processes apart from the "accidents of circumstance" and to consider the elements of the processes as solutions to the problems "posed by the conditions of form." Additionally, by comparing what was done with what could have been done, given the resources of art, we shall be able "not merely to illuminate the method of the poet, but to judge his craftsmanship as well." Finally, we shall only lose what we can well do without, "the self-mystification which results when confusions are mistaken for problems."

55. "Art and Science." In On Value Judgments in the Arts and Other Essays. Chicago and London: The University of Chicago Press, 1976, pp. 293-306. See 10.

Sets forth a program for developing scientific knowledge of art, after first comparing the state of knowledge in the arts (in which, at the present time, progress is "horizontal," with many approaches producing few significant consequences) with that in the sciences (in which progress is "vertical," with many significant consequences springing from relatively few approaches) and then distinguishing among theoretical (e.g., math and physics), practical (e.g., ethics and politics) and productive (the arts, useful and fine) sciences in terms of the kinds of principles upon which each is based (see 45).

From an examination of the history of theories of art, we discover that knowledge of art is not only possible, but abundantly available, though rarely built upon or extended. To advance such knowledge as we have, we must recognize 1) that while theorists often use similar terms (because of "nature of language"), they use those terms differently ("because of the nature of their thought"); 2) that there cannot be contradiction except within the same system of reference or inference; 3) that words in use are modified by the contexts in which they appear and by their function within that context; 4) that the meaning of words in use is always determinate; 5) that a problem is always relative to its formulation, as is the solution, and 6) that formulations are necessarily finite. Thus, no single theory can embrace all truth, and no single method can be the one right method.

With these principles established, Olson goes on to examine the causes of philosophic variation in 1) the systems of inference employed and 2) the kinds of subject-matter discussed. Once we understand that our terms, distinctions, assumptions, and methods of reasoning not only allow us to express our meaning but determine the meanings we can express, we are fitted for the task of separating the true from the false in our critical heritage and of building our knowledge upon solid foundations. Vertical progress in the science of art is contingent, finally, upon developing "every valid approach," upon knowing how to discover a problem and to "formulate it precisely, upon constructing and testing our interpretations of works, and upon drawing on relevant findings in other sciences. By developing the science of art, we shall acquire more genuine knowledge, and "we shall know something more about man."

56. "A Conspectus of Poetry, Part I." Critical Inquiry, 4 (Autumn, 1977), 159-80.

In this first installment of a long essay published in two parts in successive issues of Critical Inquiry, Olson initiates his discussion of the formal principles underlying various kinds of poems, one which moves steadily from the most basic to the most complex forms and seeks to arrange them in an order of increasing complexity.

Proceeding inductively and empirically, he identifies features relevant to form and then arrives at definitions of poetic forms. To remove ambiguity from the term "form," Olson explains exactly what he means by it: form is that towards which all other forms, structures, and functions within the text tend, that which includes the others, and that for the sake of which they are present.

Because he is interested in moving from the simple to the complex, and because the latter build upon or are variously constructed from the elements of the former, Olson looks first at severely restricted areas of expression, taking as his examples two brief propositions, one command, one haiku poem, and a revised version of the first line of Tennyson's "The Eagle." At the command we reach a point where "language reaches beyond meaning to constitute an action," where the nature of the act must be understood (not simply the grammatical and logical aspects of the statement). The two poetic examples offer us indivisible simulated actions (i.e., acts of perception), and from these we can imagine other poems dealing with other indivisible activities (insulting, praising, etc.), indeed, with any single activity, as well as with every emotional response.

To complicate his argument further, Olson examines "Dirce," "O Western Wind," "Night," "Spring Day," and "On Seeing a Hair of Lucrezia Borgia," distinguishing between the first two and the last three in terms of our relation to the speakers. To the last three we respond as the speaker responds, because we have "been placed imaginatively in the condition" of the speaker, whereas to the first two we respond to the "thoughts, feelings, and actions of others." The differences in our responses to these poems can be attributed to different causes of emotion, and in the remainder of this essay, Olson examines those causes. (Briefly, since every emotion is felt about some object on some ground and in some frame of mind, and since emotions have as their ground "some sensation or memory, or some image of imagination, or some opinion," the ways poets can produce emotional response are determined by these conditions.) At the end, Olson notes that in poems like "Dirce" and "O Western Wind" our responses are based on conjectures relating to the nature of the action, to the character and intention of the agent, and that we judge these actions much as we do those in real life, except that "our judgments are in no way affected by reflections on our self-interest." This essay concludes with the observation that what has been said about images and principles of response will obtain in longer and more complex forms of poetry also, whatever additional materials and principles may enter into their structural integrity.

57. "A Conspectus of Poetry, Part II." Critical Inquiry, 4 (Winter, 1977), 373-96.

Extends and completes the argument begun in the previous issue of Critical Inquiry (see 56, immediately above), moving from single, elementary actions and the principles upon which their effects are based to more complex kinds of action, with each stage building upon the elements of the preceding stage, until we reach the maximum forms, the grand plots of tragedy and epic.

From single, momentary, indivisible actions, Olson moves to poems in which a succession of moments is bound together in a unity. At this point, we are no longer concerned with the probabilities entailed by the depiction of the momentary, but with the probabilities of motion and change determined by the character, emotion, or circumstances of the agent engaged in the activity and, hence, with the conditions of discovery and reversal. Thus, Olson considers next the kinds of magnitude possible to actions, again from the simplest to the most complex, using particular works to illustrate the progression, as follows: 1) "The Eagle"--the single action of a single person in a single situation (the magnitude of a speech); 2) "The Bishop Orders His Tomb"--serveral people interacting, though only one person speaks (the magnitude of a scene); 3) Sohrab and Rustum--the interaction of several agents in an action of greater compass than that of Browning's poem (the magnitude of an episode); and 4) Hamlet or the Iliad--an action of greater compass than that of Arnold's poem and containing a number of episodes (the magnitude of a grand plot).

Although literary forms can clearly be distinguished in terms of magnitude of action, magnitude (measured not by the length of the work, but by how much has to be done to complete the action) is essentially a quantitative matter, and full definition requires the specification of the qualitative differences of forms as well. Thus, Olson goes on to discuss the serious and the comic in great detail, identifying the circumstances necessary to the production of each and further differentiating among the ridiculous, the absurd, the tragic, and the heroic.

To complete his account, Olson considers, first, differences in how poems depict action (identifying the various possibilities of disclosing information--and, hence, controlling emotional responses--in the dramatic, narrative, and mixed modes of representation) and, second, differences occasioned by the kinds of diction employed (giving emphasis to clarity, obscurity, metaphor, etc. and noting that diction is determined by "what is probable for the speaker and his circumstances").

Having established "what a poem may imitate, how it may imitate, and the means which it may employ in imitation," Olson has provided a "general basis for the discrimination of all forms of imitative poetry." Throughout, Olson has been concerned with imitative works, and at the end he briefly distinguishes between these and didactic works and brings the whole essay to conclusion by noting that if we have discovered no single definition of poetry (and learned why there can be no single definition), we have "seen the growth of one species out of another" and "have found nothing that can limit that process of growth." "What the word poetry can fully mean only the poets can tell us."

58. "Morality and Art." *Religious Humanism*, 11 (1977), 69-77.

Develops a complex argument concerning the relations between art and ethical behavior, in which the characteristics of art conducive to moral behavior are identified. To Olson, literature has the capacity to extend our experience and increase its depth, to show us the "causes and consequences of human action, thought, and feeling," to arouse proper emotions in us in the proper degree and in response to the proper objects, and to enable us to contemplate spectacles of human character, action, and passion apart from self-interest. What all this can mean for moral behavior becomes clear when we consider the grounds of acting well. In order to do so, we must be able to see the consequences of good and bad action, to distinguish the good from the bad, and to hold firmly to the course of the good. The person who is disabled from acting well exhibits deficiency in one or more of these three conditions. By setting before such a person vivid images of good and bad (the grounds of his opinions and, hence, emotions) in abstraction from his immediate self-interest, thus obliging him to separate the good from the bad and to choose the good (emotional response in the form of hope or fear being such a choice), we can free him from narrow self-concern. And literature is preeminently suited to these tasks.

In the conclusion of the essay, Olson observes that deviation from ethical behavior among artists and the connoisseurs of art can be accounted for by recognizing that of the three conditions of ethical behavior, art can give us only the first two. It can induce us to take correct action, but it cannot make us act. The third condition "involves a habit of moral choice and action upon it."

E. REVIEWS

59. "A Defense of Poetry." *Poetry: A Magazine of Verse*, 50 (April, 1937), 54-56.

Reviews F. O. Matthiessen's *The Achievement of T.S. Eliot*, praising it as a serious and comprehensive study, one, however, that, for all its virtues, would have contributed more substantially to the advance of criticism if its author had steadily borne in mind what he clearly articulates in his preface, i.e., that the poem, not the poet or reader, is the proper object of critical inquiry. In fact, the subject of his book is not the poem, but the poet, and the result of his pervasive identification of the work with the artist is that the study of character replaces the study of poetry.

60. "Recent Literary Criticism." *MP*, 15 (February, 1943), 275-283.

Examines the critical principles expressed either directly or by implication in three books that, taken together, fairly represent the range of critical production "in our age": *The Intent of the Critic* (edited by Donald Stauffer and containing essays by Edmund Wilson, Norman Foerster, John Crowe Ransom, and W. H. Auden); *The Language of Poetry* (edited by Allen Tate and containing essays by Philip Wheelwright, Cleanth Brooks, I.A. Richards, and Wallace Stevens), and *How to Read a Poem* (by I. A. Richards). Each work is considered in turn, so that the essay takes the form of a series of book reviews.

After briefly summarizing each of the essays in The Intent of the Critic, Olson notes that all four, their professed and ostensible differences notwithstanding, exalt parts to "the universality of the whole" and employ the same critical method, one based on a form-matter (ultimately, a style-content) dichotomy and allowing only combination and division as principles of argumentation or inference. Form is usually determined exclusively in stylistic terms, and matter is reduced to subject matter. Reasoning is analogical, and, as a consequence, these critics are unable to come to close quarters with many particulars of individual texts or to discuss works in terms of "principles peculiar to species of literature."

Most of what Olson says about these essays applies equally well to those in The Language of Poetry. Nevertheless, the essays in this collection, while employing the critical method found to be inadequate in the first book, are distinguished by their common tendency to treat poetry as a kind of knowledge, "a kind of statement of knowledge." Thus, the enormous diversity of poetic expression is subsumed by a single principle: poetry becomes, in effect, a "verbal instrument by which truths may be stated." By a circuitous route we are brought back to a diluted form of Roman and Hellenistic rhetoric by these critics.

In the concluding section of this essay, Olson takes issue with Richards's conception of multiple meanings, which derives from the view that words are systematically ambiguous, and insists that meaning may be "manifold, but never multiple," because the very nature of signification requires words in use to be both selective and restrictive. Finally, Olson observes that Richards's project is not really "dialectical"--in spite of his claims--but "stoutly lexicographical," founded as it is on the "enumeration, distinction, and correlation of the senses of words independently of their appearance in any philosophic or poetic context."

61. "Mr. Creekmore's Treasury." Poetry: A Magazine of Verse, 82 (August, 1953), 281-82.

Praises Hubert Creekmore's A Little Treasury of World Poetry, an anthology of poems in translation representing thirty-one languages and thirty-five centuries, for the scope and judiciousness of its selection, the whole volume reflecting the wise choices of an editor aware of the problems inherent in "representation" and familiar with the "practice, theory, and history of translation."

62. "The Schoolroom Poets." Poetry: A Magazine of Verse, 84 (May, 1954), 98-100.

Reviews George Arms's The Fields Were Green: A New View of Bryant, Whittier, Holmes, Lowell, and Longfellow, with a Selection of Their Poems, finding his attempts to restore some lustre to the tarnished reputations of these poets unsuccessful, largely because, as a defense counselor, he is convinced that his clients, their occasional virtues notwithstanding, are culpably affined with poetic standards that are at some considerable remove from those postulated as definitive of excellence in all poetry by modern--i.e., "new"--criticism (and accepted as such by Arms).

63. [Untitled] Bulletin of the Atomic Scientists: A Magazine of Science and Public Affairs, 15 (February, 1959), 92-93.

In this playful review, Olson diminishes the "argument" of C. Day Lewis's The Poet's Way of Knowledge (that, because poetry is faithful to the "observed facts of human behavior" and is, in addition, "an experience in itself," it both reflects and expresses a "special kind of knowing") by demonstrating that even though Lewis kicks the stuffing out of those who would say him nay his victory can occasion no tumultuous cheering, inasmuch as his opponents are nothing but straw men into whom he has diligently crammed, not arguments, but the self-same fibers that out of them he has kicked. Addressing the analogies by which Lewis "establishes" relations between the "scientific process and the poetic" (both science and poetry search for a means of communication, use metaphor, and "grope in the dark until they have found what they are looking for"), Olson says through the quizzical voice of the "Scarecrow of Oz"--a straw man with a brain--that a syllogism should have a distributed middle term, that "two affirmative premises in the second figure of a syllogism can prove nothing" (or anything), that, even if we reject the notion that "poetry is nothing but an end in itself," we are not obliged to treat it as a special kind of knowing, and that arguments from analogy, "however extended, cannot prove identity." In his own, more humane and tolerant voice, Olson praises Lewis for his effort to defend poetry and for insisting on the "human significance of poetry." Olson concludes by berating the Scarecrow for saying that Lewis has proved nothing, for clearly "his poetry proves him a poet, and his defense of poetry, an earnest man who values poetry very highly." (On Olson's copy of this review, the following title, in Olson's hand, appears": "Waltz of the Straw Men.")

F. POEMS

64. "Last Night." Poetry: A Magazine of Verse, 32 (May, 1928), 81.

    This and the following poem appear in the same issue of Poetry under the title "Soft Music."

65. "Towers of Sleep." Poetry: A Magazine of Verse, 32 (May, 1928), 82.

66. "Waters." Poetry: A Magazine of Verse, 36 (July, 1930), 175-76. Reprinted in Poetry, 37 (November, 1930), 112-13. Also reprinted in The New Poetry: An Anthology of Twentieth-Century Verse in English. Ed. Harriet Monroe and Alice Corbin Henderson. New York: Macmillan, 1943, pp. 428-29.

67. "The Quarry." Poetry: A Magazine of Verse, 36 (July, 1930), 176-77.

68. "Body of Man Compared to a Tree." Poetry: A Magazine of Verse, 36 (July, 1930), 177-78.

69. "Garden-Piece." Poetry: A Magazine of Verse, 36 (July, 1930), 178. Reprinted in Poetry, 37 (November, 1930), 113.

70. "Dirge for the White Bird." *Poetry: A Magazine of Verse*, 36 (July, 1930), 179.

71. "The Gift." *Poetry: A Magazine of Verse*, 36 (July, 1930), 180.

72. "Angleworms." *Poetry: A Magazine of Verse*, 36 (July, 1930), 181.

73. "Lazarus." *Poetry: A Magazine of Verse*, 36 (July, 1930), 182.

74. "Last Night." *Poetry: A Magazine of Verse*, 39 (October, 1931), 1-6.

This and the following poem appear in the same issue of *Poetry* under the title "Thus Revealed."

75. "Essay on Deity." *Poetry: A Magazine of Verse*, 39 (October, 1931), 6-8. Reprinted in 11, 13 and 15. Also reprinted in *Scholastic*, 28 (February 8, 1936), 12. Also in *Great Poems of the English Language*. Ed. Wallace Alvin Briggs, with a supplement of recent poetry selected by William Rose Benet. New York: Tudor, 1937, pp. 1452-54. Also in *The New Poetry: An Anthology of Twentieth-Century Verse in English*. Ed. Harriet Monroe and Alice Corbin Henderson. New York: Macmillan, 1943, pp. 426-28. Also in *Modern Religious Poems: A Contemporary Anthology*. Ed. Jacob Trapp. New York: Harper and Row, 1964, pp. 141-43.

This poem won the Guarantor's Prize in 1933.

Poems

76. "Talisman of Words." _Poetry: A Magazine of Verse_, 41 (October, 1932), 23-25. Reprinted in 11.

This poem and the next four poems appear together in volume forty-one of _Poetry_ under the title "A Group of Five."

77. "Prelude to Despair." _Poetry: A Magazine of Verse_, 41 (October, 1932), 25-26. Reprinted in 11.

78. "The Ghostly Spring." _Poetry: A Magazine of Verse_, 41 (October, 1932), 27. Reprinted in 11.

79. "To Music." _Poetry: A Magazine of Verse_, 41 (October, 1932), 28-29.

80. "Song: When Shall This Weight Be Cast." _Poetry: A Magazine of Verse_, 41 (October, 1932), 29.

81. "Novel in Pictures." _Poetry: A Magazine of Verse_, 42 (July, 1933), 181-89. Reprinted in 11 and 15.

82. "Wishes for His Poem." _Poetry: A Magazine of Verse_, 44 (April, 1934), 26-27. Reprinted in 11, 13 and 15.

This poem and the following four poems appear together in volume forty-four of _Poetry_ under the title "Preludes and Impromptus."

83. "Legend." _Poetry: A Magazine of Verse_, 44 (April, 1934), 27-29.

84. "Prologue to His Book." Poetry: A Magazine of Verse, 44 (April, 1934), 29-30. Reprinted in 11 and 15.

85. "Madrigal." Poetry: A Magazine of Verse, 44 (April, 1934), 30. Rperinted in 11, 13 and 15.

86. "Sonnet: This Is the Thing that Was Not Born to Die." Poetry: A Magazine of Verse, 44 (April, 1934), 31.

87. "Elegy at the End of Summer." In Thing of Sorrow (11). New York: Macmillan, 1934, pp. 30-31. Reprinted in The Best Poems of 1934. Sel. Thomas Moult. New York: Harcourt, Brace and Co., pp. 49-50.

88. "Voice Heard from the Third Planet." Saturday Review of Literature, 11 (March 2, 1935), 514. Reprinted in 12 and 15.

89. "Winter Marketplace." New Republic, 82 (May 1, 1935), 335. Reprinted in 12 and 15.

90. "Colloquy." Scholastic, 28 (February 8, 1936), 12. Also in 11. Reprinted in 15.

91. "Angel of the Annunciation." Poetry: A Magazine of Verse, 48 (August, 1936), 239-40. Reprinted in 12, 13 and 15.

This poem and the following five poems appear together in volume forty-eight of Poetry under the title "The Cock of Heaven."

Poems

92. "Soul's Journey." _Poetry: A Magazine of Verse_, 48 (August, 1936), 240-41. Reprinted in 12.

93. "The Cock of Heaven." _Poetry: A Magazine of Verse_, 48 (August, 1936) 241-42. Reprinted in 12 and 15.

94. "The Assumption." _Poetry: A Magazine of Verse_, 48 (August, 1936), 242-43. Reprinted in 12 and 15.

95. "No. 10 Blucher Street." _Poetry: A Magazine of Verse_, 48 (August, 1936), 243-44. Reprinted in 12, 13 and 15. Also reprinted in _Anthology of Magazine Verse for 1936 and Yearbook of American Poetry_. Ed. Alan F. Pater. New York: The Poetry Digest Association, 1937, p. 112.

96. "A Clock Striking at Midnight." _Poetry: A Magazine of Verse_, 48 (August, 1936), 244-45. Reprinted in 12.

97. "Sonnet: I have Served Thee, Give Me Mine Hire, O Lord." _Poetry: A Magazine of Verse_, 56 (April, 1940), 7.

This poem and the following five appear together in volume fifty-six of _Poetry_ under the title "Devil in Crystal."

98. "The History." _Poetry: A Magazine of Verse_, 56 (April 1940), 6.

99. "Encounter of Travelers." _Poetry: A Magazine of Verse_, 56 (April, 1940), 5. Reprinted in 12.

100. "Liber de Causis." Poetry: A Magazine of Verse, 56 (April, 1940), 4. Reprinted in 12, 13 and 15.

101. "Abailard Sleeps at His Book." Poetry: A Magazine of Verse, 56 (April, 1940), 3. Reprinted in 12, 13, and 15.

102. "Episode." Poetry: A Magazine of Verse, (April, 1940), 1-2. Reprinted in The Best Poems of 1940. Sel. Thomas Moult. New York: Harcourt, Brace and Co., pp. 107-08.

103. "Spectre and Substance." The Chicago Daily News (December 4, 1940).

104. "The Statue." Furioso II, 4 (Summer, 1947), 30. Reprinted in 13 and 15. Also reprinted in Illinois Poets: A Selection. Ed. E. Earle Stibitz. Carbondale, Illinois: Southern Illinois University Press, 1968, 170-71.

105. "Winter Nightfall." Furioso II, 4 (Summer, 1947), 32-33. Reprinted in 13 and 15. Also reprinted in Heartland: Poets of the Midwest. Ed. Lucien Stryk. DeKalb, Illinois: Northern Illinois University Press, 1967, 171-72.

106. "The Mirror Men." Chicago Review, 3 (Summer, 1948), 5. Reprinted in 13 and 15. Also reprinted in The Chicago Review Anthology. Ed David Ray. Chicago: The University of Chicago Press, 1959.

107. "Ars Poetica." Chicago Review, 3 (Summer, 1948), 5. Reprinted in The Chicago Review

Anthology. Ed. David Ray. Chicago: The University of Chicago Press, 1959.

108. "The Rebellion." Poetry: A Magazine of Verse, 73 (December, 1948), 144-45. Reprinted in 13 and 15.

109. "Ice-Age." Poetry: A Magazine of Verse, 73 (December, 1948), 146-49. Reprinted in 13 and 15.

110. "Pavane for the New Year." Poetry: A Magazine of Verse, 73 (December, 1948), 150.

111. "Last Autumnal." The Tiger's Eye, 9 (October, 1949), 23. Reprinted in 13, 14, and 15.

112. "Horror Story." The Tiger's Eye, 9 (October, 1949), 24. Reprinted in 13 and 15.

113. "The Midnight Meditation." Measure: A Critical Journal, 2 (December, 1950), 49-51. Reprinted in 13 and 15. Also reprinted in Heartland: Poets of the Midwest. Ed. Lucien Stryk. DeKalb Illinois: Northern Illinois Universty Press, 1967, pp. 175-78.

114. "Poem." Measure: A Critical Journal, 2 (December, 1950), 52. Reprinted in 13 and 15.

115. "Childe Roland, Etc." Poetry: A Magazine of Verse, 81 (October, 1952), 59-60.

Reprinted in 13 and 15. Also reprinted in *The Oxford Book of American Light Verse*. Ed. William Harmon. New York: Oxford University Press, 1979, p. 450.

116. "Ballad of the Scarecrow Christ." *Poetry: A Magazine of Verse*, 82 (April, 1953), 1-6. Reprinted in 13 and 15. Also reprinted in *Art and Craft in Poetry*. Ed. James T. Lape and Elizabeth Baymore Lape. Boston: Ginn and Co., 1967.

This poem and the following four appear together in volume eighty-two of *Poetry* under the title "Five Poems."

117. "Plot Improbable, Character Unsympathetic." *Poetry: A Magazine of Verse*, 82 (April, 1953), 6-7. Reprinted in 13, 14, and 15. Also reprinted in *Heartland: Poets of the Midwest*. Ed. Lucien Stryk. DeKalb, Illinois: Northern Illinois University Press, 1967, pp. 173-74; and in *The New Pocket Anthology of American Verse from Colonial Days to the Present*. Ed. Oscar Williams. New York: World Publishing Co., 1955, p. 393.

118. "The Fountain." *Poetry: A Magazine of Verse*, 82 (April, 1953), 7-8. Reprinted in 13, 14, and 15.

119. "The Night There Was Dancing in the Streets." *Poetry: A Magazine of Verse*, 82 (April, 1953), 8-9. Reprinted in 13 and 15. Also reprinted in *The New Pocket Anthology of American Verse from Colonial Days to the Present*. Ed. Oscar Williams. New York: World Publishing Co., 1955, p. 394; and in *Heartland: Poets of the Midwest*. Ed. Lucien Stryk. DeKalb,

Illinois: Northern Illinois University Press, 1967, pp. 174-75.

120. "Jack-in-the-Box." Poetry: A Magazine of Verse, 82 (April, 1953), 9-10. Reprinted in 13, 14, and 15. Also reprinted in The New Pocket Anthology of American Verse from Colonial Days to the Present. Ed. Oscar Williams. New York: World Publishing Co., 1955, pp. 394-95; in Heartland: Poets of the Midwest. Ed. Lucien Stryk. DeKalb, Illinois: Northern Illinois University Press, 1967, pp. 172-73; and in Illinois Poets: A Selection. Ed. E. Earle Stibitz. Carbondale, Illinois: Southern Illinois University Press, 1968, pp. 169-70.

121. "A Farewell." In The Poetry of Dylan Thomas. Chicago and London: The University of Chicago Press, 1954. (see 4). Reprinted in 14 and 15. Also reprinted in A Garland for Dylan Thomas. Ed. George J. Firmage. New York: Clarke and Way, 1963, p. 95; and in Art and Craft in Poetry. Ed. James T. Lape and Elizabeth Baymore Lape. Boston: Ginn and Co., 1967.

122. "Crucifix." Virginia Quarterly Review, 30 (1954), 227-28. Reprinted in 13, 14, and 15. Also reprinted in Modern Religious Poems: A Contemporary Anthology. Ed. Jacob Trapp. New York: Harper and Row, 1964, pp. 129-31; and in Poems from the Virginia Quarterly Review, 1925-67. Charlottesville: University Press of Virginia, 1969, pp. 172-73.

123. "Able, Baker, Charlie, Et Al." In Modern Writing. Ed. William Phllips and Phillip

Rahv. New York: Avon, 1954, pp. 238-39. Reprinted in 13, 14, and 15. Also reprinted in _Shake the Kaleidoscope_. Ed. Milton Klonsky. New York: Pocketbooks, 1973.

124. "The Altar." _Hudson Review_, 8 (Winter, 1956), 578-79. Reprinted in 14 and 15.

125. "The Cry." _Hudson Review_, 8 (Winter, 1956), 578. Reprinted in 14 and 15.

126. "In Defense of Superficiality." _New Yorker_, 33 (October, 1957), 46. Reprinted in 14 and 15. Also reprinted in _The New Yorker Book of Poems_. New York: Viking, 1969.

127. "London Company." _Virginia Quarterly Review_, 33 (1957), 503-04. Reprinted in 14 and 15.

128. "Knight with Umbrella." _New Yorker_, 33 (February 1, 1958), 72. Reprinted in 16. Also reprinted in _The Fireside Book of Humorous Poetry_. Ed. William Cole. New York: Simon and Schuster, 1959.

129. "The Last Entries in the Journal." _Poetry: A Magazine of Verse_, 91 (March, 1958), 232-47. Reprinted in 14 and 15.

130. "A Valentine for Marianne Moore." _Poetry: A Magazine of Verse_, 91 (March, 1958), 348-49. Reprinted in 14 and 15.

131. "The Voice." _Poetry: A Magazine of Verse_, 91 (March, 1958), 349.

Poems

132. "The Exegesis." *Poetry: A Magazine of Verse*, 91 (March, 1958), 350. Reprinted in 14 and 15.

133. "For the Demolition of a Theater." *Poetry: A Magazine of Verse*, 91 (March, 1958), 351. Reprinted in 14 and 15. Also reprinted in *Illinois Poets: A Selection*. Ed. E. Earle Stibitz. Carbondale, Illinois: Southern Illinois University Press, 1968, p. 169.

134. "Preview, Informal." *Hudson Review*, 11 (Spring, 1958), 96-97. Reprinted in 14 and 15.

135. "Mobile by Calder." *Hudson Review*, 11 (Spring, 1958), 96. Reprinted in 14 and 15. Also reprinted in *Poetry and the Visual Arts*. Ed. D. G. Kehl. Belmont, California: Wadsworth, 1975.

136. "A Dream for a Sad Lady." *Hudson Review*, 12 (Fall, 1959), 405. Reprinted in 15.

137. "Mirror." *Hudson Review*, 12 (Fall, 1959), 404-05. Reprinted in 15.

138. "Directions to the Armorer." *New Yorker*, 35 (November 14, 1959), 191. Reprinted in 15. Also reprinted in *Some Haystacks Don't Even Have Any Needle and Other Complete Modern Poems*. Ed. Stephen Dunning, Edward Lueders, and Hugh Smith. Glenview, Illinois: Scott Foresman, 1969, p. 99.

139. "At a Military Ceremony." Chelsea, 8 (October, 1960), 52. Reprinted in 15. Also reprinted in Illinois Poets: A Selection. Ed. E. Earle Stibitz. Carbondale, Illinois: Southern Illinois University Press, 1968, p. 171.

140. "Ice-Skaters." Poetry: A Magazine of Verse, 97 (November, 1960), 63-66. Reprinted in 15. Also reprinted in Sprints and Distances: Sports in Poetry and the Poetry in Sports. Ed. Lillian Morrison. New York: Thomas Y. Crowell, 1965, pp. 145-47; and in A Literature of Sports. Ed. Thomas Dodge. Lexington, Massachusetts: D. C. Heath and Co., 1980.

141. "Conversation Between a Mirror and the Sea." Poetry: A Magazine of Verse, 97 (November, 1960), 66. Reprinted in 15.

142. "The Graveyard by the Sea." Poetry: A Magazine of Verse, 97 (November, 1960), 67-71. Reprinted in 15.

143. "The Impersonation." Hudson Review, 13 (Winter, 1960-61), 578. Reprinted in 15.

144. "Argument about the Decoration of the Punch Table." New Yorker, 37 (December 30, 1961), 24. Reprinted in 15.

145. "The Attack on the Jungle Train." In Noble Savage. Ed. Saul Bellow, Keith Bobford, and Aaron Asher. Cleveland: World Publishing, 1962, pp. 67-68. Reprinted in 15.

Poems

146. "Exhibition of Modern Art." *Poetry: A Magazine of Verse*, 101 (October, 1962), 89-93. Reprinted in 15.

147. "Exposition of the Quarrel of the Birds." *Poetry: A Magazine of Verse*, 102 (August, 1963), 317-18. Reprinted in 15.

148. "Old Story, New Hero." *Poetry: A Magazine of Verse*, 102 (August, 1963), 318-19. Reprinted in 15.

149. "Taxco." *Poetry: A Magazine of Verse*, 102 (August, 1963), 319-22. Reprinted in 15.

150. "Poet to Reader." *Virginia Quarterly Review*, 39 (Autumn, 1963), 587-88. Reprinted in 15.

151. "Daguerreotype of Chopin." *Virginia Quarterly Review*, 40 (Summer, 1964), 401-03. Reprinted in 16. Also reprinted in *Poems from the Virginia Quarterly Review, 1925-67.* Charlottesville: University Press of Virginia, 1969, pp. 174-76.

152. "Directions for Building a House of Cards." *Virginia Quarterly Review*, 40 (Summer, 1964), 403-04. Reprinted in 16. Also reprinted in *Poems from the Virginia Quarterly Review, 1925-1967*. Charlottesville: University Press of Virginia, 1969, p. 177.

153. "Nightfall." *Virginia Quarterly Review*, 40 (Summer, 1964), 404. Reprinted in 16. Also reprinted in *Poems from the Virginia*

Quarterly Review, 1925-1967. Charlottesville: University Press of Virginia, 1969, p. 178.

154. "Souvenir of the Play." Virginia Quarterly Review, 40 (Summer, 1964), 405. Reprinted in 16. Also reprinted in Poems from the Virginia Quarterly Review, 1925-1967. Charlottesville: University Press of Virginia, 1969, p. 179.

155. "City." Virginia Quarterly Review, 40 (Summer, 1964), 405-06. Reprinted in 16. Also reprinted in Poems from the Virginia Quarterly Review, 1925-1967. Charlottesville: University Press of Virginia, 1969, p. 180.

156. "Olson's Penny Arcade." Chicago Review, 17 (1964), 19-23. Reprinted in 16.

157. "Wild Horse." In Art and Craft in Poetry. Ed. James T. Lape and Elizabeth Baymore Lape. Boston: Ginn and Co., 1967. Reprinted from 14.

158. "Spring Ghost." In Illinois Poets: A Selection. Ed. E. Earle Stibitz. Carbondale, Illinois: Southern Illinois University Press, 1968, pp. 168-69. Reprinted from 11.

159. "Inscription for the Tomb of Man." In Illinois Poets: A Selection. Ed. E. Earle Stibitz. Carbondale, Illinois: Southern Illinois University Press, 1968, p. 171. Reprinted from 11.

Poems

160. "A Restaurant in South-East Asia." Chicago Review, 24 (Winter, 1973), 23-24. Reprinted in 16.

161. "Puerto Vallarta." Chicago Review, 24 (Winter, 1973), 22-23. Reprinted in 16.

162. "Punch and Judy Songs." In Shake the Kaleidoscope. Ed. Milton Klonsky. New York: Pocketbooks, 1973. Reprinted from 14.

163. "Last Warning." Forum, 22 (Summer-Fall, 1977), 13.

164. "History-to-be and History Already." Chicago Review, 28 (Winter, 1977), 152-53.

165. "Rottenrock Mountain." South Carolina Review, 10 (April, 1978), 4-6.

166. "Russian Doll." New Yorker, 55 (July 30, 1979), 77.

167. "Merry Christmas." New Letters, 46 (Spring, 1980), 85.

168. "In Despair He Orders a New Typewriter." The American Scholar, 49 (Summer, 1980), 334-35.

169. "Volcan de Agua." Poetry: A Magazine of Verse, 136 (July, 1980), 211-13.

170. "A Clock." New Yorker, 57 (March, 2, 1981), 42.

G. PLAYS

171. *The Shepherd and the Conqueror*. In *The Cock of Heaven*. New York: Macmillan, 1940, pp. 65-67. Reprinted in 13 and 14. (See 12).

172. *Faust: A Masque*. *Measure: A Critical Journal*, 2 (Summer, 1951), 298-319. Reprinted in 14.

173. *The Sorcerer's Apprentices*. *Western Review*, 21 (Autumn, 1956), 5-14. Reprinted in 14.

174. *The Carnival of Animals*. In *Plays and Poems, 1948-1958*. Chicago: The University of Chicago Press, 1958, pp. 55-76.

This radio play in verse won the joint award of the Academy of American Poets and the Columbia Broadcasting System in 1957.

175. *The Illusionists*. In *Plays and Poems, 1948-1958*. Chicago: The University of Chicago Press, 1958, pp. 79-120.

176. *A Crack in the Universe*. *First Stage*, 1 (Spring, 1962), 9-33.

177. *The Abstract Tragedy: A Comedy of Masks*. *First Stage*, 2 (Summer, 1963), 166-86. Reprinted in 16.

H. NOTES AND LECTURES

178. "Aristotle on Art." Lecture presented on Tuesday, October 10, 1978, at Phillips University in Enid, Oklahoma as part of a symposium entitled "Aristotle and the Greek Experience."

Argues that Aristotle's treatment of art is determined by the entire body of his philosophy. After elucidating what constitutes scientific knowledge for Aristotle (the specification of attributes inhering necessarily in subjects) and distinguishing among sciences according to the inherence of different attributes in different subjects through different causes, Olson considers Aristotle's division of the sciences into three basic categories or groups, the theoretical, the practical, and the productive, noting, among other things, that each science has a peculiar end in view, respectively, knowledge (e.g., math and physics), action (e.g., ethics and politics), and a product (the useful and fine arts). Although in Aristotle's scheme art can be discussed under any of these sciences, only a poetics is equipped to examine products in themselves. Moreover, unlike natural objects (trees, horses, oysters, etc.), which have an internal principle of development, artificial objects require for their realization the imposition of some form upon a material not predisposed to assume any given form. Thus, since for Aristotle definition is a statement of the nature of the whole, concrete object produced by a certain art, and since no artificial whole can be constructed unless some form is imposed by some means upon some matter for some end, adequate definition of the whole demands the specification of its formal, material, efficient, and final causes, the last being the most important, being that for the sake of which the others are present. Olson concludes his talk by showing how the *Poetics* follows the pattern of reasoning that he has outlined and by reminding the audience that Aristotle's method can be extended to deal with developments in art since his time.

179. "Dylan Thomas." In *Twentieth-Century Literary Criticism: Excerpts from Criticism of the Works of Novelists, Poets, Playwrights, Short Story Writers, and Other Creative Writers, 1900-1960*. Ed. Dedria Bryfonski and Phyllis Carmel Mendelson. Detroit: Gale Research Co., 1978, p. 470.

Reprints parts of three paragraphs from chapter two ("the Nature of the Poet") of *The Poetry of Dylan Thomas*. In these passages Olson describes Thomas's two chief limitations, i.e., his restriction to a certain range of lofty emotion and his restriction to one poetic character. Thomas is a poet of sublimity, and although he can feel great emotion for others, he "cannot stand in another's skin." When he does not achieve the sublime, "he fails."

180. "Harriet Monroe." Talk given on May 7, 1980, at the Joseph Regenstein Library (University of Chicago) on the occasion of the opening of the exhibit "Poetry Magazine: A Gallery of Voices."

In this unpublished talk, Olson pays fond and warm tribute to Harriet Monroe, the founder and longtime editor of Poetry: A Magazine of Verse. He devotes the bulk of his remarks to an assessment of the quality of the magazine that survives her and is still informed by her principles and to a portrait of the quality of the woman who established the first real outlet for poets during a time when "American poetry was undergoing a revolution or rather a series of revolutions." By means of vivid scenes and significant anecdotes, Olson captures the distinctive traits that reveal her essential character. She was tireless in her search for new talent, unflagging in her support of "flagging older talent," sympathetic to both traditionalists and "avant-gardists," wisely intolerant of all dogmas, convinced as she was that "poetry had to encompass all human experience," rich in "good counsel" and, what is more rare, receptive to the "good counsel of others." In all, a woman "kind and stern, generous and frugal." Although, like anyone who accomplishes something truly impressive, she did not escape "detraction" (especially from "wounded egos, ignorance, and prejudice"), Olson marvels, in retrospect, that "so much energy...goodness, indeed greatness, could be housed in so small and frail a body." For Olson, she remains the best practical critic he ever met and one for whom his "love and esteem--in the long physical absence, and sustained only by memory--have grown and deepened."

II
SECONDARY MATERIALS

I. BOOKS

181. Lucas, Thomas E. *Elder Olson*. New York: Twayne Publishers, 1972.

Contents

Provides a sympathetic and intelligent assessment of Olson as a theorist, practical critic, and creative artist. Lucas's judgments achieve authority as a result of their being based on a careful and sensitive reading of the plays and poems and on a thorough understanding of the principles and assumptions underlying Olson's arguments. In short, Lucas earns the right to assert that Olson is "the finest theoretical critic writing today" and that he "will eventually find a place in the first rank of American poets." To those unfamiliar with Olson's work and those from whose familiarity time has worn off the memory of the Grecian precision with which Olson defines and resolves issues, the book will be extremely useful.

Lucas begins his study with a review of Olson's conception of criticism as a philosophical discipline, which is always part of a larger system of thought, and of pluralism, which is based on the recognition that there are a variety of valid critical and philosophic methods. In the next three chapters (2-4), Lucas focuses on literary theory, giving particular attention to Olson's "extensions of Aristotle's thought" and method, his distinctions among kinds of plot, his analyses of character, thought, manners of representation, and the technical resources of language, his delineation of the relationship between morality and art, and his investigations into comedy, tragedy, and the shorter forms, especially the lyric. The chapters on practical criticism (5-7) stress Olson's studies of drama and of Pope, Stevens, Marianne Moore, and Dylan Thomas. To Lucas, the practical essays illustrate Olson's "theories in operation" and provide "models for practical critics."

In the concluding chapters, Lucas examines and evaluates Olson's achievement as both poet and playwright, devoting attention to each collection of poems (with the exception of _Olson's Penny Arcade_, which postdates _Elder Olson_) and to each of the plays, especially _A Crack in the Universe_ and _The Abstract Tragedy_. Although Olson has written in a variety of styles and forms, Lucas is convinced that his finest productions "are of the type that he calls 'the imagistic lyric of ideas.'" These are "poems which present circumstances (primarily depicted in images...) which evoke specific thoughts and feelings which attend the possibility of their truth."

The "whichiness" of the last sentence notwithstanding, Lucas's prose is generally perspicuous, supple, efficient, and exact.

In sum, Lucas's book provides a useful overview of Olson's achievement as a critic and poet and a healthy corrective to the frequently splentic or dyspeptic animadversions of his detractors. Reviewed in *Criticism*, 15 (Fall, 1973), 366-68 (See 355).

J. ESSAYS, REVIEW ARTICLES, AND EXTENDED NOTICES

The entries in this category are arranged alphabetically by author.

182. Adams, Hazard. _The Interests of Criticism: An Introduction to Literary Theory_. New York: Harcourt, Brace and World, Inc., 1969, pp. 113-46. (Discussion of "Chicago criticism" occurs on pp. 134-41.)

In a section on "Chicago, neo-Aristotelian criticism," reviews what Crane and McKeon have to say on the subjects of imitation and representation and then takes up Olson's attack (most notably in the essay on Empson) against those critics who focus chiefly on the language of poetry, determining that Olson's argument makes "a telling criticism of New Critical practice," but not of its theory, which is concerned not so much with words as with the power of language to constitute reality in a symbolic form. Notes also that in directing attention to what the "words point to" (i.e., what they enable us to infer about, say, character and thought), Olson leaves unsettled the "degree of actual being" that can be attributed to what the poem evokes in our minds. Like Crane, Olson seems inclined to find the justification of the poem only in its "emotive effect." Thus, the poem finally neither represents experience--since, as Olson says, "what is imitated is different from the imitation of it"--nor organizes experience in "constitutive symbols."

183. "Allewaert, René. "Aristote a Chicago; La Nouvelle Criticism." _Etudes Anglaises_, 14 (1961), 211-24.

Using _Critics and Criticism_ and _The Verbal Icon_ as his principal texts of reference, attempts to define the nature of the squabble between the "Chicago Aristotelians" and the "New Critics" and then, once the issues have been joined, to determine which of the contending parties has the better case.

Allewaert admires the energy and sensibleness with which Crane, Olson et al. seek to reduce the confusion in critical discourse by reminding us that the aim of criticism is not to multiply hypotheses, but to take advantage of and to refine the sound principles and methods that we have inherited, and by insisting on the application of rigorous standards of demonstration to critical argumentation. Nevertheless, when he turns to the theory and practice of the "Chicago critics," he discovers the very same sort of "a priorism" that they attack in their opponents, an exclusive emphasis on concrete wholes and the purely formal elements of texts which restricts the range of their inquiry, and a refusal to make use of all the techniques and principles that linguistics, psycho-analysis, anthropology, etc. have made available to us and that the "New Critics" skilfully adapt to literary studies. In the end, he rules in favor of the "New Critics" and accepts the validity of Wimsatt's charge that the "Chicago" critics are guilty of committing the "fallacy of the neo-classic species."

But, lest we think for a moment that he has forgotten the importance of being a

Frenchman, he puts the trial in perspective by viewing it as an example of _un dilemme permanent de la pensée americaine._ Americans are always coming down on the side either of consolidation or of discovery; they are either instructing the public in the classical tradition (Chicago critics) or furnishing the public with new instruments of knowledge (New critics). Given such a choice (and only such a choice), he nods _naturellement_ in the direction of discovery and new instruments. Of Olson specifically, he acknowledges that his attacks against Empson and Robert Penn Warren are just, but, missing the point and allowing wonder to do the work of refutation, he wonders whether Olson's Aristotelian attachment to moral choice, moral action, in his analysis of "Sailing to Byzantium" as a certain kind of lyric, would be of any use in a discussion of most modern works, which are concerned with _being_, not _action_. Concludes the whole piece with the sort of Gallic mysticism that in some quarters passes for intellectualism: "truth comes and goes ceaselessly; it is one and many at once, but one can hold it neither for long nor for himself alone."

184. Altieri, Charles. "The Qualities of Action: A Theory of Middles in Literature." _Boundary 2: A Journal of Post-Modern Literature_, 5 (1977), 323-50.

In a section of his essay that attempts to explain why the "new critics" ignored or neglected "action," says that Wimsatt's "The Chicago Critics" (see 225 below) is an "unsuccessful reply" to the "penetrating critiques" of the new critics by Olson and Crane. He then examines Olson's distinction between speech as meaning and speech as action, noting in conclusion that, irony upon irony, because Olson himself ignores the "cognitive effects" resulting from reflection on literary actions and "is content" with an "essentially affective theory" of how literary actions evoke emotional responses, it is Cleanth Brooks, not Olson, who articulates what can genuinely be called a "dramatistic theory of literary truth."

185. Battersby, James L. "Elder Olson: Critic, Pluralist, and Humanist." Chicago Review, 28 (Winter, 1977), 172-86.

Presents, in what is ostensibly a review of On Value Judgments in the Arts and Other Essays, a description and assessment of Olson's achievement as a critic over the last forty years, giving particular attention to his analyses of the causes of variation in philosophic and critical reasoning and to his contributions to the three primary branches of literary inquiry, poetics, hermeneutics, and criticism. Especially useful are those sections of the essay in which Battersby speaks directly to the charges often levelled at Olson and other so-called "Chicago" or "Neo-Aristotelian" critics by more or less sympathetic commentators, for example, the charge that these critics are guilty of viewing and judging all works according to a priori generic criteria, or the charge that they really approve of only one critical method. Admits to writing as a "partisan, as a friend of the court," but also demonstrates that criticism, as pursued by Olson, is a rigorous, intellectually demanding enterprise, one which can lead to genuine knowledge.

186. Beardsley, Monroe C. and Sam Hynes. "Misunderstanding Poetry: Notes on Some Readings of Dylan Thomas." College English, 21 (1960), 315-22.

Looks at four approaches to the "Altarwise by owl-light" sequence of sonnets as examples of interpretive methods that, of necessity, fail to explicate Thomas's meaning, each approach exhibiting how, when faced with obscurity, a serious critic can go "seriously and thoughtfully wrong." Among the four they list "The Error of the Imposed System; or The Runic Method of Explication (the other three have equally catchy titles: "The Anti-explication Error," "The Error of Piecemeal Plucking," and "The Error of Hasty Plucking"), the principal perpetrator of which is Olson, who imposes a coherent meaning on the sequence by reading it in terms of the Hercules Constellation, thus manifesting in unadulterated form the sort of "a priori approach to explication" that he has elsewhere (in the Thomas book even) eloquently attacked. Admitting that Olson's system is applied with "remarkable consistency," they ask, rhetorically, whether there is "any evidence that these poems have anything at all to do with the constellation Hercules."

187. Borklund, Elmer. Contemporary Literary Critics. New York: St. Martin's Press, 1977, pp. 396-401.

Presents a brief but useful overview of Olson as a critic, giving particular attention to his "pluralism" (i.e., to his analyses of the principles and assumptions determining the kinds of problems that can be entertained and the kinds of terms in which such problems can be addressed) and to his practical criticism, especially of the lyric and of drama, buttressing each section of the article with liberal quotations from Olson's writings. Although interested primarily in adequately representing Olson's views, he occasionally assesses what he describes, remarking of "The Dialectical

Foundations of Critical Pluralism," for example, that this "extraordinarily complex and rewarding essay displays a kind of thinking about thinking which has rarely been attempted by any critic, modern or otherwise." Prefaces his account with a brief biographical sketch and a selected list of publications.

188. Burke, Kenneth. "The Problem of the Intrinsic (as Reflected in the Neo-Aristotelian School)." In _A Grammar of Motives_. Englewood Cliffs, New Jersey: Prentice-Hall, Inc., 1945, pp. 465-84. Reprinted in _Aristotle's Poetics and English Literature_ (see 19).

In response to essays published in the _University Review_ (1942) by R.S. Crane, Norman Maclean, and Elder Olson (whom Burke calls--and he is the first to do so--"Neo-Aristotelians"), argues that since every critic "begins with a more or less systematically organized set of terms by which to distinguish and characterize the elements of the poem he would observe," since, in short, particular statements about a poem are "deduced" from the terminology the critic employs, criticism cannot really "start from scratch" without presuppositions, cannot really be "inductive," as these critics claim. Also takes issue with Maclean and Olson for asserting that "great art...is always in the last analysis _sui generis_." If they were right, we could have "no statements about the lyric as a genus." Moreover, despite their emphasis on particular works, these critics regularly use "a vocabulary wider in reference than the orbit of the given form...." Concludes by observing that it is not enough to consider a poem solely "in terms of its 'perfection' or 'finishedness,' since this conventionalized restriction of our inquiry" to the "intrinsic" could not possibly tell us "all the important things about its substance."

189. Burke, Kenneth. "The Serious Business of Comedy." _New Republic_, 160 (March 15, 1969), 23-27.

In a long review of _The Theory of Comedy_, "an unusually able and superior work," carefully traces the outline of Olson's complex, variously branching argument, giving emphasis to Olson's distinction between the comic, a quality, and comedy, a form, and to his definition of comedy modelled after Aristotle's definition of tragedy. Although greatly admiring the utility of Olson's definition, wonders whether, in seeing comedy as a type of work effecting a _katastasis_ (i.e., relaxation) of concern, he is not disposing of _catharsis_ in comedy too quickly and whether, given his emphasis, he needs to distinguish further between the "kind of relaxation that is due to _relaxed_ conditions and the kind that runs counter to _tense_ conditions." Remarks that the second half of the book, in which the theory is applied to particular cases, "abounds in gratifyingly acute comments," and while admitting to a "hankering after" a theory that has room for "comic catharsis," concludes by expressing his admiration for a book that commands "attention."

190. Cambon, Glauco. "Between Aristotle and Plato." _Poetry: A Magazine of Verse_, 102 (June, 1963), 198-201.

Reviews six books, including Olson's _Tragedy and the Theory of Drama_, all reflecting a concern with how the space between the gesture of Plato, pointing up, and the gesture of Aristotle, pointing down, in Raphael's The School of Athens (a space containing all Western thought and art) has been filled in. Finds in Olson's book echoes of the issues that occupied the attention, not only of Plato and Aristotle, but the Italian Cinquecento critics as well (as documented in the books on the criticism of the Italian Renaissance by Bernard Weinberg and Baxter Hathaway, also reviewed in the article). Thus, in dealing with plot, character, and dialogue, Olson confronts problems "hotly debated" by his Italian ancestors; in asserting that action has precedence over language, he recalls Guarini and Angelo Ingegneri. Beyond noting similarities between Olson and his forebears, Cambon praises his skilful, pragmatic approach to the construction of King Lear, Macbeth, and Agamemnon, but discovers irony in his refusal to consider language as "essential," especially since he is at his best when he is examining "speeches in their contextual relevance."

191. Crane, R.S. "Two Essays in Practical Criticism: Prefatory Note." University Review, 8 (1942), 199-202.

Introducing the two pieces that follow his article, Crane compares the principles and assumptions underlying the practical criticism of Norman Maclean ("An Analysis of a Lyric Poem") and Elder Olson ("'Sailing to Byzantium': Prolegomena to a Poetics of the Lyric") with those guiding the interpretive procedures of the most influential modern commentators, namely, T.S. Eliot, I.A. Richards, Cleanth Brooks, John Crowe Ransom, and Allen Tate, all of whom are, in the broad sense, Coleridgeans, in that, for all their differences, they commonly assume that "poetry is a single essence." Moreover, that essence is determined by finding analogies to poetry in some part of human experience--e.g., in language, mind, speech--of general significance, and then showing how the particular terms applicable to poetry--e.g., extension and intension--participate in the universal scheme. In their hands, a poem "ceases to be a concrete object of a particular sort deliberately ordered to a specific artistic end by the poet" and becomes an "exemplar of principles broader in their relevance than poems or any given kind of poems." Olson and Maclean, on the other hand, focus on the poem itself in its "wholeness and particularity as a structure of mutually appropriate parts." Thus, in contradistinction to these other critics, Olson and Maclean choose to identify the parts of a work and the principles of their interrelation independently of any "a priori assumptions about the nature of poetry in general."

192. Daiches, David. "A Major Contribution to Modern Criticism." Times Higher Education Supplement [London], August 27, 1976.

In a review of On Value Judgments in the Arts and Other Essays that is sensitively responsive to the subtlety and complexity of Olson's thought, to the range of his critical voices, and to the rigorous sharpness of his distinctions, rates this collection of essays "one of the three outstanding books produced by the ['Chicago'] movement." (Critics and Criticism and Crane's The Languages of Criticism and the Structure of Poetry are the other two). Looking at the essays in chronological sequence, Daiches notices that Olson "grows more genial as he grows older," though "no less rigorous in the development of his arguments." Says that, taken together, the essays "constitute a major contribution to criticism." To Daiches, no summary of Olson's views can be "adequate" to the "dialectical rigour" of his arguments," and he notes, in conclusion, that the provocative effect of Olson's arguments on the "careful reader" is such that he "must rethink" all his critical assumptions once he "puts the book down."

193. Frye, Northrop. [Untitled] *Shakespeare Quarterly*, 5 (1954), 78-81.

In this review of *Critics and Criticism*, Frye quickly sets forth the theoretical principles and assumptions of the "Chicago" critics and the order in which the essays are presented and then concentrates on those issues particularly relevant to the criticism of Shakespeare, focusing on Weinberg's discussions of the criticism of Robortello and Castelvetro, on Keast's and Maclean's separate essays on *King Lear*, and on Olson's broad division of literature into two mutually exclusive classes, the didactic and the mimetic. To Olson, since these forms are constructed acording to different principles, they must be judged differently. Argues that Olson's view is inconsistent with that of Sidney, for whom the mimetic and didactic are "complementary" and "inseparable" aspects of the same thing, and with the practice of Renaissance poets and playwrights, Shakespeare's perhaps most notably. In the reaction of Olson and his colleagues to the "new critical" reduction of a "stage play to a tissue of verbal ambiguities," they fall into the opposite error, i.e., confusing not *praxis* and *lexis*, but *praxis* and *mythos*, thus failing to recognize that a "well constructed imitation of an action...has a *dianoia* or thought-form as well as an event-form," that this *dianoia*, the "total internal idea of the poem," inheres in both "mimetic and didactic poetry." "Inner meaning" is coextensive with and, thus, part of the action. Nevertheless, his reservations notwithstanding, Frye says that the "learning and acuteness" of the collection as a whole make "it indispensable for the serious student of criticism."

194. Gray, J.M. "Aristotle's Poetics and Elder Olson." Comparative Literature, 15 (Spring, 1963), 164-75.

Taking seriously Olson's insistence that a proper understanding of an intellectual system can only be achieved by examining it within the terms of its own logical and linguistic framework and attempting to hoist Olson on his Aristotelian petard, Gray proposes to show how the inconsistencies in Aristotle's presuppositions and method carry over into and, thus, diminish the value of Olson's critical theory (as expressed principally in "An Outline of Poetic Theory," "The Poetic Method of Aristotle," and the essay on Empson).

From his own reading of Aristotle, supported by the timely assistance of Gerald Else's word by word analysis of the Poetics, Gray argues: 1) that no justification is supplied by Aristotle or Olson for applying the form-matter distinction to the discussion of poetry; 2) that language is the matter of poetry only as an unwarranted assumption by analogy with natural things; 3) that Aristotle and Olson use the terms "productive science" and "mimesis" inconsistently (for example, from the notion that the cause and productive processes of artificial objects are similar to those of natural objects, there can be no derivation of the idea that imitation is a copy or likeness of another thing); 4) that if the emphasis is put on imitation as a process, then questions relevant to object, means, and manner of imitation are not implicit in the term; 5) that there is nothing peculiarly inductive about the method by which Aristotle arrives at definitions; and, finally, 6) that there is nothing in the term "imitation," considered in the sense of similarity of form, to justify the assumption that an "imitation will have a single defining function or effect." Concludes by suggesting that the failure of Olson's poetics can be attributed, not to his misreading of Aristotle, but "to his misunderstanding of Aristotle's significance as a philosopher." Aristotle contributed massively to the "greatness of classic Greek culture." But his greatness "is historical greatness, and not justification for founding a modern theory of literature and criticism on an ancient philosophy which in itself was never directly concerned with aesthetics."

195. Hernadi, Paul. Beyond Genre: New Directions in Literary Classification. Ithaca and London: Cornell University Press, 1972, pp. 35, 99-104, 158, 172, 178.

Devotes considerable space to a description and assessment of Neo-Aristotelian poetic theory, concentrating on the writings of Crane and, especially, Olson, who has most forcefully expressed what Hernadi takes to be the "most important single tenet" of the "Chicago" group, i.e., that words are subordinate to their functions. Then focuses on the contributions of Olson and Crane to genre studies, suggesting that they deviate from Aristotle--who was concerned with the "whole of literature as a mimetic act"--in their division of literature into a "mimetic and a didactic genre." After reviewing Olson's careful discussion of the different ends to which the parts of didactic and mimetic works are ordered and his precise distinction between speech as meaning (lexis) and speech as action (praxis), notes (apparently failing to read what he has just written) that he sees no reason why we should treat the speech of a character in the Iliad any differently from the speech of a character in The Divine Comedy. Goes on to examine Olson's remarks on the magnitude of action in different forms and on comedy and tragedy. Determines that Olson's analyses of comedy and tragedy betray "an unwarranted evaluative prejudice," since they assume that "all mimetic works are either 'serious' or 'comic.'" Finally, in spite of Olson's sharp separation of the ridiculous from the ludicrous and his careful delineation of several comic plot forms, insists that Olson's theory is based only "on the punitive aspect of genre," and as a consequence, he "fails to account for the joyous, festive, gay, and playful elements permeating all but the most bitter...manifestations of the comic."

196. Holbrook, David. Llareggub Revisited: Dylan Thomas and the State of Modern Poetry. London: Bowes and Bowes, 1962, pp. 85-115.

In a chapter entitled "Critical Self-Deception," delivers a blistering, no-holds-barred, slap-'em-by-the-side-of-the-head Philippic against Thomas's barbarisms of language and against those critics who have been charmed and disarmed by the ecstatic bawling of the child-poet who, from the vantage point of infantile egocentrism, demands universal approval and protection from the realities of life. Singles Olson out as a critic representative of those taken in by the Welsh con-man, quoting regularly from his book on Thomas passages that betray a deluded sense of Thomas's poetic accomplishments. Olson is further castigated for suggesting that Thomas's language is essentially symbolic, not metaphoric, thus contributing in some not entirely clear way to the disesteem of the view that "metaphors are the fibre of language." From various sections of Olson's work, Holbrook takes sentences and shards of sentences to compile a "quotation" exhibiting Olson's argument and then brings this hodge-podge to judgment before the tribunal charged with punishing faulty logic. Olson is elsewhere accused of indulging in "undigested Aristotelianism" and of carrying to Thomas's _hwyl_ (ecstasy) an answerable style. For the most part, however, Olson, because he is seen as representative, is used as a sparring partner to keep our author in trim for his fight with Thomas, though Holbrook too frequently abuses either himself or the shadow cast fitfully on the wall by his own visible darkness.

197. Holloway, John. "The New and the Newer Critics." In _The Charted Mirror: Literary and Critical Essays_. London: Routledge and Kegan Paul, 1960, pp. 187-203. Reprinted from _Essays in Criticism_.

Attempts to take a moderating position between the views of the "neo-Aristotelians" and the "new critics." Recognizes that in their attacks against the "new critics" and the myth, ritual, and psychoanalytic critics, the "neo-Aristotelians" score some telling points, noteworthy among which are Olson's observations on Empson's failure to realize that what is interesting in substance is not necessarily "complex or ambiguous in treatment" and that "full meaning" is not a function of the interactions of words, considered independently of thought and character, but argues that in their castigation of efforts to extract meanings and themes from works, the "neo-Aristotelians" exhibit a blindness to the fact that some literary "masterpieces" do have "moral patterns as their predominant reality." Considers next their positive contributions to criticism, giving emphasis to what they say about concrete poetic wholes, the unifying principle of form, and plot as a system of incidents arranged to provide pleasure by arousing and allaying emotions. Takes issue, however, with the idea that literary art is distinguished by "a high order" of peculiar "emotional pleasure." To Holloway, art is characterized by "an unusually comprehensive vision of an imagined situation or train of events," any reduction of the reading experience to a sequence of emotions being "a dangerous simplification," an error exactly the converse of that--the stressing of the "intellectual side of communication"-- committed by Brooks, Empson, et al. Going briefly outside Critics and Criticism, notes that although Olson's "remarkable discussion" of Dylan Thomas's "Altarwise by owl-light" sonnets makes the "whole sequence clear," his analysis does not appear to develop or spring from the notion that the organizing principle of the work is "a peculiar sequence of emotions." Concludes by observing that our involvement with characters makes possible other and more important emotions than those stressed by the "neo-Aristotelians" (the emotions, for example, which "come through comprehension and contemplation") and that the "Chicago inquiry" requires for its completion a consideration of "imagery, poetic texture," and, hence, "themes."

198. Johnson, S.F. "'Critics and Criticism,' A Discussion: The Chicago Manifesto." JAAC, 12 (December, 1953), 248-57.

In a hostile review of Critics and Criticism, accuses the "Chicago critics" of being "severely refutative of other methods" and "merely assertive" of their own. Finds something to attack in works written by each of the members of the group but devotes most space to essays by Crane and Olson, giving substantial attention to Olson's views on the subordination of diction to artistic function in the essay on Empson. By means of selective quotation, misemphasis, and flat denunciation, Johnson assembles an indictment that charges these critics with 1) preaching a pluralism that they do not practice, 2) celebrating the virtues of an inductive method for arriving at definitions of species, while rigidly deducing definitions from the Aristotelian formal cause, 3) deviating from their professed concern with poetry as poetry by determining the nature of the poetic object according to a postulated intention in the author and an effect on the audience (i.e., with making the formal cause dependent upon the efficient--author--and final--audience--causes), 4) taking a "low view" of the importance of language, 5) advocating the specification of distinctive kinds of works and then enrolling all works under two broad, subsumptive classes, the didactic and the mimetic, and 6) making the "uniqueness of the poetic object" "independent of language." In all, these critics exhibit not only inconsistency but a shocking disregard (indeed, derogation) of virtually all the positive advances that have been achieved in critical studies by such myth, ritual, and genre critics as Frye, Wheelwright, Fiedler, Chase, and Fergusson and, especially, by the "new critics" who have made it impossible for any serious student of literature to deny "the significance of verbal patterns in literature." If there were such critics as those described by Johnson, they could not survive, with their self-respect intact, his excoriation.

199. "Crane, R.S. "A Reply to Mr. Johnson." JAAC, 12 (December, 1953), 257-65. (This entry is placed out of the alphabetical sequence, so that the reader may see Crane's response to Johnson in its proper context.)

In this response to Johnson's critique of Critics and Criticism (see 198, immediately above), Crane regrets that the author neglected the first duties of a reviewer (i.e., to address "in a serious and learned way" what actually was said in the work under consideration and then either to applaud the fruits of inquiry or to show how what went wrong might have been set right) and chose instead to attack the book as a whole in the service of "various doctrines about literature and critical method" to which he had prior commitments, thus making the whole enterprise a polemical exercise in partisan apologetics. However much he may personally regret the aim of the review, Crane feels that he is under no obligation to allow Johnson's handling of evidence to pass by without public scrutiny. To further his rhetorical strategy and to preclude genuine debate, Johnson has manipulated evidence in several not entirely subtle ways, for example, by suggesting that his "damnatory statements are so obvious that they require no proof," by wrenching numerous passages from their contexts and, thus, destroying their specific meaning and value within whole arguments, by suppressing qualifying statements, by treating historical generalizations as value judgments, by insisting that in spite of what a writer says he actually holds the opposite view, etc. All these devices of "rhetorical reviewing" are serviceable, but they do not contribute to the advancement of inquiry. In addition to identifying specific instances of Johnson's use of these devices, Crane also manages to restore to intelligibility and cogency the arguments that had been misrepresented by Johnson, to reinvest with clarity, at least, the views of the "Chicago critics" on such issues as pluralism, form-matter relationships, the function of language in poetry, and so on.

200. Johnson, S.F. "A Counterstatement by S.F. Johnson." _JAAC_, 12 (December, 1953), 265-67.

Briefly responding to Crane's response to his review of _Critics and Criticism_ (see 199, immediately above), Johnson essays to give him some of his own by accusing Crane of writing a "rhetorical review" of his review. Also, misreading Crane's distinction between "internal" and "external" bases of refutation, avers that Crane seems to rule out any criticism of the "Chicago" position that does not assume the validity of its principles. Reasserts, in conclusion, his judgment that the "Chicago critics" are pluralists in name only, adding that he is not alone in thinking so, as recent essays on these critics by Wimsatt and Vivas testify.

201. Kershner, R.B., Jr. _Dylan Thomas: The Poet and His Critics_. Chicago: American Library Association, 1976, pp. xii, 4-5, 6, 7, 52, 70, 77-81, 88, 91, 92, 96, 98, 125, 136, 163, 169, 170, 207, 208-09, 214, 218.

Comments on various aspects of Olson's book on Dylan Thomas, offering a mixed assessment of the whole (Olson's analyses are variously "idiosyncratic," "controversial," "brilliant," "reasonable," and "ambiguous"). Devotes most attention to Olson's exegesis of Thomas's sonnet sequence, which, based as it primarily is on "arcane lore" relating to pagan and Christian interpretations of the Hercules constellation, has occasioned considerable resistance from critics, a substantial number of whom believe that Olson, in spite of his opposition to the mechanical application of symbolic codes to specific poetic works, has imposed a symbolic system on the sequence. Although agreeing with much of what Olson says in his analysis, Kershner finally concludes that "the sort of God Thomas comes to" is left "ambiguous by Olson." Finds illuminating Olson's discussion of the kinds of complexity found in Thomas's poetry and his definition of the "pseudo-dramatic dialogue."

202. Kinneavy, James Leo. A Study of Three Contemporary Theories of the Lyric: A Dissertation. Washington, D.C.: The Catholic University of America Press, Inc., 1956, pp. 1-69.

Devotes chapter one, "Elder Olson: The Lyric as Choice," to a discussion of Olson's approach to the lyric. Assumes throughout that in the two essays dealing with Yeats's poem ("'Sailing to Byzantium': Prolegomena to a Poetics of the Lyric" and "An Outline of Poetic Theory") Olson is defining, not a particular kind of lyric (which is what Olson is doing), but lyric poetry generally, though in a note Kinneavy admits that Olson's references to three types of lyric activity in The Poetry of Dylan Thomas, published after his study had been written, may render what he says about Olson "obsolete." Examines Olson's approach, which is based upon a consideration of all the causes that converge to produce the emotional effects of species, in the light of his own distinctly different assumptions about the lyric and the requirements of definition. Kinneavy postulates a concept of genre determined by "kinds of meanings or references" and assumes a distinction between form, which is comprised of only three types (expository, dramatic, and narrative), and genre, which specifies the object referred to by the poem, the referential "reality" of the poem. Charges Olson with deviating from Aristotle's methodology, with confusing action (the "reality referred to") and plot (the "imitation itself"), art and life, and end and means. Detects real differences in the two essays on Yeats's poem, noting that the earlier essay ("Prolegomena") stresses argument and stasis, and the later essay ("Outline"), moral choice and dynamism. Concludes by finding the later essay superior to the earlier, since it presents a view of the poem that conforms more readily to "reality."

203. Klotz, Volker. [Untitled] Anglia, 88 (1970), 130-35.

In this review of Tragedy and the Theory of Drama, Klotz questions the appropriateness of the "general application" of Aristotle's Poetics to genres other than drama by the "Chicago Neo-Aristotelians" but admits that since Olson's topics are tragedy and dramatic theory his study cannot be faulted for its Aristotelianism. Unlike most German theorists, Olson examines drama, not only as a literary form, but also as a production for the stage. Klotz presents a summary account of the book and then says that Olson's enquiry could be called a "neutral production esthetics," neutral because it is free of rigid dogma, and production esthetics because it locates the subject in the "sequence of the production process," in the developing problems of the working dramatist. Asserts that Olson occasionally uses "quasi-scholastic argumentation" and leaves unquestioned many "norms and definitions." Nevertheless, he concludes by saying that this is an "important book that should find a German publisher."

204. Krieger, Murray. "Creative Criticism: A Broader View of Symbolism." Sewanee Review, 58 (Winter, 1950), 36-51.

Considers the strengths and weaknesses of the "Chicago" and "New" critics prior to advancing his own views, which make use of the insights of both "schools." Krieger gives prominence to several of Olson's essays, especially "An Outline of Poetic Theory," the "most cogent" exposition of the neo-Aristotelian approach "to date." After reviewing the principal tenets of "Chicago" criticism--at one point referring to the object of imitation (the formal cause) as the material cause and to the means of imitation (the material cause) as the formal cause--Krieger avers that the "Chicago" critics indulge in circular reasoning (demanding an emotional effect, "searching it out," and then judging a work by "its conformity to this effect"), that they are indifferent to language "with its ambiguous and connotative levels," that they are purely formalistic in their emphasis on the relations of the parts to the whole, and that they have recourse to an "extra-poetic ideal" in their appeal to pleasure. While granting the legitimacy of much in the "Chicago" attack against the "new critical" tendency toward thematic reductionism, Krieger asserts that Cleanth Brooks and others have provided us with valuable insights into contextual ambiguities and highly "complex and paradoxical themes." If the differentiating feature of art is that it presents an organization of experience in all its complexity as a result of the artist's struggle to make his medium answerable to the "shadings and intricacies of felt life" and, thus, to create an "essential significance which lies immanently within the object," then criticism should "proceed structurally as well as linguistically to get at the unique integrity of experience."

205. Krieger, Murray. The New Apologists for Poetry. Minneapolis: The University of Minnesota Press, 1956, pp. 73n, 93-98, 148-55, 195-96, 210, 211, 215, 216.

Contains two long sections on the "Neo-Aristotelians," in both of which Olson figures as one of the chief spokesmen for the theoretical principles and assumptions of the group. Krieger asseverates that in his attack against the "new critical" inclination to reduce criticism to a mere commentary on language, Olson, who emphasizes the subordination of language to other poetic elements and all elements to the synthesizing principle of form, has a "blind faith in the...unclouded referentiality of the language of poetry" and fails to realize that the art product can only emerge "from the struggle of the artist with his medium." In moving from an examination of the "unique formal structures" of particular works to the development of a general theory of poetry based on the definition of species in terms of "the effect aroused in us," these critics become entangled in inconsistency, since the "claim for uniqueness is incompatible with their consciousness of classes." Moreover, by defining a poetic species in terms of a peculiar emotional effect and then judging the value of each work according to its approximation of the effect, Olson and the others engage in circular reasoning and are as Platonic as the critics they attack, inasmuch as they put faith in an a priori and extra-poetic ideal (i.e., the arousal of a peculiar kind of pleasure), one, alas, founded on a "strikingly obsolete psychology." This piece of demolition work would be devastating, if it were not so thoroughly tainted with misunderstanding.

206. Lesser, Simon O. "'Sailing to Byzantium': Another Voyage, Another Reading." <u>College English</u>, 28 (January, 1967), 291-310.

Asserts that Olson, though writing with a "brilliance" that gives his ideas authority, completely misreads Yeats's poem in his "'Sailing to Byzantium': Prolegomena to a Poetics of the Lyric," and that most of the blame for his misunderstanding can be attributed to his method, which leads him to disregard the "emotional content" of literature and our "emotional responses to it." Summarizes Olson's interpretation and then observes that the whole "chain of reasoning" on which it is based is wrong, inasmuch as the "happy conclusion" it reaches (the old man joyfully works out his problem with the unsuitableness of age to "that country") is founded on patently erroneous readings of the first three stanzas, especially one (Olson here fails to see that "all"--including the old man--are caught in the "sensual music,") and three (Olson here misses the point that the old man "prays for death"). The poem is not a "happy one," coming to culmination in some form of noble joy or exultation, as Olson claims, but a desperately sad one; it is a "cry of agony," and in the last stanza the old man refers to a form of reincarnation only to make us "feel his present despair."

Devotes the second half of the essay to speculations on the cause of Olson's deviant reading. Olson's shortcomings as an interpreter, we discover almost immediately, can be traced to his approach. His "formalism" is inappropriate to poetry, because it deflects attention from the "rag-and-bone shop of the heart" and emphasizes, instead, the world of "tidy, antiseptic abstractions." Olson "domesticates" the poem, reducing perhaps his own anxiety, but only at the cost of denying the "primary process thinking" that all poetry--and especially lyric poetry--reflects. Olson may wish to suppress awareness of how the sight of the young in one another's arms can arouse desire and envy, but by so doing, he is "betrayed by his approach and the unknown emotional factors playing upon him" into a massive misreading of the poem.

207. Maud, Ralph. "Dylan Thomas Astro-Navigated." Essays in Criticism, 5 (1954), 164-68.

Asserts that in spite of the five chapters of exposition describing Thomas's poetic "universe," his symbolism, his handling of the devices of language, his dramatic voice and so on, the long chapter on the "Altarwise by owl-light" sonnets dominates The Poetry of Dylan Thomas and can be considered as Olson's "major original contribiution to Dylan Thomas criticism." Maud finds Olson's phrase by phrase analysis of the sequence in terms of the movements of the stars "uncalled for and unrewarding," such correspondences as can be discovered between the peregrinations of the Hercules constellation and the details of the text being the inevitable result of bringing into conjunction "a willing mass of zodiacal data" and a "suggestive poem." In an attempt to give weight to his general charge, Maud offers an alternative reading of the first two lines of the first sonnet, one elucidating how these lines, as well as the whole poem, demand "a Christian, rather than a Herculean, interpretation."

208. Mazzaro, Jerome. "Critical Discontents." Sewanee Review, 86 (Winter, 1978), 139-46.

In this review of On Value Judgments in the Arts and Other Essays, Mazzaro summarizes Olson's views on critical method and the causes of critical conflict and then extols the merits of the title essay and "The Dialectical Foundations of Critical Pluralism," the "volume's richest pieces." Still, Olson's methodology has its "blindnesses," for working within the rigors of Olson's method inevitably involves the separation of the reader from "his idiosyncratic feelings." Avers in conclusion, by way of summing up his reaction to the collection of essays, that knowledge in art "exists as play," not as "problem solving," and "for critics to restrain this play is dangerous not to art but to the criticism involved."

209. McLaughlin, Charles A. "Two Views of Poetic Unity." University Review, 22 (1956), 309-16.

Discusses the different views of poetic unity advanced by the "New Critics" (chiefly Brooks and Wimsatt) and the "Chicago critics" (chiefly Crane and Olson) and then, to illustrate the practical powers and limitations of the two approaches, considers how each group of critics would interpret

Frost's "Stopping by Woods on a Snowy Evening." For the "New critics" unity is "an attribute of the mind of the poet or speaker" made manifest through devices of "the poetic medium" and characterized by the "reconciliation of opposites" inherent in the subject matter, whereas for the "Chicago critics" unity is at once an "attribute of the object imitated" and an "attribute of the effect that unified actions are capable of producing." Unlike the "New critics," who are interested in differentiating poetry from science in terms of the special kind of tension or balance among "meanings, attitudes, or interpretations" possible to poetic communication, the "Chicago critics" distinguish among kinds of poems in terms of achieved effect. As a consequence of their different assumptions, these critics would read Frost's poem either as a "dialectical progression" from local tensions to "ultimate implications," the details of the poem at their "fullest symbolic stretch," or as a dramatic exhibition of moral choice effecting "pleasurable admiration." Concludes by observing that the analytic methods of the two groups of critics speak to different aspects of literature and that we should not be dismayed by apparent conflict but grateful for the varieties of methods that "are available to enrich our reading of poetry."

210. Offen, Ron. "Portrait of the Artist (As a Musing Critic)." Hyde Park Herald, June 14, 1972, 12.

Interviews Olson, inquiring about the process of composition (it begins with "clear, auditory images," followed by rhythms, phrases, and feelings, until "it's rather like being in a hurricane in a feather factory"); about his revisions (not unusual for Olson to make "35 drafts of a poem" before being satisfied with it); about the quality of poetry today (there has never been a time "when so many poets possessed such high technical skills"); about the relationship of his poetry to his criticism (the classroom is a "kind of laboratory" in which he tests the theories informing his poems, his discoveries then filtering "back into the poetry"), and about his work habits (cannot write poetry while working on criticism but can work "on several different poems at the same time").

211. Oppel, Horst. "Elder Olson als Dramatiker." Neueren Sprachen, 4 (April, 1959), 153-64.

Presents an assessment of Olson's production as a playwright based on the four major plays written by 1959: Faust: A Masque, The Sorcerer's Apprentices, The Carnival of Animals, and The Illusionists. American drama generally includes a deep symbolic setting for its energetic realism, but Olson develops the symbolic backgrounds into actual allegories that regularly show us how little man has done with his world. In The Sorcerer's Apprentices man competes with and loses to the robot, and in both The Carnival of Animals and The Illusionists men become material, and happiness, as it is socially regulated, excludes the arts and sciences. And although Faust: A Masque borrows from Goethe (and others), Olson deliberately creates a one-dimensionality that brings devices of modern art to mind and that suggests a kind of "regressive evolution." But here, as elsewhere, Olson is principally concerned with "self-interpretation" and with the dangers implicated in the modern thirst for knowledge in science and technology. What Olson creates finally is a "literary laboratory" that shadows forth the "modern laboratory of the world." As a dramatist,

Olson's chief strength is his metaphorical imagination, which he uses to expose "the ways in which man has degraded himself."

212. Phelan, James. Worlds from Words: A Theory of Language in Fiction. Chicago and London: The University of Chicago Press, 1981, pp. 8, 9, 13, 14, 152, 155-83.

For the purposes of his inquiry, Phelan highlights what Olson has to say about the function and importance of language in literature (especially in "William Empson, Contemporary Criticism, and Poetic Diction"), namely, that if the task of criticism is to show how the various elements of a text combine to produce a "single, though complex effect," then language is the least important of such elements, since it is determined by everything else. Chapter five, "Verbal Artistry and Speech as Action: Elder Olson and the Language of Lolita," undertakes to test Olson's view of language, as well as his own similar view, against Nabokov's Lolita, a work in which the language appears to provide pleasure in itself, independently of its contribution to the artistic intention or the final end of the work. Phelan first differentiates his position, which distinguishes between the linguistic and nonlinguistic aspects of a "speech-event," from Olson's, which distinguishes between speech as meaningful and speech as action, and then, after admitting that both he and Olson agree that the language is successful in proportion to its contribution to "an intention" and that inferences about characters and situations are what language has importance relative to, argues that his distinction allows greater flexibility than that of Olson, since it recognizes that in some situations only certain language will serve the purpose. To Phelan, specific words are sometimes crucial to the artistic effect. Nevertheless, in subjecting Olson's and his own more "flexible" conception of language to the challenge of Lolita, he discovers that an account of Nabokov's style in terms of its contribution to the final end simply "does not exhaust our pleasure in it." Both views of language must be revised, since neither is sufficiently capacious to accommodate Nabokov's use of language.

213. Phillips, M.J. "The Poetry of Dylan Thomas." Chicago Review, 8 (Fall, 1954), 12-18.

Asserts that The Poetry of Dylan Thomas successfully diminishes the force of two charges leveled at the "Chicago critics": that they give little evidence of the appropriateness of their theoretical machinery to the tasks of practical criticism and that their prose is positively gothic, beyond intelligibility. Olson's book is perspicuous and thoroughly practical. Argues, moreover, that, for all its practicality, the study also extends and clarifies Olson's theory and that it is additionally valuable for its detailed investigations into the technical problems involved in the construction of poems. Proceeds to go through the book chapter by chapter, providing a capsule account of each and regularly praising Olson for liberally illustrating his points with quotations from Thomas's poems. Calls Olson's reading of the "Altarwise by owl-light" sonnets "one of the marvels of interpretation of our age." Finishes off his review by registering one or two demurrers concerning what he takes to be Olson's equation of excellence with difficulty and his defense of Thomas's obscurity. Wonders, finally, why, if "there are no 'rules' or 'laws' of art," as Olson says, such a fuss is made about the "post-Aristotelian system of lyric species or subspecies" in Olson's criticism.

214. Ransom, John Crowe. "The Bases of Criticism." Sewanee Review, 52 (1944), 556-71.

Ostensibly written in response to Hoyt Trowbridge's essay in praise of the critical method of the "Chicago critics" (see 222 below; Trowbridge's article immediately precedes this one in the Sewanee Review) and in opposition to essays of practical criticism by Norman Maclean ("An Analysis of a Lyric Poem") and Elder Olson ("'Sailing to Byzantium': Prolegomena to a Poetics of the Lyric"), Ransom's piece merely takes the occasion of these essays to argue for the subordination of argument and syntax to imagery and dystax (i.e., the terms of the poem that are not logical) in poetic structures. Olson "seems dialectically tougher than Maclean," but both of these hopelessly "academic" critics tend to see the poem as existing for the argument, instead of the other and correct way about (i.e., with the argument existing for the poem). They try at once to "stretch paraphrase" until it will "hold the poem" and to "trim" the poem until it "will get into the paraphrase," failing to realize, in their concern with logical relations, that the "imitation element," the "free natural imagery," is "the thing which gets excluded from the argument." Having found the "faults" of Maclean and Olson by filtering their views through his lenses, their problems through his, Ransom presents his own superior case: that whereas logical argument is the "formal cause," the "public front" of poetry, "imagery" is the "final cause," and that poetry is a "mode of discourse" which distinguishes itself from the scientific mode by using language that is elliptic or dense with imagery to "throw into relief the dystax of the poem." (In Ransom's scheme, the "dystax is as proper to the poem as the syntax is proper to the argument.") Thus, Olson and Maclean can tell us something about argument, but nothing about what is genuinely valuable in a poem or what is truly distinctive of poetry.

215. ________________. "Humanism at Chicago." Kenyon Review, 14 (1952), 647-59.

Describes the "Chicago critics," in what is ostensibly a review of Critics and Criticism, as humanists who gave up the hard questions and turned for comfort to a program of studies sanctioned by the ancient authority of Aristotle, from whose handbook they have deviated not a tad, if we make allowances for some slight adjustments to cover Shakespeare, lyric poetry, and modern drama and fiction. Ransom sees them throughout the first section of his essay as uncritical celebrants of antique and, thus, "antiquated" doctrines, making their "adaptations" within the boundaries delimited by the Text (as the loveable uncles who appear at all formal occasions wearing spats and, though conspicuously dotty, have the amused, tolerant, and condescending respect of all for their charming loyalty to outmoded fashions). Ransom then reviews what in his opinion Aristotle has to offer, in the doctrinal line, under the headings of plot, character, thought, and diction, pointing out in passing that few of Aristotle's tenets are applicable to Shakespearean drama or modern literature. As an alternative to the "Chicago" program, Ransom concludes with a proposal to consider each poem, not as one object, but as three objects: one made up of plot or argument; one created by the words in their impetuous reach beyond mere "denotation," and one brought about by a meter that mediates between the other two and, thus, allows an "intimation of the Platonic Ideas." The "Chicago" preference for plot over poetry is given "closest and clearest" expression by Olson, "their best man in a long hard fight at close quarters." Throughout the essay Ransom neglects the primary concern of the "Chicago critics" with Aristotle's method and obliges them to participate in a dispute about doctrines, about such matters, for example, as whether plot is more important to literature than poetry, a dispute in which they neglected to engage.

216. Booth, Wayne C. "On the Aristotelian Front." _Kenyon Review_, 15 (1953), 299-301. (This entry is placed out of the alphabetical sequence, so that the reader may see Booth's response to Ransom in its proper context.)

Levels the following charges at Ransom's review of _Critics and Criticism_ (see 215, immediately above): that instead of reading the "Chicago critics'" essays in the light of the specific principles and assumptions governing their arguments, he _translates_ their views into a different idiom, preserving the terms of their discussions but losing the intellectual framework only in relation to which their statements have determinate meaning and value; that in spite of their rigorous defense of _pluralism_, he persistently accuses them of being dogmatic Aristotelians; that he makes these critics out to be firm supporters of the _doctrines_ of the _Poetics_ who wish only to add codicils to Aristotle's "handbook" so that more recent works may be rendered submissive to its authority, whereas they everywhere betray an awareness of the limitations of the doctrines of the _Poetics_ and only wish, for some practical purposes, to apply Aristotle's _method_--which is permanently useful--to a variety of forms for which Aristotle made, and could have made, no accommodation; that throughout the review he assumes that these critics mean by _plot_ and _diction_ what he means by _structure_ and _texture_, whereas the terms are not interchangeable; and, finally, that he treats the whole book from the perspective of his own theoretical commitments.

217. Ransom, John Crowe. "Reply by the Author." _Kenyon Review_, 15 (1953), 301-04.

In this response to Booth's critique (see 216, immediately above) of his review of _Critics and Criticism_, avers that only twice did he, indulging in "a little foolish clowning," fail to tell the "whole truth" about the "Chicago critics." Acknowledges, first, that he did not emphasize the pluralism of these critics, a failure partially justified by the fact that, while professing pluralism in theory, they are actually preoccupied with "their Aristotelianism" and, hence, as "monistic" as those whom they attack. And admits, second, that he was wrong to accuse all the Aristotelians of a pious attachment to the "idea of action" (even when, as in a lyric poem, the "sequence" is not an action, but an argument), but claims that his remarks do apply to Olson, who, in his efforts to define the species of lyric to which Yeats's "Sailing to Byzantium" belongs, betrays his unswerving fidelity to Aristotle by referring to the chief part of the poem as an act of moral choice. Wearing his own pluralist hat at a jaunty angle, Ransom says in conclusion that Olson's reading provides one way "to set about figuring the logical organization of a lyric, but it is an Aristotelian and now a quaint way."

218. Reichert, John F. "'Organizing Principles' and Genre Theory." Genre, 1 (January, 1968), 1-12.

Attempts to isolate the shortcomings inherent in Olson's (and Crane's) division of literary works into the broad categories of the mimetic and the didactic on the basis of final causes and in Sheldon Sacks's similar division--indeed it is an extension of the one advanced by Crane and Olson--of prose fiction into satire, apologue, and represented action. The categories are represented as mutually exclusive by these critics, although there is nothing in the nature of literature, "considered abstractly," or in the existent instances of literary production to convince us that the arousing and allaying of emotions (characteristic of mimetic works) and the exemplification of a thesis (characteristic of didactic works) are mutually exclusive ends, or that the ends proposed as distinctive of the three types of prose fiction cannot be or are not incorporated into the same work. Briefly considers Tom Jones and Gulliver's Travels (works which Crane and Sacks cite to illustrate their views) as examples of prose fiction that effectively accommodate both didactic and mimetic readings. The classes, upon the definition of which all subsequent discussion of individual texts depends, are, according to Reichert, neither "exhaustive nor mutually exclusive." The dangers implicit in reliance on such categories for practical analysis are that works will be prematurely assigned to inappropriate genres and that, as a consequence, "effects achieved in works but not anticipated by the 'genre definition'" will not be recognized.

Concludes by inviting the reader to be aware that "no pre-conceived unifying principle" will be sufficiently adequate to the work before him.

219. ________________. "More than Kin and Less than Kind: The Limits of Genre Theory." In _Theories of Literary Genre_. Ed. Joseph P. Strelka. University Park and London: The Pennsylvania State University Press, 1978, pp. 57-79.

Examines the "theoretical weight" that the genres "have been asked to bear" by the theories of Crane, Olson, Sheldon Sacks, Frye, and Tzvetan Todorov. Taking issue with the attempts by Crane and Olson to extrapolate a "general theory" from Aristotle's remarks on tragedy, especially with their division of literature into two general classes, the mimetic and the didactic, Reichert argues that there is nothing to prevent a work from satisfying the demands of both classes, from both propounding a doctrine and exciting and arousing emotions. And what is true of the "non-exclusivity" of the classes postulated as mutually exclusive by Crane and Olson is also true of Sacks's extension of their views into prose fiction with his distinctions among satire, apologue, and represented action, since a single work could be examined with reference to all three types. Each of these critics, in asking genre to do more than is within its power, is in danger of categorizing a work prematurely and of "ignoring" effects in a work "not anticipated by the definition of genre."

220. Sastri, P.S. "The Poetics of the Lyric and Olson's Approach." _Literary Criterion_, 9 (Winter, 1969), 70-77.

Attempts to out-Olson Olson in his reading of Yeats's "Sailing to Byzantium" in the light of Aristotelian categories. Accuses Olson of denying to the poem a "mimesis of action" and insists that the "mimesis of dianoia" is also a form of praxis (Sastri's hard terms aside, his sense _seems_, oddly, to run not against but with the grain of Olson's position). Having established to his satisfaction the limitations of Olson's understanding of Aristotle, Sastri devotes the bulk of the essay to "showing" the weaknesses in Olson's interpretation of the poem that result from his "refusal to look into the structure of the poem" (i.e., the structure conceived by Sastri as unified "by the idea of music"). Asserts that because the old man has "only a desire to become the 'artifice of eternity,'" he does not and cannot arrive at Byzantium. He is "just sailing" to Byzantium, where a "fusion of beauty with music" may be achieved, once the "process of sailing" is completed. Claims that Olson is wrong to think that the final stanza resolves the conflict and that the golden bird's song is of the "divisions of eternity," for at the end we find simply a "new desire" to sing the "divisions of time, of the temporal process." Where argument with argument might fight, here claim after claim merely asserts its right. Sastri boxes sometimes with the shadows of Yeats and Olson, sometimes with the substance of his own case.

221. Sutton, Walter. _Modern American Criticism_. Englewood Cliffs, New Jersey: Prentice-Hall, Inc., 1963, pp. 152-74.

Presents, in a chapter entitled "The Neo-Aristotelians," a brief overview of "Chicago" criticism, devoting most space to summaries of the essays in _Critics and Criticism_, a book that might, not improperly, be called "an anti-New Critical symposium." Following each capsule account of the essays selected for review, Sutton offers a few evaluative comments. As far as Olson is concerned, he focuses chiefly on "An Outline of Poetic Theory" and the Empson essay, taking issue with Olson's typical "neglect of language" (i.e., with his view that language--the medium of poetry--is determined by everything else) and with his statement that strictly speaking a mimetic poem "has no meaning at all." Missing the radical significance of what Olson says, Sutton observes that since poetry and imaginative literature are "language products," literature "necessarily communicates meanings, and that since form is discerned only through its medium, the uses of language "determine form." To account for the fact that "Neo-Aristotelian criticism" had "no wide appeal," Sutton offers in evidence its inadequate "imitation theory," its genre approach (which tends to produce "sterile categorization"), its deductive and a priori method (despite its championing of the inductive and a posteriori), and its demotion of the importance of language.

222. Trowbridge, Hoyt. "Aristotle and the 'New Criticism.'" Sewanee Review, 52 (1944), 537-55.

Argues intelligently and persuasively that the "Chicago critics" have developed a "new technique" of literary criticism, one expressing "bold, incisive, and revolutionary ideas," and one founded on the recognition that two fundamentally different approaches to poetry have prevailed in the history of criticism: the integral, dialectical approach originating with Plato and concerned with the nature and degree of poetry's participation in some more comprehensive norm or value and the differential, inductive, and empirical approach originating with Aristotle and concerned with the specification of the principles responsible for the integrity of concrete artistic wholes. The "Chicago critics" develop the latter method, which is peculiarly suited to the task of providing a criticism of poems as poems. After quickly differentiating the aims of Plato from those of Aristotle, Trowbridge provides a brief overview of criticism "since the Greeks," seeing it as one "long attempt to achieve Aristotle's results [a criticism that is specifically literary] by the use of Plato's method," the general historical tendency reflecting a consideration of poetry in terms, successively, of ethics (Horace and his sixteenth-, seventeenth-, and eighteenth- century followers, such as Sidney, Dryden, Pope, and Johnson), of psychology (Longinus, Coleridge, and, in the twentieth century, Cleanth Brooks), and of style or "mode of discourse" (Greek and Latin rhetoricians and their modern "new critical" counterparts, for example, Allen Tate). Each of these essentially Platonic, extrinsic, a priori approaches is examined and then contrasted with the "Chicago" Aristotelian approach, as exemplified specifically in the writings of McKeon and Olson. (Olson's essay on "Sailing to Byzantium" is cited to illustrate the point that the "program of the Chicago school," far from leading to a "sterile formalism" that mechanically applies Aristotelian doctrines to emergent forms, emphasizes the need to discover artistic principles by means of "inductive analysis.") Concludes by remarking that the "Chicago critics" are certainly right in their insistence that both the Platonic and the Aristotelian methods have their distinctive powers and limitations and that their criticism, because it is principally addressed to the artistic integrity of the product itself, makes possible a criticism "genuinely literary," makes poetics (the "science of poetry as poetry") possible.

223. ______________________________. [Untitled] Comparative Literture, 3 (1951), 356-64.

Reviews three popular anthologies of modern literary criticisim (The Critic's Notebook, edited by R.W. Stallman; Critiques and Essays in Criticism, 1920-1948, also edited by R.W. Stallman; and The Foundations of Modern Literary Judgment, edited by Mark Schorer et al.), the editors of which not only represent "new criticism" as the dominant mode of literary imquiry, but also agree on the "high value" of its theoretical principles. Trowbridge questions not the prevalence but the value of "new criticism," noting that it has no satisfactory answers to the objections raised against it by such scholars as Douglas Bush, who discover in the readings of the "new critics" "unhistorical distortions" of the meanings of terms and phrases, and by the "Chicago critics," especially Crane and Olson, who detect radical weaknesses in the principles and assumptions on which these critics base their interpretive procedures. Rehearsing the arguments of Crane and Olson (particular attention is given to Olson's essay on Empson, his "An Outline of Poetic Theory," and his "Recent Literary Criticism"), Trowbridge observes that the "new critical" assumption that "all poetry is essentially one" precludes distinctions among kinds, leads to the evaluation of all poems by a uniform standard of excellence, and makes impossible the "treatment of a poem as anything but an instance of universal poetry." Furthermore, in making a particular use of language or diction the distinctive characteristic of poetry, these critics assume what cannot be demonstrated, restrict analysis to but one of the causes of any poem, and give preeminence to the least essential element of poetry. Finds the "neo-Aristotelian" approach of the "Chicago critics" the "most attractive" alternative to the "new criticism," though he admits that such critics as Burke and Trilling are also enriching current critical thinking and doing so by refusing, unlike the "new critics," to reduce all literature to "a drab abstraction" or to identify "poetics with linguistics." To Trowbridge, "new criticism" is a "cul-de-sac," and he is certain that the "future of criticism...lies in a different direction."

224. Vivas, Eliseo. "The Neo-Aristotelians of Chicago." _Sewanee Review_, 61 (January, 1953), 139-49. Reprinted in _The Artistic Transaction and Essays on Theory of Literature_. Columbus: The Ohio State University Press, 1963, pp. 243-59.

Focuses, in this review of _Critics and Criticism_, not on the "practical" essays or the "historical and contemporary studies" of other critical systems, but on the "positive doctrines" of the "Neo-Aristotelians," as expressed principally in McKeon's "The Philosophic Bases of Art and Criticism" and Olson's "An Outline of Poetic Theory" and "A Dialogue on Symbolism." Applauds the labors but rejects the doctrines of the "Chicago" critics, offering before the court of critical inquiry several objections. If the first task of a poetics is to define a work as a unique concrete whole, a distinct synthesis of parts ordered to a peculiar effect, then, according to Vivas, it seems 1) that _imitation_ "is a very poor term to achieve that end" (since it leaves out of account the creative process, the poet's creative act by which he "adds to what his senses gave him"); 2) that pleasure can neither define the end of poetry nor distinguish among poetic kinds (since pleasure, "qua pleasure," considered independently of the objects that arouse it--which is not how these critics consider it, of course--is "all of one kind"); 3) that their manner of analysis, founded on the discrimination of poetic species, is "open to question" (since an "inductive definition of species in the process of change" is impossible), and, finally, 4) that the "methodologoical relativism" advocated by these critics is "self-stultifying" (since if it has any value at all, it applies not only to their own work but to their analyses of other critical systems, seen as they are through "Chicago" lenses). His reservations and objections notwithstanding, Vivas says in conclusion that no serious critic "can ignore the challenge of the Neo-Aristotelians of Chicago."

225. Wimsatt, W.K. "The Chicago Critics: The Fallacy of the Neoclassic Species." Comparative Literature, 5 (Winter, 1953), 50-74. Reprinted in The Verbal Icon: Studies in the Meaning of Poetry. Lexington, Kentucky: University of Kentucky Press, 1954, pp. 41-65.

Fires repeated salvos at the "Chicago critics," especially Crane, McKeon, and Olson, directing his heaviest artillery at their principal tenets, which are, alas, the most vulnerable. Although claiming persistently to be pluralists (i.e., tolerant of a diversity of critical positions and methods) and Aristotelians only for strictly pragmatic purposes (i.e., so that they can attend to certain questions and problems), they everywhere manifest an intolerant rejection of all modern approaches concerned with verbal analysis and with "wholes" determined, not by genres, but by the "value principle of variety in unity or the reconciliation of opposites," wholes, i.e., naturally and practically related to the discussion of the "technical principles of ambiguity, polysemy, paradox, and irony." To their intolerance are joined a dogmatic commitment to their own views and a desire to develop their Aristotelianism into a "comprehensive critical method." Moreover, in treating the poem as a "literal, non-verbal artifact," they fail to realize that a poem is not a product; "if it is anything at all," it is a "verbal discourse." The concrete wholes that they claim to study are only such wholes as are indicated by the "superficially inspectable shapes of works or by genre definitions," but wholeness is not merely a form, but "a form arising out of a certain kind of matter, an organization of meaning in words." Theirs is, finally, a "neoclassic criticism by rules of genre." Takes issue with the legitimacy of their distinction between mimetic and didactic works and develops a case designed to show that they are themselves guilty of the intentionalism and affectivism for which they chastise others, for in spite of their professed interest in the study of poems, not their origins or results, their most important terms are "pleasure and purpose." Affectivism is apparent in their emphasis on pleasure. But what happens, Wimsatt asks rhetorically, to the Aristoteliain "thing" or "artifact," if _pleasure_ is stressed? On the other hand, the genetic fallacy is evident in their regular appeal to the intentions of the author. Wimsatt notes that they confuse form "in the object" with form "in the mind of the maker," and he brings his commentary to an end by remarking that "they expect too much of their system and too little of their own capacity to read poems and respond to them"; in their efforts to construct a "strictly self-contained" definition of poetry, they are the "Scaligers, not the Aristotles, of modern criticism." (In its first publication the essay did not include "The Fallacy of the Neoclassic Species" in the title.)

K. REVIEWS

The entries in this category are arranged chronologically under each book reviewed.

Thing of Sorrow

226. Walton, E. L. Books, 7 Oct. 1934, p. 23.

Asserts that Olson's Thing of Sorrow "is by no means a book to be neglected, for Mr. Olson has a real gift, especially in the handling of unusual rhythms." (This review was not to be found in the libraries I consulted. I quote Walton's remarks as they appear in Thomas E. Lucas's Elder Olson; see 181.)

227. S., G.M. "Thing of Sorrow: A Poet Who Offers the Spiritual Tonic Society Needs." Boston Evening Transcript, 10 Oct. 1934, p. 2.

Calls Thing of Sorrow a "distinguished first volume," which, along with Paul Engle's American Song, carries us beyond the "whining" and "unintelligible" verse of the past decade and "sounds a positive note" that finds the "struggle of life exhilarating." Praises the poems for their "exquisite phrasing" and their reflection of the poet's "veneration for the art of poetry." Eagerly awaits more from this poet "brave enough" to depart from the kinds of poetry produced by his "immediate poetic ancestors."

228. Jack, Peter Monro. "A Poet of Lyrical Distinction." New York Times Book Review, 14 Oct. 1934, p. 25.

Discerns in Olson's Thing of Sorrow "a promise of authentic lyrical talent" and an ambition to find language commensurate with his subject. Also recognizes that in its preoccupation with "style" and a "not unpleasing melancholy" the poetry is that of a young man. Comments positively on Olson's penchant "for the metaphysical" and negatively on his "expatiations," his tendency to progress without advancing, but notes in summation that this first book, "though slight," has the "signs of distinction."

229. Benét, William Rose. "Round About Parnassus." Saturday Review of Literature, 27 Oct. 1934, p. 247.

Refers to Olson, in this review of Thing of Sorrow, as one of "the most interesting of the younger American poets," who in making the active mind the center of his interest "sets metaphysics before us again." Olson's work commands attention for its "metaphysical properties" and its clear, immediate, though subtle, expression. Olson writes with "so rare a distinction" that he "awakens new hope for American poetry."

230. [Anon.] "Impotent Sorrow." Christian Science Monitor, 14 Nov. 1934, p. 12.

Declares that in Thing of Sorrow Olson, "whether intentionally or not," has fashioned out of the subject of sorrow a beauty that is joyful and "furnished unmistakable evidence of sorrow's impotence."

231. [Anon.] "Poetry." [London] Times Literary Supplement, 29 Nov. 1934, p. 859.

Observes that Olson's verse in Thing of Sorrow has the "virtue, both in its vision and its intonation, of the depths he invokes." Singles out "Essay on Deity," "The Ghostly Spring," and "Spring Ghost" as especially moving in their evocative power.

232. Stroebel, Marion. [Untitled] Chicago Daily Tribune, 14 Dec. 1934, p. 12.

Favorably reviews Thing of Sorrow, observing that Olson "has as sensitive an ear as any lyric poet writing today." (I have taken Stroebel's remarks from Thomas E. Lucas's Elder Olson; see 181. The bibliographical data is probably incorrect. At any rate, I could not locate Stroebel's review on the page or in the issue of the Tribune cited above.)

233. [Anon.] [Untitled] The Booklist, Dec. 1934, p. 124.

Brief notice of Thing of Sorrow, giving publication data and describing the book as a collection of "short-lined lyrics" notable for "exquisite phrasing and quiet imagery" and expressive of a "pensive mood" under the control of a "fine sense of objectivity."

234. Walton, Eda Lou. "An Interesting New Poet." Nation, 9 Jan. 1935, p. 54.

Sees the Olson of Thing of Sorrow as a poet of masterful technical competence, one, however, working within a narrow range of concern (i.e., that change evokes, defines, and destroys beauty, thus making all things "things of sorrow") at a level of presentation somewhere between that of the "fully sensuous" poet and the "true mystic," though he is a mystic only to the extent that, like any "modern thinker," he is "aware of the Bergsonian philosophy of fluctuating emotions and shifting ideas." Judges Olson to be a "bit literary" and lacking in "fiery intensity," yet, all the same, "worth reading and worth watching."

235. Emerson, Dorothy. "Poetry Corner: Elder Olson." Scholastic, 28 (February 8, 1936), 12.

Indicates that "many people thought that Olson should have won the Pulitzer Prize last year for Thing of Sorrow" and then, after quoting "Essay on Deity" and "Colloquy," in illustration of his "characteristic mood" and "musical phrasing," observes that his poems "are so perfect of their kind that one feels Mr. Olson to be among the very best...poets in this country."

236. Kunitz, Stanley J. "The Enchanted Pilgrim." Poetry: A Magazine of Verse, 45 (February, 1935), 279-82.

Reviewing Thing of Sorrow, Kunitz praises Olson for exhibiting the "rarest of gifts: the innocent eye" (what is seen is seen so clearly that "he needs merely to name it...for us to share his delight"). Also praises his technical "dexterity" in the management of rhythms and in the use of "dissonances to break up the rhyming pattern" and his ability to "fabricate" intricate and economical poems "about a node of meaning" (he never mistakes an "afflatus for an idea"), but also notes that the range of his ideas is "yet too limited," with too many poems playing "variations on the old theme of the sorrowful heart and its paradoxical freight of sweetest songs."

The Cock of Heaven

237. Holmes, John. "Poems and Things." Boston Evening Transcript, 7 Oct. 1940, p. 11.

Briefly reviews several recent books of poetry, including Olson's The Cock of Heaven, a more "ambitious book" than his earlier Thing of Sorrow, which had a "richer lyrical value than almost any book of its time." Observes that in his second book of verse Olson has extended his range "technically, spiritually, and artistically." Yet, for all its many excellences, Holmes believes that the book will appeal to a "limited number of people," because it lacks that "simplicity" sought in poetry.

238. [Anon.] [Untitled] New Republic, 102 (October 14, 1940), 534.

In a brief notice, calls Olson's The Cock of Heaven a poem of "epic proportions" that is "technically smart, but unoriginal."

239. Jolas, Eugene. "Poets and Poetry: Goodbye to Yesterday." Living Age, 359 (October, 1940), 195.

Describes the Olson of The Cock of Heaven as a "metaphysical poet," who writes "vigorously in many styles." Finds his work noteworthy for its rich imagery, profound erudition, and lyric power.

240. Jarrell, Randall. "A Job Lot of Poetry." New Republic, 102 (November 11, 1940), 667-68.

Praises Olson's The Cock of Heaven in such terms that even a stone would feel the insult. Summarizes the "conception" of the work--the wanderings of the Magi who forever seek a Messiah--runs through an extensive list of poets (primarily Yeats, Donne, Eliot, Hopkins, MacLeish) whom Olson has endeavored to imitate, and then refers to the whole as a kind of fairy tale produced by an author belonging to "a simpler age," an author who sports a "sword-cane" and an "opera cloak" and who could be found "applauding passionately the first performance of Hernani."

241. [Anon.] Poetry." Time, 18 Nov. 1940, pp. 91-92.

Describes Olson's The Cock of Heaven as a "craftily written" work on "a major theme" (i.e., that for sin-soaked man salvation is a consummation never to be attained, though devoutly to be wished), a work that for "purely literary excitement" should "rank as the poetic book-of-the-year." Qualifies this ostensible praise almost immediately by saying that the poem, in spite of Olson's praiseworthy efforts to give his subject fresh power, produces in the "reader's conscience" very little "agitation."

242. Rago, Henry. "Symmetry of Frustration." Poetry: A Magazine of Verse, 57 (1940), 214-17.

Praises Olson's The Cock of Heaven as a "tour de force," rich in "skillful undertones and delicate fluencies of sound," though at times less than economical in the range "of resources" that it manipulates.

Lists among Olson's virtues his "swift and neat" handling of plot, his competence at "really distinguished parody," and his "intellectual gift for sharp aphorism," but feels that his "contrivances" produce no "authentic impact." Looks forward to a more "direct speech" from Olson, now that he may "consider himself proved" as a poet.

243. Jack, Peter Monro. "New Books of Poetry." New York Times Book Review, 9 Feb. 1941, p. 18.

Reviewing Olson's The Cock of Heaven, as well as several other books of poetry, says that this book, with its range of verse forms and emotions, "is far beyond Olson's first book" and an auspicious token of even better books to come.

244. [Anon.] [Untitled] Atlantic Monthly, February, 1941, p. 286.

Quickly summarizes the legend upon which the text is a commentary and then notes that The Cock of Heaven, though "obscure in parts," contains many passages "of great power and passion" presented in a rich variety of styles.

245. Untermeyer, Louis. "Yeats and Others." Yale Review, 30 (Winter, 1941), 378-85).

Reviews, among other works, Olson's The Cock of Heaven, which is "nothing if not ambitious." Although the work is regarded by Olson as a single poem, Untermeyer finds "eighty well-separated" pieces, with the parts "greater than the whole." The individual lyrics, striking for their "vigor" and "dexterity" (when Olson is not imitating "Donne," "Blake," or "Pound") move from "the fiercely ironic to the quietly mystical."

The Scarecrow Christ and Other Poems

246. Joost, Nicholas. "Auden and Olson: The Transformation of One, the Emergence of the Other." Chicago Sunday Tribune, 27 Mar. 1955, p. 12.

In a review of Auden's The Shield of Achilles and Olson's The Scarecrow Christ, observes that Olson deserves notice from a "wider public" and then highlights a few poems indicative of Olson's range, giving special attention to "Crucifix," a "fine poem because it fuses Olson's integrity of art and feeling."

247. McDonald, Gerald D. "Poetry." Library Journal, 80 (April, 1955), 8B.

Brief notice summarizing the contents of The Scarecrow Christ.

248. Bogan, Louise. [Untitled] New Yorker, 30 Apr. 1955, p. 125.

Reviewing The Scarecrow Christ, Bogan notes that Olson is "open to moments of terror and horror" and that "immensity weighs upon him." Praises his often "startlingly precise" diction and imagery and his remarkable skill "with strict and formal lyric forms."

249. Rodman, Selden. "The Content and the Form." New York Times Book Review, 22 May 1955, pp. 10-11.

Reviews seven recent books of poetry, including Olson's _The Scarecrow Christ_, in which the learned weight of "literary allusion" diminishes the "emotional impact" of poems that in general betray a fine ear and a mind with something to say. Singles out "Last Autumnal" as an example of Olson's "admirable maturity and simplicity."

250. Ciardi, John. [Untitled] _Nation_, 11 June 1955, p. 508.

Notes briefly, in a review of _The Scarecrow Christ_, that Olson is a poet "about whom too little is heard" and that the poems in this collection "should certainly take any reader."

251. Untermeyer, Louis. "Disciplined Fantasists." _Saturday Review_, 18 June 1955, p. 21.

Calls Olson, in this review of _The Scarecrow Christ_ and other books of verse, "one of the more disciplined and distinctive fantasists" of our day, one who in going beneath "surface sanctimony" is actually "penetrating" and "painfully revealing," especially in the third and best section of this uneven book, in which "unusual concepts" are combined with "appropriately powerful images."

252. Carruth, Hayden. "Seven Books in Search of a Customer." _Poetry: A Magazine of Verse_, 86 (June, 1955), 168-72.

On the basis of the pieces collected in _The Scarecrow Christ_, judges Olson to be, not a "metaphysical poet," as some might be inclined to think, given the "conviction" that informs the "pure thought" of his poetry, but a "high romantic, a Byron of the intellect," whose best poems are his "reflective lyrics," such as "Cry Before Birth," "Wishes for His Poem," and "The Midnight Meditation." The book contains many "poems which no one should be willing to overlook."

253. Jarrell, Randall. "Recent Poetry." Yale Review, 44 (June, 1955), 598-608.

In a review of several volumes of poetry, Jarrell says that the poems in The Scarecrow Christ are best when Olson "deliberately assumes a manner and the properties that go with it"; otherwise, when he writes in his own style, the poems seem to be "a stagey, exaggerated mixture of other people's poetry."

254. Barrett, Alfred, S.J. [Untitled] Catholic World, 181 (August, 1955), 398.

In a brief review of Auden's The Shield of Achilles and Olson's The Scarecrow Christ, observes that Catholic theology has served "as inspiration for the poet figures in these volumes by two of America's most difficult writers of verse"; sees Olson as a poet who "writes a powerful line which appeals to head and heart" and likens the title poem, because of its "force and shock value," to Dali's cubistic "Crucifixion."

255. Flint, F. Cudworth. [Untitled] Virginia Quarterly Review, 31 (Autumn, 1955), 648-56.

Reviewing The Scarecrow Christ, along with several other volumes of verse, Flint remarks on Olson's "metaphysical bent" and on a diction similar to that of Yeats, though "displayed in a more capricious line." Like Yeats, Olson inclines to a "cyclical view of reality," but if Yeats's cycles "whirl about" historical "personages," those of Olson--so Flint's riddle goes--"operate in a universe of particulars which contains those implied in the fact of Chicago."

256. Fisher, John A. "Six Younger Poets, a Review." _Mandala_, 1 (1956), 131-34.

Reviews six books of poetry, including _The Scarecrow Christ_, in which the "lines pile up through the book, full of poetic thought but not poetry." Suggests, with more verve than sense, that if Olson had been "more swept away by contemporary enthusiasms" and had employed some of "the 'new' critical methods he scorns," his "lines might have had a more natural sound."

The Poetry of Dylan Thomas

257. Korg, Jacob. "A Changed Dylan Thomas." _Nation_, 24 Apr. 1954, pp. 260-61.

Declares, in this review of _The Poetry of Dylan Thomas_, that in addition to describing with care the techniques employed by Thomas and clarifying the "awesome dimensions of his art," Olson provides an "interesting defense" of Thomas's obscurity and, in the major section of the book, constructs a subtle reading of the sonnets based on "recondite astrological lore" that, while raising perhaps as "many questions as it answers," compels the reader to believe that he has "discovered the key to an understanding of these poems."

258. Clinchy, Evans. "'Under Milk Wood' Typically Thomas." _Hartford Times_, 1 May 1954.

Says that The Poetry of Dylan Thomas (which is reviewed along with Under Milk Wood) contains much that is "valuable and illuminating" concerning the tasks of criticism and Thomas's "ideas on art." Considers Olson's analyses of the poems "helpful," but a trifle too "academic." Acknowledges that Olson has performed a "considerable service," but insists that the "true" Dylan Thomas is found "beyond the realm of criticism," in the poems and the recordings.

259. Fitts, Dudley, "The Bard of Wales." Saturday Review, 1 May 1954, p. 30.

Welcomes the appearance of The Poetry of Dylan Thomas, representing as it does the first "considerable attempt to evaluate the whole range" of Thomas's verse, a pleasant relief from the plethora of "mawkish" elegiac tributes occasioned by Thomas's untimely death. Suggests that because Olson is a poet first and a critic second he is "able to do justice to his subject" and calls his "brilliant" analysis of the "Altarwise by owl-light" sonnets "a model of responsible criticism."

260. Engle, Paul. "A Brilliant Study of Thomas's Poetry." Chicago Sunday Tribune, 2 May 1954, p. 6.

Praises Olson's The Poetry of Dylan Thomas for its "utility and brilliance"; it is a work which not only offers insights into the poems immediately under discussion, but also, especially in the sections on Thomas's techniques of language and his management of symbols, casts "a revealing light on poetry in general." Faults Olson slightly for occasionally deviating into the jargon of "the academe," but in the end observes that it is the sort of book "for which poets are grateful."

261. Russell, Francis. "Twisting Counterpoint of Thought." Christian Science Monitor, 6 May 1954, p. 11.

Briefly reviews The Poetry of Dylan Thomas and Thomas's Under Milk Wood, calling Olson's work "informative" and "as adequate an introduction to Thomas as can be found." Notes, however, that when exegesis has done its best work, we are still left, not with a "heightened awareness of the ultimate life processes," as Olson claims, but with real confusion, with "lyric crossword puzzles."

262. Joost, Nicholas. "And He Sang in His Chains like the Sea." Commonweal, 14 May 1954, p. 151.

Finds in Olson's The Poetry of Dylan Thomas a compellingly convincing answer to the accusation that the so-called "Chicago critics," despite their "formidable theoretical equipment," are unable to provide an "esthetic" capable of handling "fresh creative work," for Olson demonstrates that a sufficiently "broad understanding of Thomas's poetry" can be achieved, not by the methods employed by "the mythopoeic, the sociological, and the ontological (or new) critics," but by the flexible adaptation of the method developed by Aristotle to new forms. Thanks Olson for providing a "fitting tribute to Dylan Thomas," one that carries us back to "the object, the poem, not to ourselves."

263. [Anon.] [Untitled] Booklist, 15 May 1954, p. 354.

Briefly notes that in <u>The Poetry of Dylan Thomas</u> Olson has supplied the reader with an "enlightening introduction" to the complex and "often baffling" poetry of Thomas. Olson's "most exacting criticism" is displayed in his analysis of the "Altarwise by owl-light" sonnets.

264. Scott, W.T. "Poet of a Lost Eden Recaptured in Wales." <u>New York Herald Tribune Book Review</u>, 23 May 1954, p. 4.

Asserts, in a review concerned primarily with Thomas's <u>Under Milk Wood</u>, that Olson's <u>The Poetry of Dylan Thomas</u> is a "general study" modestly and "decently done."

265. Ferling, Laurence. "Recent Books of Poetry." <u>San Francisco Chronicle</u>, 13 June 1954, p. 21.

Sneering behind his smile or smiling within his sneer, Ferling (Ferlinghetti?) observes that <u>The Poetry of Dylan Thomas</u> displays the sort of "close criticism" that is "perfectly suited for use by professors and students at graduate seminars" and asserts that Olson can be correct in his judgment that Thomas's sonnets are his best poems only if one assumes a necessary positive correlation between value and complexity.

266. Keister, Don A. "Two Critics Appraise Dylan Thomas' Poetry." 13 June 1954. (This item was taken from a "review clipping" that did not cite the publication or the page.)

Briefly reviews Thomas's <u>Under Milk Wood</u> and Olson's <u>The Poetry of Dylan Thomas</u>, calling the latter an "indispensable book" for the reader of Thomas's poetry, one that examines many of the "most important poems" and "throws much light on their notorious obscurities."

267. Schott, Webster. "Stage Lost a Great Potential Dramatist in the Untimely Death of Dylan Thomas." Kansas City (Missouri) Star, 15 June 1954.

In a review of Thomas's Under Milk Wood and The Poetry of Dylan Thomas, states that Olson's study cannot be "praised too highly." Summarizes Olson's estimate of Thomas's genius and then remarks that the book is "full of insights into Thomas's meaning and method."

268. Tomlinson, Charles. "Scholarship and Dylan Thomas." Spectator, 20 Aug. 1954, p. 235-36.

Manages in a brief review of The Poetry of Dylan Thomas to discharge a full pint of toxic waste. Notes, for example, that although Olson is called a scholar and a critic on the "book-wrapper," he exhibits nothing "that is recognisably scholarship or criticism" in the development of his argument. He relies throughout the book on the "old academic" baggage of "themes and periods," none of it relevant to the business of "serious literary evaluation." Avers in conclusion that Olson, far from making a case for Thomas's "greatness," scarcely establishes that he was "in any exact sense a poet at all."

269. Fraser, G.S. "Grasping a Whole." New Statesman and Nation, 18 Sept. 1954, p. 330.

Treats Olson's The Poetry of Dylan Thomas as at least in part a tactical assault in the neo-Aristotelian campaign against those critics who give preeminence to verbal analysis, calling the chapter on the "Altarwise by owl-light" sonnets a "triumph of the non-verbal," the structural approach. Rehearses the argument of this chapter, taking issue from time to time with Olson's readings of particular lines. Ends his review, however, on a note of praise: what Olson "does for Thomas's grand structures...makes us forgive him for what he fails to do in detail."

270. Brown, Alan. "Books Reviewed." Canadian Forum, 34 (September, 1954) 140.

Dances about The Poetry of Dylan Thomas for a while trying to find something really witty to say about American ingenuity and the fruits of same (about, for example, the adeptness with which Americans take apart alarm clocks and atoms), before settling down to describe the contents of the book, to smile patronizingly at Olson's exegetical wizardry, and, finally, to express--in it would be impossible to determine what tone exactly--his "considerable respect for systematic work, coupled with awe and amazement at the approach."

271. White, William. [Untitled] Bulletin of Bibliography, 21 (September/December, 1954) , 103.

Calls The Poetry of Dylan Thomas a "major contribution to understanding a complex and often obscure modern poet." The book is "sensitive and perceptive," and it concludes with a "searching interpretation" of the "Altarwise by owl-light" sonnets.

Reviews

272. Christopher, Sister Mary, R.S.M. [Untitled] Catholic World, 180 (November, 1954), 159-60.

Calls Olson's The Poetry of Dylan Thomas a "balanced evaluation and an understanding critique" of Thomas's poetry and then presents a summary overview of the contents of the book.

273. [Anon.] [Untitled] 13 Dec. 1954. (This item from a French publication was taken from a "review clipping" that did not cite the publication or the page.)

Briefly summarizes the nature of Olson's approach to the poetry of Thomas in The Poetry of Dylan Thomas and directs the reader especially to the chapter that makes sense of sonnets previously taken to be hopelessly obscure.

274. Eberhart, Richard. "Time and Dylan Thomas." Virginia Quarterly Review, 30 (1954), 475-78.

Notes, in this review of The Poetry of Dylan Thomas, that Olson's "sane, moderate, and temperate approach" establishes confidence in his judgments and recommends the chapter on the "Altarwise by owl-light" sonnets to anyone "who wishes a crib to the ten sonnets." Disagrees with Olson's preference for the "hardest, most prolix poems." ("Ballad of the Long-Legged Bait," for example) and suggests that those which reveal their meaning fairly directly, such as "In my Craft or Sullen Art," will best satisfy the test of time.

275. Maud, Ralph N. [Untitled] Western Humanities Review, 8 (1954), 165-66.

Acknowledges that Olson makes "many useful observations" in his "ambitiously comprehensive book," _The Poetry of Dylan Thomas_, but declares that his "phrase by phrase" explication of the "Altarwise by owl-light" sequence in terms of the Hercules constellation--apparently the book's "raison d'etre"--exhibits such "forced ingenuity" that we "lose all sympathy with the critic." His treatment of the sonnets "undermines our confidence in the whole."

276. Thompson, Marjorie. "The Twentieth Century." _Year's Work in English Studies_, 35 (1954), 221-22.

Briefly reviews _The Poetry of Dylan Thomas_, remarking that the "broad essentials" of Thomas's poetry are delineated in an "admirably clear and satisfying manner" and that Olson's analyses of metaphor and symbol and his comments on melodrama and tragedy are "very helpful."

277. [Anon.] [Untitled] _St. Louis Globe-Democrat_, 2 May 1954.

States, in this brief notice of _The Poetry of Dylan Thomas_, that readers owe "an immense debt of gratitude to Elder Olson" for untangling the perplexities of Thomas's poetry. Assumes that the study will rise in value "as Thomas's adherents increase."

278. [Anon.] "Interpretations of Dylan Thomas." [London] _Times Literary Supplement_, 7 Jan. 1955, p. 10.

Examines _The Poetry of Dylan Thomas_ and Derek Stanford's _Dylan Thomas: A Literary Study_, observing that Stanford concentrates in his more modest study on texture, whereas

Olson emphasizes structure, the "dramatic plotting" of the poems "as wholes." Asserts that Olson's study is a "triumph of structural analysis" and that he is the first critic to make "coherent sense of two of Thomas's most difficult poems," the "Altarwise by owl-light" sequence and the "Ballad of the Long-Legged Bait," but suggests that Olson's formal method often makes Thomas a "tidier poet" than he finally is. And asks whether, even if the poems have the sort of logic that Olson's ingenuity detects in them, Thomas should not be "condemned" for his reliance on an "arbitrary...riddling technique." Observes, finally, that Olson's subtlety sometimes carries him beyond or around what Stanford, in his modest way, notices directy.

279. Ghiselin, Brewster. "Some Help for the Readers of Dylan Thomas." _Western Review_, 19 (Winter, 1955), 145-47.

Finds Olson's _The Poetry of Dylan Thomas_ to be a "useful" but "uneven" book, the first three chapters, on Thomas's poetic "character and his gift," being the least satisfactory because too little attention is devoted to what causes the reader the most trouble, "the meaning and function of the specific symbols of Thomas's poetry." Nevertheless, these chapters contain "much solid exposition and argument." Asserts that although it is possible to quibble with some of Olson's interpretations, there seems to be "no flaw in his conclusions" about the "development of meaning" in the poetry taken as a whole. Calls the latter part of the book a "courageous and successful attack upon the most difficult of Thomas' poems" and his reading of the "Altarwise by owl-light" sonnets "enormously illuminating."

280. A., A. [Untitled] Personalist, 36 (1955), 213-14.

Notes that The Poetry of Dylan Thomas is characterized by "learning, planning, and a sense of responsibility" to the reader and the poet and that even seasoned readers of modern poetry "will profit" from this volume, especially from the discussions of the complexities of Thomas's symbolism and of the "Altarwise by owl-light" sonnets.

281. Ghiselin, Brewster. "Critical Work in Progress." Poetry: A Magazine of Verse, 87 (1955), 118-19.

Declares that everything in Olson's "too brief book," The Poetry of Dylan Thomas, is designed to "encourage and facilitate" an intelligent understanding of Thomas's poetry, evaluation, though certainly present, regularly being subordinated to defining an approach to the poetry that "will make it fully accessible." Says that the book would have been "of nearly perfect usefulness," if each chapter had been as "full and well-proportioned" as the one on the sonnets, and hopes that a "strengthened" and "truly complete" second edition is in progress.

282. White, William. [Untitled] Papers of the Bibliographical Society of America, 49 (1955), 90-93.

Calls The Poetry of Dylan Thomas an "illuminating study" and then examines William H. Huff's "Bibliography," which is appended to Olson's book. Although really a "checklist," it is, with all its "faults," a "valuable" list.

Reviews

283. Thompson, Marjorie. "The Twentieth Century." _Year's Work in English Studies_, 42 (1961), 259.

In this review occasioned by the publication of the paperback edition, says that _The Poetry of Dylan Thomas_ "remains the most helpful and perceptive guide to Thomas."

Plays and Poems, _1948-1958_

284. Engle, Paul. "Liveliness in Poetry." _Chicago Sunday Tribune_, 4 Jan. 1959, p. 3.

Calls _Plays and Poems_ a "fortunate addition" to our literature because it "extends the range of writing" and then remarks that both the plays and the poems included in the volume are characterized by "liveliness" and lyrical power, the poems often leading you "gently down [a] path" and "quietly rattling the teeth in your head."

285. Ray, David. [Untitled] _University of Chicago Magazine_ (April 1959), 25.

Thoughtfully reviews _Plays and Poems_, giving particular attention to the plays, in which he finds, among other things, "sharp and pithy images," trenchant wit ranging from the "burlesque" to the "metaphpysical conceit," and philosophic thought that probes "deeply and eloquently into man's experience and fears." Compares Olson's work, in terms of its artistic achievement, with that of MacLeish, Eliot, Orwell, Wilbur, Yeats, and Huxley. Of his poetry, observes that the art is always "silently at work" creating verses of striking "intensity and beauty" and images and concepts of such immediacy that they have the force of "objects within the range of our touch."

286. Hazel, Robert. "The New Volumes." Poetry: A Magazine of Verse, 94 (August, 1959), 346-50.

After providing brief summaries of the five plays included in Plays and Poems, Hazel says that only a "fool would not find these plays interesting," though their attraction is, finally, "of ideas, not actions." Moves next to a consideration of the poems, which, taken together, form a whole "more fertile and powerful" than the recent volumes published by Olson's contemporaries and "cast him in a flattering light among them." Singles several poems out for particular notice, notably "Crucifix," which betrays a "large mind," "The Pole," which is a striking "instance of philosophical statement," and "A Valentine for Marianne Moore," which is a "splendid" direct address and "deserves to be famous." Concludes by noting that if Olson occasionally yields to "momentary sentiment," he is generally the poet of "impressive passions and intellections." Because he persistently "brings mind to art," we "need Olson to continue to produce."

287. Dickey, James. "The Human Power." Sewanee Review, 67 (1959), 509-11.

Sees Olson as the "most gifted" of the "Chicago" critics and as a distinguished poet. In this review of Plays and Poems, Dickey says that the five plays in the volume are "ingenious" and "amusing," but not commensurate in "originality" or "lasting effectiveness" with the poems. Characterizes the best poems as "models of difficult thinking made profoundly clear," as works reflective of a capacity to display the "Great Questions" in powerful relation to "the actual circumstances of everyday life." Concludes by saying that he cannot understand why, considering the quality of his work, Olson's poetry "is not better known."

Tragedy and the Theory of Drama

288. Dorsch, T.S. "Literary History and Criticism: General Works." Year's Work in English Studies, 42 (1961), 19-20.

Briefly describes the issues addressed and the plays discussed in Tragedy and the Theory of Drama and then says that the book is "sensible enough" but a "bit thin," coming no closer to "first principles" than many another book on tragedy. (But see 293 below)

289. Pritchard, J. P. [Untitled] Books Abroad, 36 (Summer, 1962), 319.

In a short review of Tragedy and the Theory of Drama, remarks that Olson has produced a "stimulating and profitable book," one free of the "pedantic style" that seems to be the distinctive signature of the "Chicago" critics. While extending and "corroborating" the premises of the Poetics, Olson also displays an "independent, penetrating mind."

290. Heffner, Hubert C. [Untitled] Quarterly Journal of Speech, 49 (February, 1963), 87-89.

Welcomes the appearance of Tragedy and the Theory of Drama, a study with which no student of the drama should be unacquainted, because it economically and forcefully establishes the principles of drama and explains "how they operate." Agrees with Olson's view that dialogue is subordinate to both plot and representation and considers his analysis of the problems involved in the creation of incidents the best he has seen "in any study." Objects slightly to the application of the term tragedy to "O'Neill's Mourning Becomes Electra, but ends by acknowledging that he is indebted to Olson for his "packed study," at once lucid in style and cogent in argument.

291. Gudas, Fabian. [Untitled] Modern Drama, 6 (May, 1963), 107-08.

Briefly reviews Tragedy and the Theory of Drama (along with George Steiner's The Death of Tragedy), noting that it is the "latest and most complete effort" in the "Chicago Critics'" campaign to show how Aristotelian "principles and distinctions" can be "refined, expanded, and supplemented into a full and coherent literary theory." (Of course, Olson's project, concerned as it is with the making part and not the reasoning part of poetics, is essentially Humean.) Concludes by summarizing the contents of the last half of the book, giving emphasis to Olson's analysis of the tragic effect and his discussions of particular plays.

292. de Schweinitz, George. [Untitled] Western Humanities Review, 17 (Spring, 1963), 191-92.

Drives his admiration of Tragedy and the Theory of Drama to an "O altitudo"; praises the book--one is almost obliged to say--"to the hilt," finding it to be "consistently keen-minded, intellectually spare, and verbally agile," "historical and holistic as well as eminently practical and germane to modern culture." Gives special attention to Olson's discussion of plot and to the immediate relevance of his theoretical principles to the writing and interpretation of tragic drama.

293. Dorsch, T.S. "Literary History and Criticism: General Works." Year's Work in English Studies, 47 (1966), 21.

Notes the appearance of the paperback edition of Tragedy and the Theory of Drama and remarks that the chapters on such general issues as plot, character, and dialogue contain useful "concrete illustrations" and that the "practical" chapters are "sensitive studies" of particular plays and playwrights." (See 288 above)

Collected Poems

294. Palmer, David. "Poetry." Library Journal, 88 (December, 1963), 4768.

In the venerable "loved him-hated her" tradition of reviewing, Palmer goes through each of the five sections of Olson's Collected Poems finding either beauties or faults: one part of the collection is rich in "clichés," another, "well consummated," and so on. Opines that Olson "writes about" rather than "expresses the reality" of his subjects.

295. Carpenter, Margaret Haley. "Poetry of Note." Chicago Sunday Tribune, 12 Jan. 1964, p. 8.

Of Collected Poems says that the volume "deserves an honored place on the shelf of contemporary poetry" and gives particular emphasis to Olson's variety and "vitality" and to the striking "blend of the emotional and intellectual" in his poetry. The collection evinces a poet of "strength, originality, and mature stature."

296. Faverty, Frederic E. "Lyricism and Philosophy." Chicago Literary Review, 7 Feb. 1964, p. 7.

Briefly reviews Olson's Collected Poems and Babette Deutsch's Collected Poems, 1919-1962, comparing the output of these two distinguished poets. Notes the range of "subject matter and treatment" in Olson's work and, in view of his success with "lighter themes," regrets that the collection contains so few poems like "Childe Roland, Etc." and "Exhibition of Modern Art," even though he recognizes that Olson should be judged primarily as a poet of philosophic meditation, as one who is at his best when presenting "dialogues of the mind with itself." Compares two of Olson's poems with two by Deutsch and concludes that the basic difference between them is that Olson is "inspired" by "philosophical, aesthetic, and moral problems," whereas Deutsch is "inspired by particular things or people."

297. Sorrentino, Gilbert. "Some from the forge, some slightly forced." Book Week (Washington Post-Time-Herald), Mar. 1964, pp. 6, 19.

Reviews four books of poetry, including Olson's Collected Poems, which he finds "a strangely uneven book," etiolated at time by "archaic syntax and verbiage" but characterized in general by a "remarkable intelligence" and by a rich variety of "moods and interests." Notes that Olson is preoccupied with the "a-lyrical poem" and that such an interest leads him to "narrative" and away from the "problems of poetry *per se*." Judges the book to be "more than competent," though at bottom it deals with issues somewhat dated "at this time of groundbreaking and upheaval in American poetry."

298. Rosenthal, M.L. "Sharp Glimpses of Reality." *New York Times Book Review*, 8 Mar. 1964, pp. 4, 37.

Reviews books of poetry by Kenneth Rexroth, Elder Olson (*Collected Poems*), and Daisy Aldan, observing that both Rexroth and Olson, though respected and admired, have not been the favorites of the critics. Detects in Olson's work, in addition to "occasionally wearying spirals of thought" that "belie his best instincts as a poet," two lines of continuity, one characterized by a "keen brooding sensitivity and a fine perfection of melodic line" and the other by trenchant commentary moving between "bitter allegory" and "broad satire," between attempts "to get at the basic nature of man" and expressions of zestful "buffoonery" springing from a "profound sense of things gone wrong." Remarks, in summation, that, "taken together," the poems are "not quite in concentrated focus," but that, taken one by one, "they yield not only hard gems but plain human revelations."

299. Fitts, Dudley. "Between the Sirens and the Muse." *Saturday Review*, 2 May 1964, pp. 34-36.

In a review of several volumes of poetry, discerns in Olson's *Collected Poems*, along with "civility" and "substantial accomplishment," a certain "hollow portentousness" and "prophetic fuss" (though he admits that few of the volumes examined contain material pressing "upon the heels" of the work of Olson and a handful of other poets).

300. [Anon.] "No Ideas But in Things." [London] Times Literary Supplement, 7 May 1964, p. 396.

Examines books of poetry by William Carlos Williams, Elder Olson (Collected Poems), and William Dickey, giving most attention to Williams. Of Olson, says that when he is not "ruthlessly academic" or writing "poetic diction," he is imitating Donne, Hopkins, Eliot, or Yeats, perhaps deliberately but certainly boringly.

301. Carruth, Hayden. "Among Friends." Hudson Review, 17 (Spring, 1964), 149-57.

Examines fifteen books of poetry, including Olson's Collected Poems, which allows us "a good view of his work, most of which is admirable," though many of Olson's ideas are "conventional" and "derivative." Qualifies the negative by declaring that Olson has an "easy flow of language" and often endows the conventional with vitality when he makes it inhere vividly in the "particular experience." Praises his experiments with "dramatic and novelistic methods in verse" and his eye for descriptive detail, the poems about the rural north being "among the most genuine things in the book."

302. Garrett, George. "The Naked Voice." Virginia Quarterly Review, 40 (Spring, 1940), 326-29.

Reviewing Collected Poems, says that this "impressive volume," representing the "range and consistency" of Olson's poetry over the years, attests to his "considerable achievement" and partly atones for his poetry not being "widely anthologized" in "those periodic social registers of the literati produced by poets who have stopped producing." Considers Olson's poetry to be solidly based on "critical theory"; his poems are literary "in the best sense," are products of an intellectual who finds "abstractions as real as a toothache," but they are remarkable chiefly for their expression of a true poetic voice, one not always "pleasing" but certainly "serious, cerebral, introspective, and often anguished." Beyond Olson's "integrity and courage," his wit, irony, and deep feeling, however, Garrett feels the absence of something, perhaps "joy" or "charity." Still, Olson's voice is "clear" and "honest," and his poems "are true poems."

303. Hathaway, Baxter. [Untitled] Epoch, (Spring, 1964), 275-79.

Briefly reviews Collected Poems, noting that many of the poems are "deservedly well-known" and that there is almost always in Olson's poetry "a commitment to the truth he knows."

304. Hecht, Roger. "Intelligence and Care." Poetry: A Magazine of Verse, 104 (June, 1964), 275-79.

Remarks, in this review of Collected Poems that Olson's strength as a poet "is the toughness of his intelligence." For all their many virtues, the poems are not flawless; they are too often "abstract with...a vengeance." Nevertheless, at his best, Olson "induces the common reader to peruse the entire poem at one gulp" (he said, looking with a hard swallow).

305. Brown, Ashley. "Poets of a Silver Age." Sewanee Review, 72 (Summer, 1964), 518-26.

Remarks in this review of Collected Poems that although Olson, following the lead of Aristotle, conceives of his poems as imitations of actions, he achieves some of his most striking effects through his adroit handling of alliteration, assonance, and rhythm, as in "Ballad of the Scarecrow Christ." Refers specifically to only two additional poems, "A Nocturnal for His Children" and Olson's version of Valery's Le cimetière marin, both of which he finds impressive, the former as one of the best poems on the subject of man's post-Christian "response to the abyss of infinite space," and the latter as a "brilliant" translation of the subtle effects of the original.

306. Weeks, Robert Lewis. "Rimes and Cunning Rhythms." Prairie Schooner, 38 (Fall, 1964), 281-82.

Comments briefly on books of poetry by Henry Rago, Elder Olson (Collected Poems), and William Dickey. Believing that to make a rhyme is to commit a crime, inasmuch as rhyme (ingeniously spelled rime throughout) "always leads a poet away from what he might have said," Weeks, lifting bluster onto his shoulders, asserts that Olson manages "rime" more adroitly than Dickey and is indeed a "fine poet when he forgets all about rime and traditional forms," though not nearly so accomplished a poet as Rago, who "doesn't use much rime."

307. Hamod, H. Samuel. [Untitled] Cresset, 28 (October, 1965), 25.

Briefly reviews Collected Poems, noting that Olson produces a poetry "of the intellect" that contains images "precisely tempered and framed" and that he is never "emotional and lyrical to a fault," though he perhaps goes "too far in the other direction" (i.e., the intellectual direction).

American Lyric Poems: From Colonial Times to the Present

308. Moore, Geoffrey. "American Literature." Year's Work in English Studies, 45 (1964), 355-56.

Asserts that Olson has put together a "personal" rather than a "representative" anthology of poems, one including a "good many poets" (e.g., Edward Coote and Richard Realf) who would not "normally be found" in a collection of American lyrics. It is an "unusual" book, marred by "a number of printing errors."

309. Nicholl, Louise Townsend. [Untitled] Spirit (January, 1965), 180-81.

In this short review of American Lyric Poems, summarizes the introduction, which "at too great length defines" the lyric, and then comments on the selections, remarking that the "earlier lyrics" give the anthology "its special value." The special value of the review is here exhibited in epitome: "The incomparable Anne Bradstreet begins it, and the amazing Edward Taylor, and then come on in breath-taking continuity Joel Barlow...Melville, Whitman and Dickinson, and on and on to Hart Crane and Wallace Stevens nearer by."

310. Stafford, William. "Weighed and Found Wanted." Poetry: A Magazine of Verse,

106 (September, 1965), 429-33.

Reviews Olson's American Lyric Poems, along with seven other anthologies of poetry, praising it highly for its inclusion of works by some lesser known poets (by virtue of the richness of Olson's selections the reader can participate in locating "the tradition and its abiding interest") and for its introduction, an expert discussion of the lyric that "illuminates the form" and sharpens the reader's understanding of "other kinds of poems" as well.

Aristotle's Poetics and English Literature: A Collection of Critical Essays

311. Satin, Joseph. [Untitled] College English, 27 (April, 1966), 582-83.

Briefly examines the first four volumes published by the University of Chicago Press in the Patterns of Literary Criticism series, including the anthology of essays introduced and edited by Elder Olson, Aristotle's Poetics and English Literature. Praises Olson's selection, which manages "to avoid including inferior" pieces "in order to pad out" the book, and his introduction, the "thrusts" and "insights" of which are by themselves "enough to justify his book."

312. Hatlen, Theodore W. [Untitled] Quarterly Journal of Speech, 52 (October, 1966), 301-02.

Sees Olson's "careful hand" throughout Aristotle's Poetics and English Literature, which is noteworthy for its "excellent" introduction and its judicious selection of essays, but wonders why pieces by Kitto, Else, Myers, and Arrowsmith are not represented and why so few essays deal with the "emotional and humane content of drama" and so many deal with the "intellectual and rhetorical aspects of dramatic theory."

313. [Anon.] [Untitled] Dietsche Warande en Belfort, 111 (December, 1966). (This entry is based on a "review clipping" that did not include page numbers.)

Refers to Olson's Aristotle's Poetics and English Literature as the most interesting work in the series of "Gemini Books" on literary criticism. Summarizes the contents of the collection, calling particular attention to Olson's introduction and to the last three essays (by Olson, Bernard Weinberg, and Richard McKeon) and observing that the best commentators on Aristotle are American academics.

314. [Anon.] [Untitled] Choice, 3 (February, 1967), 1126.

Briefly summarizes the contents of Aristotle's Poetics and English Literature, noting in passing that Olson's introduction is "excellent," that the work usefully supplements Herrick's The Poetics of Aristotle in England, and that it is "a valuable item for large collections of literary criticism."

315. Waters, L.A., S.J. [Untitled] The Modern Schoolman, 45 (November, 1967), 63-64.

Fails to understand the criteria underlying the selection of essays in Aristotle's Poetics and English Literature, but "supposes" that, since the book ends with essays by Olson and McKeon, it is put together so that the dog-wagging tail of Chicago pluralism may display its talents.

Sees the whole collection as an opportunity for Olson to present an "up to date" version of Chicago pluralism, which seems to make "valid aesthetic judgments depend on their being Aristotelian in terminology rather than on their being semantically or psychologically justified."

316. Maxwell, J.C. [Untitled] Notes and Queries, NS 15 (March, 1968), 119-20.

Observes that Aristotle's Poetics and English Literature is an "odd collection" bearing a misleading title, since virtually all the essays in it, including Olson's introduction, eschew any reference to English literature. Comments briefly on each of the essays and notes that, as a group, they are uneven in quality and significance, ranging from the intellectually sophisticated (Olson, McKeon) to the jejune or trifling (Thomas Taylor, Quiller-Couch). Devotes the last paragraph to the notation of typographical errors.

The Theory of Comedy

317. [Anon.] [Untitled] Yale Review, 58 (Summer, 1969), 28-32.

In this review of The Theory of Comedy, the author occasionally drops the mask of amused tolerance for a crazed uncle's bizarre, if innocuous views on comedy, which are about as pertinent to the real issues as a tea cozy is to guerrilla warfare, to snarl in his own voice that Olson cuts his way through a tangle of verbal thickets only to deliver such trivial news as "art can never have a greater value than life, for it is ultimately measured by the values of life." Persistently makes Olson the purveyor of tired irrelevancies by reducing his arguments to banal apothegms and regularly sweeps the board of all complications with peremptory condescension, asserting, for example, in response to Olson's argument concerning the validity of directing the Aristotelian method to comedy, that his analysis in terms of causes applies better "to a bed or a statue than to a verbal expression." Presents Olson's case in *disjecta membra* and has good sport with the pieces. Fails to give any clear sense of Olson's argument.

318. Knauf, David. [Untitled] *Quarterly Journal of Speech*, 55 (October, 1969), 341-42.

In this review of a book which is called *The Theory of Comedy* but which, judging on the basis of the reviewer's confusing and derisive description of its contents, bears only a clownish resemblance to a work of the same title by Elder Olson, Knauf carps and nips at the author, "the most dogmatic of the Chicago neo-Aristotelians," for abandoning "careful argument, "scrupulous... scholarship," and "inventive exegesis"--i.e., all the palliatives that in the past rendered wrongheadedness tolerable--to produce a book of "rigid" and "unrewarding" formal analysis based on barbarously simple "neoclassic assumptions about human emotion and behavior." Sees bumbling practical analysis courting the assistance of theoretical clumsiness in the second half of the book. In short, Knauf finds a pack of snarling dogs at which to hurl, with lustful self-satisfaction, his cut-out of Olson.

319. Masinton, Charles G. [Untitled] *Modern Drama*, 12 (December, 1969), 329-30.

Briefly summarizes the argument of *The Theory of Comedy*, giving detailed attention to Olson's Aristotelian definition of comedy, and notes that Olson's approach enables us to focus "on the esthetic form of a play and not its subject matter." Concludes by saying that this "excellent" book "is a major contribution to the old problem of deciding just what comedy is."

320. L., H. [Untitled] Comparative Literature, 22 (Summer, 1970), 286-88.

Welcomes The Theory of Comedy for its theoretical slant and its clarifying focus on comedy as a genre, not as a "sense of life." Olson's book provides a sharp contrast to the traditional "English approaches," which have resisted theory and confused issues by "intermingling comic fiction with comic drama." Summarizes the contents of the book and then asserts, in qualification of his high praise, that Olson emphasizes wit "at the expense of humor"; that he is more concerned with ridicule than with "what may well be a richer source of motivation," the element of play; that the practical application of the theory in the second half of the book seems to be a matter of adjusting texts to a priori determinations; that he slights the "conditioning circumstances of the stage," and that his criticism is "rarely graced by the charms of the Comic Spirit."

321. Raphael, D.D. [Untitled] Notes and Queries, NS 20 (February, 1973), 63-66.

Summarizes the contents of The Theory of Comedy, giving emphasis to Olson's Aristotelian definition of comedy, his distinction between the ludicrous and the ridiculous, and his descriptions of the four basic types of plot found in comedy. Judges the work to be a "really valuable contribution to the study of comedy," noteworthy at once for its general theory and for its illustrative analyses of specific plays, especially those by Shakespeare and Molière. Recognizes that Olson would have been a less acute theorist than he is if he had not "soaked himself in the _Poetics_," but asserts that his writing is far more "impressive when he gets away from Aristotle and speaks his own thoughts."

Olson's Penny Arcade

322. Portis, Rowe. [Untitled] _Library Journal_, 100 (August, 1975), 1424.

Briefly describes the contents of _Olson's Penny Arcade_ and then, mistaking insipidity for dash, accuses Olson of inflicting upon us a poor imitation of Wallace Stevens.

323. Schoen, John E. [Untitled] _Literary Tabloid_, (October, 1975), 26.

Gives the reader, in this brief review of _Olson's Penny Arcade_, his unqualified recommendation of Olson's work, which exhibits "a variety of form and feeling...not even approached by many contemporary poets" and depicts "universalities in a totally individual way." Reaches beyond the reach of the most ambitious superlatives in an effort to locate terms answerable to his estimation of Olson's achievement, only to find: "The perfection, the truth, the thrust of every poem leaves the reader powerless at its climax. Every poem is an experience."

324. [Anon.] [Untitled] _Booklist_, 15 Dec. 1975, p. 548.

Summarizes the contents of *Olson's Penny Arcade*, a collection of poems exhibiting the virtues characteristic of Olson's "traditionally styled" poetry: "wit," "profundity" and absence of "excess."

325. [Anon.] [Untitled] *Choice*, 13 (March, 1976), 72.

Remarks that *Olson's Penny Arcade* contains a "strong" play, *The Abstract Tragedy*, which is replete with those qualities distinguishing "all of Olson's work:" "vigor, intensity, and keen insight." Finds the poems of less "consequence," with the exception of "Knight, with Umbrella."

326. Grumbach, Doris. "Beautiful Books from University Presses." *Commonweal*, 103 (May, 1976), 340.

Remarks that the University of Chicago Press was responsible for producing this year an award-winning, "wittily designed edition of Charles [sic] Olson's *Penny Arcade*."

327. Lattimore, Richmond. "Poetry Chronicle." *Hudson Review*, 29 (Spring, 1976), 113-29.

In a review of several books of poetry says that *Olson's Penny Arcade* is an "oddly assorted volume" containing many excellent poems, as well as a verse play, *The Abstract Tragedy*, that "takes up more than half the volume." Thinks that the "Four Immensely Moral Tales" are "delightfully told" and that, of the "grimmer poems," "The Daguerrotype of Chopin" is the "finest."

Reviews

328. Lucas, T.E. [Untitled] Spirit 43 (Spring/Summer, 1976), 33-41.

Conducts the reader through the four sections of Olson's Penny Arcade, clearly and intelligently delineating the principal features of each and, through the use of substantial quotations from several poems, giving weight and authority to his praise of the "skill" of Olson's "versification" and the "depth of his thought and feeling." Presents enough samples of the range of Olson's tones and attitudes to establish the validity of his estimation of the excellence of Olson's poetry.

329. Smith, Raymond J. "Poetry Chronicle." Ontario Review, No. 4 (Spring/Summer, 1976), 104-10.

In this review of several volumes of poetry, including Olson's Penny Arcade, Smith finds The Abstract Tragedy (the one play in the book) "interesting," but much less successful than the poems, which best exhibit Olson's clear, intelligent craftsmanship, his felicity "with words, rhythm, and sound," and his ability to create works that both "reveal their meaning at once" and remain "fresh upon repeated re-readings." Says that the title poem, "a series of unconnected bits," varies considerably in seriousness and quality. Singles out "Four Immensely Moral Tales," "The Daguerrotype of Chopin," "Munich: New Year's Eve, 1936," "Reflections on Mirrors," and "Puerto Vallarta" as among the most memorable poems in this fine collection.

330. Ramsey, Paul. "Image and Essence: Some American Poetry of 1975." Sewanee Review, 84 (Summer, 1976), 533-41.

Reviewing several volumes of poetry, Ramsey calls Olson's _Penny Arcade_ a "fine book," one with the "fineness," not "of gossamer or sighs, but of ivory, of steel," and considers it a "privilege to be in the presence of so much intelligence, integrity, and fully controlled poetic skill." Comments on the details of several poems in an effort to depict the range of Olson's substantial accomplishments noting, for example, that the difficulty of making art in the absence of a sustaining "aesthetics or ethics" is "nowhere better expressed" than in "Directions for Building a House of Cards."

331. [Anon.] [Untitled] _Virginia Quarterly Review_, 52 (Summer, 1976), 80-81.

In what is ostensibly a review of Olson's _Penny Arcade_, regrets that Olson, a "transitional poet"--both modernist, in his "philosophical concerns," and post-modernist, in his mastery of motifs relating to the "chaos of the inner world"--who has produced over the years a "rich, coherent _oeuvre_," will apparently be obliged to "labor on, as Stanley Kunitz did before him, in conspicuous and unmerited isolation," unless he is awarded a Pulitzer Prize or a National Book Award, both unlikely possibilities, given Olson's "aloofness from literary politics." Of the volume occasioning these remarks, says only that it "contains the strongest and the weakest poems he has committed to print."

332. Bromwich, David. "Waving and Drowning." _Poetry: A Magazine of Verse_, 129 (December, 1976), 170-75.

Briefly reviews four books of poetry, including Olson's _Penny Arcade_, a work which betrays "enormous charm and a lively fabricating facility at the service of pastiche," though the reader is too aware at times of Olson's debts, especially to Yeats and Auden.

333. Golffing, Francis. "Four Faces of the Muse." _Southern Review_, 14 (January, 1978), 177-82.

Praises _Olson's Penny Arcade_ for its "sure grip" and "utter avoidance of triviality." Olson is at his best in the "short, gnomic" pieces. In this collection we have "a metaphysician's poetry," a "poetry of comment," but in few of the poems is there any real fusion of "imagination and language." Nevertheless, the _comment_ is variously "poignant," "brilliantly trenchant," or wryly wise. Observes that this is a poetry, not to be "patronized, but to be savored, line by line, and admired."

334. Cotter, James Finn. "Poets, Poems, and University Presses." _America_, 8 Apr. 1978, pp. 282-84.

Comments briefly on several collections of poems published by university presses, including _Olson's Penny Arcade_, which contains poems notable for their "witty and unassuming charm," though the play included in the volume, _The Abstract Tragedy_, and some of the epigrams comprising the title poem are "disappointing."

335. McGlynn, Paul D. [Untitled] _Southern Humanities Review_, 12 (1978), 78-79.

In a review of poems by Louis Zukofsky and of _Olson's Penny Arcade_, remarks that Olson is a "sensitive" dispenser "of illumination," who values "wit, precision, humanism," and the "integrity of the aesthetic object." Comments briefly on poems in each of the sections, noting at the end that this collection should put to rout the persistent and comfortable myth that poems from "Academe are inherently sterile." Judges the lyrics in section one the best, but finds the book as a whole rich in insight and replete with poems in which there is a happy coadunation of "structure and imagery."

On Value Judgments in the Arts and Other Essays

336. Masterton, G.A. [Untitled] *Library Journal*, 101 (February, 1976), 530.

Says simply that the essays collected in *On Value Judgments in the Arts and Other Essays* constitute the "gratifying record of a noteworthy career."

337. Welch, Liliane. [Untitled] *Humanities Association of Canada Review*, 27 (Summer, 1976), 303-05.

Filters Olson's *On Value Judgments in the Arts* through the parti-colored lenses of her own categories and discovers a critic who in his practical essays "exiles literature into the safe existence of monads floating in the free space of bourgeois society," who in his remarks on interpretation forgets that the term "hermeneutics" is related to the Greek god charged with carrying messages "of destiny" and that the task of the modern interpreter is "to hearken to a hidden meaning," and who everywhere manifests a "morbid fascination with science and linguistics." Asserts that this collection of essays is definitely not for those eager to witness the "historical encounter between critic and work," but for those "dull scholars" or "average readers" seeking "refuge and recuperation from the tiring industrial civilization," for throughout the text, the poet-critic "sings" wistfully his "vacation dreams" about a "never-never land of art."

338. [Anon.] [Untitled] Choice, 13 (September, 1976), 806.

Provides a brief account of the contents of On Value Judgments in the Arts, noting, in conclusion, that the essays are "witty, wide-ranging," and "closely reasoned."

339. Barfoot, C.C. "Current Literature, 1976: Criticism and New Editions, Literary History, Literary Theory, and Biography." English Studies, 58 (1977), 530-52. ("Olson," p. 549).

Simply notes dyspeptically that twenty (actually twenty-one) of Olson's "difficult, quite unyielding essays" are printed in On Value Judgments in the Arts, a collection that "demands much and gives little."

340. Ellis, John M. [Untitled] Philosophy and Literature, 1 (Spring, 1977), 248-50.

Briefly describes the contents of On Value Judgments in the Arts, indicating the number and arrangement of the essays within the text, and then makes three points, all negatively tinged. Asserts that while Olson and the other "Chicago critics," for whose theoretical position this text has "documentary value," allegedly work from "a firm theoretical foundation of philosophical concerns," they appeal to virtually no nineteenth- or twentieth-century philosophers in defense or support of their criticism; that since four of the five longest essays appeared originally in Critics and Criticism, Olson's collection adds little to what we already knew; and, finally, that his most recent essays merely amplify what was implicit in earlier statements, though the title essay seems to "add a new facet to [the Chicago] framework."

341. [Anon.] [Untitled] Journal of Modern Literature, 6 (1977, Supplement), 540.

Simply describes the contents of On Value Judgments in the Arts and then recommends "A Letter on Teaching Drama" to all who teach "the subject in the university or college classroom."

342. Rump, Gerhard Charles. [Untitled] Leonardo, 11 (Spring, 1978), 161-62.

Summarizes the contents of On Value Judgments in the Arts, the digested or capsule versions of the arguments sometimes correlating positively with Olson's actual views. Evaluative commentary is slight. The "Critical Theory" section is "most interesting," and the title essay is "the most important article."

L. DISSERTATIONS

The entries in this category are arranged alphabetically by author.

343. Baker, John Ross. "The Chicago Critics: An Inquiry into Neo-Aristotelianism." Diss. Temple University, 1977.

First examines and then attacks the principles of "Chicago" criticism, giving emphasis throughout to the writings of R. S. Crane and Elder Olson. Says that the "Chicago" critics have "adapted the four Aristotelian causes" to the analysis of literature and that, in spite of their professed interest in a variety of literary kinds, they tend to enroll all works under one or another of two principal genres, the mimetic or the didactic. Similarly, while professing to employ a method in which hypotheses are rigorously accountable to independent facts, these critics are as "a prioristic" as other critics; like the facts of other critics, theirs are determined by the "concepts of" their "theory." Runs through what these critics have to say about each of the causes entering into the production of a literary work and regularly assumes that their arguments are overwhelmed by his flat assertions. For example, after describing desultorily and inadequately the reasons why these critics subordinate language to plot, Baker remarks that this denigration of language makes it impossible for these critics to develop a theory of poetic creation. Observes at the end of the study that Wayne Booth's treatment of point of view in The Rhetoric of Fiction broadens "Neo-Aristotelian" theory, but only at the cost of transforming Crane's mimetic works into didactic ones.

344. Bashford, Bruce Wilson. "The Humanistic Criticism of R. S. Crane." Diss. Northwestern University 1970.

Examines the nature and bases of R.S. Crane's critical thought. Olson is referred to at various points, but especially in chapter two, in which what is called "Crane's "semantic theory" of critical discourse, the foundation of his "pluralism," is discussed in the context of the analyses by Olson and Richard McKeon of the causes of variation in philosophical and critical argumentation. In short, in this chapter, Bashford consults the work of McKeon and Olson "to better explicate Crane's."

345. Davis, Walter A. "Theories of Form in Modern Criticism: An Explanation of the Theories of Kenneth Burke and R. S. Crane." Diss. University of Chicago, 1969.

This study is discussed in its revised and published form below; see 383.

346. Hernadi, Paul. "Concepts of Genre in Twentieth-Century Criticism." Diss. Yale University 1967.

This study is discussed in its revised and published form above; See 195.

Dissertations

347. Lemon, Lee Thomas. "The Partial Critics: Modern Criticism and the Evaluation of Lyric Poetry." Diss. University of Illinois, 1961.

This study is discussed in its revised and published form below, see 438.

348. Searle, Leroy Frank. "Basic Concepts in Literary Criticism: Some Controversial Instances." Diss. University of Iowa, 1970.

Discusses the "process of concept formation" in literary criticism, focusing primarily on the theoretical principles underlying the writings of R. S. Crane and Northrop Frye. Much of what is said about Crane applies equally well to Olson. Crane's (and Olson's) methodological pluralism arises from a "failure to distinguish" the function of "constitutive criticism," which accounts for the intelligibility of literature by appealing to an "abstract general term," from the function of "critical classification," which seeks to describe systematic structures in literature. Asserts that the failure to discriminate between these two functions leads Crane to posit two distinct kinds of critical method (the "abstract" and the "matter of fact") that culminate in two incommensurable but equally valid "frameworks." Argues that the two kinds of method "are not alternatives, but are responses to different kinds of questions" and that, taken together, the two functions of criticism might lead to a "view of literature as a legitimate *organon*."

M. MISCELLANEOUS:

BRIEF NOTICES, CITATIONS, ETC.

The items in this category are arranged alphabetically by author.

349. Abrams, M.H. The Mirror and the Lamp: Romantic Theory and the Critical Tradition. New York: Oxford University Press, 1953, pp. 284-85, 342n48, 348n6.

Sees Olson, one of the "most thoughtful of our practicing critics," as instancing the vitality of the "heterocosmic metaphor," when, speaking of poetic truth in the article on "Sailing to Byzantium," he says that poetic statements are not true or false propositions, since they do not refer to things existing beyond the poem. To Olson, "every poem is a microcosmos, a discrete and independent universe with its laws provided by the poet." Elsewhere, in the notes, Abrams directs the reader to Olson's analysis of the "conceptual structure" of Longinus's treatise.

350. Ackerman, John. Dylan Thomas: His Life and Work. London: Oxford University Press, 1964, p. 122.

Quotes from The Poetry of Dylan Thomas Olson's remark that Thomas recaptured something of the "lost Eden" in his descriptions of the natural world of Wales, in an effort to support his own view that for Thomas childhood is the ideal age.

351. Allen, Don Cameron, ed. The Moment of Poetry. Baltimore: The Johns Hopkins Press, 1962, p. 20.

Mentions Olson as one of many poets "patronized by universities."

352. Altieri, Charles. "The Hermeneutics of Literary Indeterminacy: A Dissent from the New Orthodoxy." NLH, 10 (Autumn, 1978), 71-99.

In developing a case for viewing the literary text as constituted of actions that demand and elicit from the reader responses of both sympathy and reflection, Altieri follows the lead of Olson's "powerful Aristotelian critique" of new criticism, supplementing Olson's views with a modern "philosophical understanding of action," which allows for "a kind of cognition in reading."

353. ______________. Act and Quality: A Theory of Literary Meaning and Humanistic Understanding. Amherst, Mass.: University of Massachusetts Press, 1981, pp. 240, 260-61.

Notes that Olson explains precisely how modes of thinking can be considered as acts in "'Sailing to Byzantium': Prolegomena to a Poetics of the Lyric," and suggests that Ralph Rader, though indebted to the "Chicago Aristotelians," displays a greater awareness of "the cognitive aspects of literary experience" than do Olson and Crane in their analyses of the affective quality of plot.

Miscellaneous

354. Amacher, Richard E. [Untitled] Criticism, 15 (Fall, 1973), 366-68.

Welcomes a book-length study of Olson (Lucas's Elder Olson--see 181--is under review), a critic who has "considerably advanced our knowledge of the various genres he has treated." Considers Olson's theory of the lyric a "genuine contribution to knowledge" that deserves the special attention of "teachers and graduate students."

355. Andrews, Michael Cameron. "Hamlet: Revenge and the Critical Mirror." English Literary Renaissance, 8 (Winter, 1978), 9-23.

Cites with approval Olson's assessment (in "Hamlet and the Hermeneutics of Drama") of the state of Hamlet criticism, one in which readings of the most "fantastic order" seem to be valued more highly than those based on "solid scholarship," as if authority depended more on "novelty and ingenuity" than on "cogency of proof."

356. Auburn, Mark S. Sheridan's Comedies: Their Contexts and Achievements. Lincoln, Nebraska: University of Nebraska Press, 1977, p. 190n19.

Disagrees with Olson's view (as expressed in The Theory of Comedy) that Much Ado About Nothing is "something other than a comedy," but concurs with his insistence upon a middle category "to encompass works with happy endings which are not comedies in terms of the anxieties raised by the action."

357. Baker, John Ross. "From Imitation to Rhetoric: The Chicago Critics, Wayne

Booth, and *Tom Jones*." *Novel: A Forum on Fiction*, 6 (Spring, 1973), 197-217.

In spite of Crane's published opinion that in Wayne Booth's work he finds specific applications of the general approach to critical problems suggested in his own work, and in spite of Booth's open endorsement of critical principles articulated by Crane, Baker attempts to prove that in *The Rhetoric of Fiction* Booth not only engages in a "wholesale" revision of the "Chicago" position but also effects a "radical shift in Neo-Aristotelianism" from the "imitative" to the "didactic." Olson appears periodically as the co-sponsor, with Crane, of the basic critical tenets that Booth allegedly subverts, though Baker misreads the significance of Olson's argument against syncretism and of his point that there can only be agreement within the same system of reference, that "true interpretation is impossible when one system is examined in terms of another" system. More fundamentally, Baker fails to see that Booth and Crane, though apparently referring to the same topics, are addressing different questions. For the most part, the essay is an expense of spirit in a waste of blame.

358. Battersby, James L. *Rational Praise and Natural Lamentation: Johnson, Lycidas, and Principles of Criticism*. Rutherford, N.J.: Fairleigh Dickinson University Press, 1980, pp. 265n, 266n.

Regularly betrays an indebtedness to Olson in his analysis of modes of dialectical criticism and adapts to his own purposes Olson's postulation of a "single speaker in a closed situation" as constitutive of a minimal form of poetic action. Also, borrows from the article on Empson Olson's conception of the subordination of words to their functions.

359. Bennett, Kenneth C. "The Affective Aspect of Comedy." Genre, 14 (Summer, 1981), 191-205.

In an effort to provide a working model of the complex "actions of the mind" in response to comedy, a model that respects the developing and changing ways in which the cognitive and affective reactions to comedy intermingle, argues that Olson's conception of comedy as effecting a katastasis (relaxation) of concern is too narrow and limited, since it inevitably leads to an emphasis on "low comedy at the expense of high and romantic" comedy. Nevertheless, in spite of his rejection of Olson's view, warns the reader against making "any hasty judgment about [Olson's] critical acumen."

360. Blue, William R. [Untitled] Bulletin of the Comediantes, 32 (Spring, 1980), 87-89. See 9.

In what is essentially a review of B.W. Wardropper's essay on Spanish Golden Age comedy appended to his translation of The Theory of Comedy into Spanish, observes that although Wardropper makes "heady" claims for the validity of Olson's theory, his own analyses of plays "absolutely refute Olson's proposition" about the lack of transcendence in comedy, and that although Wardropper acknowledges that he owes much to Olson's generic distinctions, his inability to adjust Spanish comedies to Olson's categories clearly, though unintentionally, reveals the rigidity and prescriptive nature of those categories.

361. Booth, Wayne C. _The Rhetoric of Fiction._ Chicago and London: The University of Chicago Press, 1961, pp. 33n, 377n.

Cites Olson's essay on Longinus in support of the view that Longinus was not interested in distinguishing between "didactic and imaginative works" but in accounting for the "general quality of 'the sublime,'" wherever it momentarily appeared. Also directs the reader to the essays by Olson and Crane in _Critics and Criticism_ dealing with the consideration of individual works in terms of "kinds of effect."

362. ______________. _Now Don't Try to Reason with Me: Essays and Ironies for a Credulous Age._ Chicago and London: The University of Chicago Press, 1270, pp. 104n, 114n, 159.

Notes that the "best introduction" to the ways in which Aristotle's work has been abused by both his opponents and defenders is in Olson's _Aristotle's Poetics and English Literature_ and that in his own remarks on Aristotle's method and pluralistic principles he is "greatly indebted" to McKeon, Crane, and Olson.

363. ______________. "'Preseving the Exemplar': Or, How Not to Dig Our Own Graves." _Critical Inquiry_, 3 (Spring, 1977), 407-23.

In support of his view that such "complexities" as _the poem_, _the text_, or _the way to read_ "can _never_ be encompassed by a single critical language," directs the reader to several important critical studies, including Olson's "The Dialectical Foundations of Critical Pluralism," all of which provide arguments for the essential "irreducibility of...critical languages...to a single right view."

Miscellaneous

364. ______________. Critical Understanding: The Powers and Limits of Pluralism. Chicago and London: The University of Chicago Press, 1979, pp. 42n, 53, 137, 201.

Refers to Olson on several occasions, giving particular attention to his "rigorous philosophical defense of pluralism" in "The Dialectical Foundations of Critical Pluralism," a long passage from which is quoted in illustration of the point that, because language in use is both selective and restrictive in meaning, there is a strict relativity of philosophic problems to their formulation.

365. Boyce, Benjamin. The Character-Sketches in Pope's Poems. Durham, N.C.: Duke University Press, 1962, pp. 16n, 104n.

Directs the reader to Olson's analysis of "Pope's" character in "Rhetoric and the Appreciation of Pope," a study of the rhetorical principles underlying the "Epistle to Arbuthnot."

366. Brookes, Gerry H. The Rhetorical Form of Carlyle's Sartor Resartus. Berkeley and Los Angeles: University of California Press, 1972, pp. 8n, 12n, 86, 95.

Lists Olson's Tragedy and the Theory of Drama and his essays on Empson and Pope as among the works on which the "critical basis" of his own study is founded and applies Olson's distinction between speech as meaningful and speech as action to his analysis of Teufeldröckh's speech about himself in "Book Second."

367. Brown, Edward J. "New Directions in Russian Criticism." In The Frontiers of Literary

Criticism. Ed. David H. Malone. Los Angeles: Hennessey and Ingalls, 1974.

Reviews developments in Russian criticism and presents summaries of the work of such western critics as Frye, Leavis, Eliot, Richards, and those of "the Chicago School."

368. Butler, Christopher and Alastair Fowler, eds. *Topics in Criticism: An Ordered Set of Positions in Literary Theory*. London: Longman, 1971, quotation numbers 73, 118, 481. (Pages are not numbered.)

Under "Genre and Mode," quotes a passage from "An Outline of Poetic Theory" relating to the development of a distinct synthesis of parts; under "Mimesis," a passage from "'Sailing to Byzantium': Prolegomena to a Poetics of the Lyric" dealing with the power of the poet to create his own universe, and under "Criticism," a passage from "An Outline of Poetic Theory" explaining how systems of criticism "correct and supplement one another."

369. Charney, Maurice. *Comedy High and Low: An Introduction to the Experience of Comedy*. New York: Oxford University Press, 1978, p. 189.

Directs the reader to Olson's *The Theory of Comedy*, a "stimulating" book.

370. Christensen, Naomi. "Dylan Thomas and the Doublecross of Death." *Ball State Teachers' College Forum*, 4 (Autumn, 1963), 49-53.

In a poem by poem account of the meaning of Thomas's "Altarwise by owl-light" sequence, slightly reworks Olson's analysis of the sonnets, substituting her terms for his but following, in general, the line of his argument.

371. Clark, John R. Form and Frenzy in Swift's Tale of a Tub. Ithaca: Cornell University Press, 1970, pp. xiii, xiv.

After taking note of Olson's definition of didactic form in "A Dialogue on Symbolism" and his discussion of synthesizing principles of form in "The Poetic Method of Aristotle," Clark decides, against Olson's implicit advice, to examine Tale of a Tub as a mimetic, not a didactic, work.

372. Cox, C. B. "Introduction." In Dylan Thomas: A Collection of Critical Essays. Englewood Cliffs, N.J.: Prentice-Hall, 1966, p. 7.

Remarks that in The Poetry of Dylan Thomas Olson asks "the fundamental questions" and offers "particularly stimulating" analyses of the "power and strangeness of Thomas's imagination."

373. Crane, R.S. The Languages of Criticism and the Structure of Poetry. Toronto: University of Toronto Press, 1953, pp. xvii, 196, 197, 198, 200, 202, 205, 206.

Thanks Olson for aiding him in the preparation of his book and invites the reader at several points to consider the consonance obtaining between his views and those of Olson, especially concerning "concrete wholes" and the conjunction of what is "possible" and "appropriate" in the "best thought." And directs the reader to Olson's discussions of the structure of Longinus's argument in On the Sublime and of

Robert Penn Warren's reading of "The Ancient Mariner."

374. ______________. "On Writing the History of Criticism in England, 1650-1800." *UTQ*, 22 (1953). Reprinted in *The Idea of the Humanities and Other Essays Critical and Historical*. Vol. II. Chicago and London: The University of Chicago Press, 1967, pp. 157-75.

Cites Olson's discussion of Longinus and Reynolds in his introduction to the "University Classics" edition of *On the Sublime* and the *Discourses* as the kind of study that provides the basis for a "more complete and intelligible history" of criticism, since it examines critical documents "in the light" of their "internal and logical causes," not in terms of the apparent compatibility of their doctrines as isolated from their informing contexts.

375. ______________. "Philosophy, Literature, and the History of Ideas." *MP*, 52 (1954). Reprinted in *The Idea of the Humanities and Other Essays Critical and Historical*. Vol. I. Chicago and London: The University of Chicago Press, 1967, pp. 173-87.

Discussing the larger "moral and intellectual bases" of artistic forms, Crane refers to Olson's "analysis of the moral universe" of Thomas's poetry in *The Poetry of Dylan Thomas* as a fine example of how to track down the "more or less coherent" presuppositions underlying artistic creation.

376. ______________. "Every Man His Own Critic." In *The Idea of the Humanities and Other Essays Critical and Historical*. Vol. II.

Chicago and London: The University of Chicago Press, 1967, pp. 194-214.

Observes that his discussion of the ways critics often confuse plot with "quite different things" is "developed more fully" in Olson's Tragedy and the Theory of Drama.

377. ______________. "Varieties of Dramatic Criticism." In The Idea of the Humanities and Other Essays Critical and Historical. Vol. II. Chicago and London: The University of Chicago Press, 1967, pp. 215-35.

Notes that Olson's Tragedy and the Theory of Drama constitutes "an original contribution" to the theory of drama.

378. ______________. "On Hypotheses in 'Historical Criticism': Apropos of Certain Contemporary Medievalists." In The Idea of the Humanities and Other Essays Critical and Historical. Vol. II. Chicago and London: The University of Chicago Press, 1967, pp. 236-60.

Remarks that the Robertsonians tend to transform a working hypothesis, one capable of suggesting sub-hypotheses that need to "be tested independently," into what Olson calls a "subsumptive hypothesis," i.e., a "ruling hypothesis."

379. Daiches, David. Critical Approaches to Literature. Englewood Cliffs, N.J.: Prentice-Hall, 1956, p. 257n.

Calls Olson's "William Empson, Contemporary Criticism, and Poetic Diction" a "reasoned attack" against Empson's critical method.

380. ______________. English Literature. Englewood Cliffs, N.J.: Prentice-Hall, 1964, pp. 94-97, 123.

Describes the criticism of the "Chicago school" as an effort in the late 1930's to supplant literary history with literary criticism and to focus classroom teaching on the "unique form of the individual literary work" and asserts that in general the critics of this school were "more philosophically professional and intellectually sophisticated" than many of the "new critics."

381. ______________. A Third World. Sussex: Sussex University Press, 1971, p. 27.

Briefly refers to Olson as one of the younger men at the University of Chicago who was influenced by R.S. Crane.

382. Davis, Lloyd and Robert Irwin. Contemporary American Poetry: A Checklist. Metuchen, N.J.: Scarecrow Press, 1975, p. 91.

Lists five of Olson's six volumes of poetry, i.e., all the volumes except Olson's Penny Arcade, which was published in 1975.

383. Davis, Walter A. The Act of Interpretation: A Critique of Literary Reason. Chicago and London: The University of Chicago Press, 1978, pp. 55, 122, 133, 134-135.

Contains scattered references to Olson, especially to his "mimetic" definition of lyric poetry. Wants to incorporate the emphasis of such critics as Crane and Olson on "the universal principles of emotional response" into a pluralism that also includes dialectical and rhetorical conceptions of form.

384. Denham, Robert D. Northrop Frye and Critical Method. University Park and London: The Pennsylvania State University Press, 1978, pp. ix, 234n2, 237n45, 250n59.

Expresses a "large intellectual debt" to Olson, who first introduced him to the problems of criticism and who assisted him with encouragement and advice during the preparation of his book. Refers at several points to Olson' writings, particularly to his discussion of the bases of interpretive diversity in "The Dialectical Foundations of Critical Pluralism."

385. Deutsch, Babette. Poetry in Our Time: A Critical Survey of Poetry in the English-Speaking World, 1900-1960. New York: Columbia University Press, 1958, pp. 263, 346.

Speaking of the poetry of Léonie Adams, Deutsch remarks that she does not extend her range to include the "grosser or uglier" aspects of the most "private world," as does her master, Yeats, and as does Olson, "whose work is singularly close to hers in structure and texture." Also observes that it is impossible to read Olson's "Essay on Deity" without bringing Hopkins's "elaborate poem on the Virgin to mind."

386. Dixon, Peter. The World of Pope's Satires: An Introduction to the Epistles and Imitations of Horace. London: Methuen, 1968, p. 207.

Expresses his indebtedness to Olson's analysis of the rhetorical strategy of "An Epistle to Arbuthnot" and to his demonstration of how the poem establishes Pope's "moral character" (in "Rhetoric and the Appreciation of Pope").

387. Dodsworth, Martin. "The Concept of Mind and the Poetry of Dylan Thomas." In _Dylan Thomas: New Critical Essays_. Ed. Walford Davies. London: J.M. Dent and Sons, 1972, p. 108.

Finds Olson's justification of Thomas's obscurity (in _The Poetry of Dylan Thomas_) unsatisfactory, even "dangerous," because it tends to make a virtue of a real defect. To Dodsworth, Thomas's riddles lead more frequently to incomprehension than to comprehenson; they repel rather than attract the mind.

388. Eddleman, Floyd Eugene. _American Drama Criticism: Interpretations 1890-1977_. 2nd ed. Hamden, Connecticut: Shoe-string Press, 1979, p. 296.

Under the heading for Eugene O'Neill, cites Olson's _Tragedy and the Theory of Drama_, pages 237-60 (i.e., chapter ten, "Modern Drama and Tragedy," in which _Mourning Becomes Electra_ is discussed at length).

389. Edwards, Thomas R. _This Dark Estate: A Reading of Pope_. Berkeley: University of California Press, 1963, p. 140.

Directs the reader to Olson's discussion of "persona" in "Rhetoric and the Appreciation of Pope."

390. Ehrenpreis, Irvin. "The Cistern and the Fountain: Art and Reality in Pope and

Gray." In Studies in Criticism and Aesthetics 1660-1800: Essays in Honor of Samuel Holt Monk. Ed. Howard Anderson and John Shea. Minneapolis: University of Minnesota Press, 1967, p. 159.

Detects in Pope's "Epistle to a Lady," in addition to a progressive increase in the number of couplets devoted to portraits, a principle of order that Olson first discerned in the "Epistle to Dr. Arbuthnot," i.e., a sharpening of the satire as the poem advances. Directs the reader to Olson's full argument in "Rhetoric and the Appreciation of Pope."

391. ____________. Literary Meaning and Augustan Values. Charlottesville: University Press of Virginia, 1974, p. 78.

Notes that a principle of order identified by Olson ("Rhetoric and the Appreciation of Pope") in Pope's "Epistle to Arbuthnot"--"as the speech progresses, the satire sharpens"--is also present in the second Moral Essay, "An Epistle to a Lady."

392. Fairchild, Hoxie Neale. Religious Trends in English Poetry. Vol. VI (1920-1965). New York: Columbia University Press, 1968, pp. 64, 122, 246, 320, 370, 422, 428, 432-33, 439.

Quotes from a considerable number of works in Collected Poems to illustrate the themes of his various chapters, finding Olson, for example, a poet, who writes clearly and firmly in reaction to the "romantic revival of the forties"; who celebrates the "holiness of the body and the holiness of enjoying it"; who treats the whole visible world as a manifestation of the attributes of "Deity"; who prefers a colorful "temporal world to a blandly timeless heaven"; who understands all phenomena to be products "of our thought"; who doubts the utility for the post-war world of the "myth of a crucified God"; and who, finally, like other secularistic poets, such as Mark Van Doren and Yvor Winters, seems to believe "everything a Christian should believe except the Christian faith itself."

393. Fletcher, Angus. Allegory: The Theory of a Symbolic Mode. Ithaca: Cornell University Press, 1964, p. 307.

Attempts to qualify Olson's view that the order of the allegorical incident in the action is governed by the "action as doctrine" (the incident occurs because a "doctrinal subject" must have a "doctrinal predicate") by exploring the ways in which the "rigors" of "authorial control" are softened and the doctrinal effects complicated in actual allegories.

394. Florescu, Vasile. Retorica si Neoretorica. Bucharest: Academiei Republicii Socialiste România, 1973, p. 183.

Agrees with Olson's judgment that Empson's categories of ambiguity are really tropes, but tropes which lack both the usefulness and the comprehensiveness of those identified by rhetoricians in their "lists of figures."

395. Ford, James, E. "On Thinking about Aristotle's 'Thought.'" Critical Inquiry, 4 (1978), 589-96.

For clarification on the issue of "thought" in Aristotle's philosophy, invites the reader to consider, in addition to other works, Olson's essays on the Poetics in Critics and Criticism and his Aristotle's Poetics and English Literature.

396. Foster, Richard. The New Romantics: A Reappraisal of the New Criticism. Bloomington: Indiana University Press, 1962, pp. 19, 208.

Berates the "Chicago critics" for employing a "pseudo-philosophic" style in the service of "intellectual bathos" and "circular exterminations of meaning" and for developing "abstract machineries for the processing, packaging, and labeling of literary produce," citing sentences by Olson and Maclean as proof positive of his assertions. Here is high dudgeon riding proudly on fustian. Concludes by blustering that after producing "hardly anything very memorable," the Chicago factory "now seems to have shut down altogether."

397. Fraser, G.S. "Some Notes on Poetic Diction." In The Penguin New Writing. Ed. John Lehmann. Harmondsworth, Middlesex: Penguin Books, 1949, pp. 115-28.

In a sensible essay on poetic diction, takes issue, in a brief digression, with Olson's view that, because they are determined by everything else, the words "are the least important elements in the poem," arguing that criticism should "pay a very close attention to" a poet's particular diction and that Olson, a "thoughtful American critic," incorrectly assumes that we are moved not by the words but by what the words stand for. To Fraser, the "pointing is the least of it." For Olson's response to Fraser's remarks, the reader should consult "An Outline of Poetic Theory," in which Olson suggests that since both he and Fraser agree that words are subordinate to their functions, they really have no quarrel.

398. ________. "Dylan Thomas." In Vision and Rhetoric. London: Faber and Faber, 1959, pp. 211-41. Reprinted in A Casebook on Dylan Thomas. Ed. John Malcolm Brinnin. New York: Thomas Y. Crowell, 1960, pp. 34-58.

Refers to The Poetry of Dylan Thomas at several points, noting, among other things, that Olson's otherwise fine reading of "I see you boys of summer in your ruin" leaves out what is most important: the poem is not only about the boys of summer, "but by one of them." Remarks that Olson, unlike many others, who have been baffled by the poem, has worked out "a logical structure" for the "Ballad of the Long-Legged Bait." And although agreeing with the general sense of Olson's explication of the "Altarwise by owl-light" sonnets, Fraser thinks that he is more ingenious than persuasive when he insists that the ideas are mediated, in an "exact and pedantic" fashion, through a symbolism drawn from the movements of the Hercules constellation.

399. Frey, Charles. "Interpreting The Winter's Tale." SEL, 18 (Spring, 1978), 307-29.

Offers as an example of "multi-dimensional interpretation," the three "levels" of dramatic criticism specified by Olson in Tragedy and the Theory of Drama (i.e., judging a work as pleasing or displeasing, analyzing the technical features of a work, and assessing the experience of the work "according to its value as an experience").

Miscellaneous

400. Friedman, Norman. "Forms of the Plot." _Journal of General Education_, 8 (1955). Reprinted in _The Theory of the Novel_. Ed. Philip Stevick. New York: Free Press, 1967, pp. 145-66.

Distinguishes among four kinds of represented action considered independently of emotional effect--speech, scene, episode, and grand plot--borrowing his divisions from Olson's "An Outline of Poetic Theory." Notes, with Olson, that action becomes more complicated as we proceed through the sequence.

401. ______________. _Form and Meaning in Fiction_. Athens, Georgia: University of Georgia Press, 1975, pp. 18, 53, 68, 104-105, 171.

Relies regularly, in the development of his own theses, on views and principles expressed by Olson. Agrees with Olson, for example, that criticism involves the study of the artistic causes of production and that Aristotle's reasoning is "regressive," moving from the whole to be produced to the parts and their interrelationships. Argues that Olson and other "Chicago critics" are not guilty of returning to a "mechanical genre criticism," as some have charged. Summarizes Olson's discussion (in "Dialogue on Symbolism") of the ways in which action may be subordinated to idea and builds upon Olson's useful division of kinds of action into speeches, scenes, episodes, and grand plots.

402. Frye, Northrop. "Content with the Form." _UTQ_, 24 (1954), 92-97.

Reviews R.S. Crane's _The Language of Criticism and the Structure of Poetry_, calling it a work of enduring value, though, at bottom, one that does little more than expound "the norm of critical procedure." The relevance of this review to Olson is that it takes issue with the distinction between didactic and mimetic forms and with that between thought and plot in poetry, with, in short, terms and distinctions central to Olson's, as well as Crane's, criticism.

403. Galligan, E.L. "William Lynch's Theory of Comedy." South Atlantic Quarterly, 77 (1978), 189-205.

Argues that there cannot be a definition of comedy comparable in cogency and incisiveness to Aristotle's "definition of tragedy" and asserts that Olson's position (i.e., that only certain kinds of plays can be called comedies) is "ridiculous." Misses, among other things, Olson's essential distinction between comedy (a form) and the comic (a quality).

404. Goldsmith, Arnold L. American Literary Criticism, 1905-1965. Vol. III. Boston: Twayne, 1979, pp. 132-45, 191.

Devotes a chapter to the "Chicago School," in which Olson is repeatedly mentioned, especially in connection with the division of poetry into mimetic and didactic kinds and with the specification of plot as the primary part of actions, taking his quotations from "The Poetic Method of Aristotle," "An Outline of Poetic Theory," and the essay on Empson. Describes the development of the "Chicago movement"; discusses the organization and the nature of the essays comprising Critics and Criticism; reviews briefly Crane's The Languages of Criticism and the Structure of Poetry and essays of practical criticism by Maclean, Keast, and Olson, and concludes with a rehearsal of W. K. Wimsatt's diatribe, "The Chicago Critics," hailing it as an "incisive evaluation" of this "school of critics." Its bias notwithstanding, the chapter, for the most part, fairly represents many of the principles of "Chicago" criticism, though too often it has the words without the melody.

405. Grimm, Reinhold and Klaus L. Berghahn, eds. Wesen und Formen des Komischen im Drama. Darmstadt: Wissenschaftliche Buchegesellschaft, 1975, pp. viii, ix, x, xvi, xvii.

Treats The Theory of Comedy as representative of the many inconclusive works on comedy recently published in America, noting that although it aspires to supply a universal theory, its ambitions are not really fulfilled.

406. Gruber, William E. "Chekhov's Illusion of Inaction." College Language Association Journal, 20 (1977), 508-20.

Grounds his discussion of the dramatic devices by which Chekhov translates human actions into dramatic art in Olson's observations (in The Theory of Comedy) that only a "certain body of dramatic devices" is available for use and that each device can do some things and not others and certain things "better than, and other things less well than, other devices."

407. ______________. "The Imperfect Action of Comedy." Genre, 10 (1977), 115-29.

Argues that while Olson correctly recognizes that the effect of comedy is to eliminate concern, he fails to see (in The Theory of Comedy) that comedy also works against "the basis of drama, the act." Comedy is the "denial of the future," and every act, because of its orientation toward the future, carries with it grounds of concern. Further, Olson's defense of the "Epilogue" to _Saint Joan_ as necessary to comic reversal cannot be accepted, since the "Epilogue" follows a completed action and contains, in Joan's last speech, an action resonant with implications for the future.

408. Guerin, Wilfred L. et al. _Handbook of Critical Approaches to Literature_. New York: Harper and Row, 1966, pp. 195-96.

Places Olson among those modern critics who, by emphasizing "literature as an _imitation_ of human experience," may be called "neo-Aristotelian."

409. Halsband, Robert. _The Life of Lady Mary Wortley Montagu_. New York: Oxford University Press, 1956, p. 149.

Notes that Olson's "Rhetoric and the Appreciation of Pope" focuses on the "crucial aspect" of the "Epistle to Dr. Arbuthnot," the rhetorical dimension of Pope's defense.

410. Hardy, J.P. _Reinterpretations: Essays on Poems by Milton, Pope, and Johnson_. London: Routledge and Kegan Paul, 1971, pp. 92-93.

Argues that Pope's portrait of Bufo in the "Epistle to Dr. Arbuthnot" is designed, not only to establish an object of contempt and to distance Pope from any ambition similar to that of the proud patron (as Olson maintains in "Rhetoric and the Appreciation of Pope"), but also to show that, in his perversion of the "god-like role of patron," he pollutes the very "source of poetry itself."

411. Häublein, Ernst. The Stanza. London: Methuen, 1978, pp. 17, 82, 119-20.

Considers his examination of the logical relations among stanzas as comparable to Olson's "structural approach to the stanza."

412. Hayden, John O. Polestar of the Ancients: The Aristotelian Tradition in Classical and English Literary Criticism. Newark, Delaware: University of Delaware Press, 1979, p. 58.

Appeals to Olson's essay on the poetic method of Aristotle for support of the view that both induction and deduction are essential to "intellectual progress" in Aristotle's thought.

413. Heilman, Robert B. Tragedy and Melodrama: Versions of Experience. Seattle: University of Washington Press, 1968, p. vii.

At the outset of his study, recognizes that Olson is a critic whose influence on tragedy and melodrama "has already been felt" by students of the subjects.

414. ______________. "Comedy and the World." Sewanee Review, 86 (Winter, 1978), 44-65.

Argues, in this speculative essay on the civilizing power of comedy, that an "acceptance of disparateness" is essential to comedy and remarks that such acceptance is consonant with Olson's definition of the comic *katastasis*, the relaxation of concern, though Heilman cannot adopt "Olson's unfortunately trivializing view that we relax when the cause of concern is shown to be not serious." Also concurs with Olson's judgment (in The Theory of Comedy) that "so long as comedy and the comic are possible, so long will life and its values have meaning."

415. Hernadi, Paul. "Order Without Borders: Recent Genre Theory in the English-Speaking Countries." In Theories of Literary Genre. Ed. Joseph P. Strelka. University Park and London: The Pennsylvania State University Pres, 1978, pp. 192-208.

Disagrees with Olson's broad divison of works into mimetic and didactic classes and with his view of speech as action in mimetic poems ("what the poetic character says in the mimetic poem is speech and has meaning; his saying it is action, an act of persuading, commanding," etc.). To Hernadi, "poetic meaning and plot are interdependent aspects," not "competing or alternative ingredients, of literary works."

416. Holbrook, David. Dylan Thomas and Poetic Dissociation. Carbondale, Ill.: Southern Illinois University Press, 1964, pp. 35-64.

This text is a slightly revised version of Llareggub Revisited, discussed above; see 196. With the exception of a few minor changes (e.g., the omission of some illustrative quotations and some rhetorical flourishes), the portions of these texts relating to Olson are exactly the same.

Miscellaneous

417. ______________. *Dylan Thomas: The Code of Night*. London: Athlone Press, 1972, pp. 191-92.

Uses Olson's brief remarks on "A Refusal to Mourn the Death, by Fire, of a Child in London," a poem exhibiting what Olson calls Thomas's "curiously external view of pain and horror," in support of his quite different opinion that Thomas cannot find the child's reality "because he cannot find his own."

418. Holland, Norman N. *The Dynamics of Literary Response*. New York: Oxford University Press, 1968, pp. 113-14.

Looking through lenses never worn by Olson, Holland finds in Olson's reading of Macbeth's "Tomorrow" speech (in *Tragedy and the Theory of Drama*) a "half-conscious" recognition of the "symbolism of the primal scene," a symbolism unconsciously expressed by Macbeth.

419. Holman, Hugh C. "The Defense of Art: Criticism Since 1930." In *The Development of American Literary Criticism*. Ed. Floyd Stovall. Chapel Hill, N.C.: University of North Carolina Press, 1955, pp. 199-245.

Briefly discusses "Neo-Aristotelianism" as a critical movement interested in applying the "inductive-deductive method of Aristotle" to modern literary forms; quotes Olson's remarks (in "The Poetic Method of Aristotle") on how a definition of the principle of artistic form is arrived at, and then notes that the "Chicago" critics have not examined the relevance of the "psychology of the 'unconscious' and of Gestalten and of modern anthropology" to the "problems posed" by the Aristotelian method.

420. ______________. A Handbook to Literature. 3rd ed. New York: Odyssey Press, 1972, pp. 76, 114.

Lists Olson, Crane, McKeon et al. under the heading "The Chicago Critics," noting that they are pluralists and, in their practical criticism, neo-Aristotelians. Under "Pragmatic Theory," a subheading within the category "Types of Criticism," Olson, along with others, is represented as being responsible for the formulation of a "formal criticism based on Aristotle's principles."

421. Hume, Robert D. Dryden's Criticism. Ithaca and London: Cornell University Press, 1970, pp. 112, 114, 200.

Directs the reader at several points to Olson's discussions of the characteristic features of Greek, Elizabethan, and French drama in Tragedy and the Theory of Drama.

422. Iyengar, K.R. Srinivasa. The Adventures of Criticism. London: Asia Publishing House, 1962, p. 309.

In an inscrutable gesture of charmingly naive diplomacy or a mystical feat of locating the one in the many, enrolls Olson, Brooks, Richards, and Trilling in the same critical battalion, citing Olson's essay on Yeats's "Sailing to Byzantium" as one of several examples of new criticism "in action."

423. Jack, Ian. Augustan Satire: Intention and Idiom in English Poetry, 1660-1750. Oxford: Oxford University Press, 1952, p. 112n.

Calls Olson's "Rhetoric and the Appreciaton of Pope" an intriguing analysis of Pope's "forensic skill," but notes that "he is wrong in supposing that rhetoric and poetry are mutually exclusive" (here supposing himself what Olson never supposes).

424. Jones, Thora Burnley and Bernard de Bear Nicol. _Neo-Classical Dramatic Criticism, 1560-1770_. New York: Cambridge University Press, p. 12.

Observes that although Olson is certainly right when he says (in the introduction to _Aristotle's Poetics and English Literature_) that between the theories of neo-classical critics and Aristotle's poetic theory there are only superficial resemblances, he perhaps goes too far when he suggests further that the development of neo-classical criticism would have been essentially the same had Aristotle not "figured in it."

425. Jones, T.H. _Dylan Thomas_. London: Oliver and Boyd, 1963, pp. 6, 17, 31, 59, 60, 77, 107.

Refers regularly to _The Poetry of Dylan Thomas_ in his running account of Thomas's poetic development, asserting at one point in the book that Olson's is the only serious "book-length study that has so far appeared" and that his is the only interpretation "that makes complete sense" of the "Altarwise by owl-light" sonnets. In a discussion of Thomas's poetic techniques, adopts Olson's distinctions among "pseudo-drama," "pseudo- narrative," and "circumstantial ambiguity." For the rest, cites Olson only to agree with his readings of poems.

426. Karrer, Wolfgang. _Die Metaphorik in Dylan Thomas' Collected Poems_. Bonn: Herbert Grundman, 1971, p. 11.

Cites Olson's reading of "Altarwise by owl-light in the half-way house..." as an example of how interpreters have confronted the problems of metaphorical complexity in Thomas's poetry.

427. Khatchadourian, Haig. "Movement and Action in the Performing Arts." _JAAC_, 37 (1978), 25-36.

Appeals at several points in his argument to Olson's distinction (as expressed in _Tragedy and the Theory of Drama_) between the _plot_ of a play and its _scenario_ or dramatic representation only at last to conjoin what Olson had separated by talking about the representation of action by means of scenario or plot, a possibility not entertained by Olson, for whom the _scenario_ is "what represents" and the _plot_, "what is represented."

428. Kidder, Rushworth M. _Dylan Thomas: The Country of the Spirit_. Princeton: Princeton University Press, 1973, pp. 27n, 76n, 77, 80, 116, 133n, 146, 170.

Refers repeatedly to Olson's readings of Thomas's poetry, usually for the purpose of establishing a basis for his own extended comments (of Olson's view that "Where once the waters of your face" is addressed to a dried sea channel, for example, Kidder says that "Everything in the poem fits this interpretation") and occasionally for the purpose of noting an analysis different from his own or from that of, say, Tindall or Kleinman.

Miscellaneous

429. Kinneavy, James Leo. A Theory of Discourse: The Aims of Discourse. Englewood Cliffs, N.J.: Prentice-Hall, 1971, pp. 71, 80, 208, 312, 342, 390.

Directs attention to the writings of Olson and other "Chicago" critics on several occasions. Appeals specifically to Olson's "An Outline of Poetic Theory" when, in his own discussion of the "general characteristics of scientific discourse," he distinguishes between the "material object" of science (what Olson would call the "subject" of investigation) and the "formal object" of science (Olson's "subject matter," i.e., that aspect or those aspects of the subject logically and semantically determined by the terms and distinctions of the discussion) and when he comments on the method of reasoning necessarily implicated in any coherent discussion. Agrees with Olson's account of the "reductionism" of Empson's approach to poetry from the perspective of "ambiguity" and with that aspect of "Chicago" pluralism which insists that no single approach can "give an exhaustive account of a given art object."

430. Kleinman, H.H. The Religious Sonnets of Dylan Thomas: A Study of Imagery and Meaning. Berkeley: University of California Press, 1963, pp. 6, 10.

Calls Olson's The Poetry of Dylan Thomas a "sensitive appraisal of Thomas's work" and reheares the levels of symbolism to which Olson makes reference in his "exegesis" of the "Altarwise by owl-light" sequence before offering the reader his own interpretation of the sonnets as a statement of "religious perplexity" coming to rest in "spiritual certainty."

431. Koelb, Clayton. "Some Problems of Literary Taxonomy." Canadian Review of Comparative Literature, 4 (Fall, 1977), 233-44.

Observes that in The Theory of Comedy Olson makes the valid point that we have no single coherent concept of comedy "but rather a series of concepts."

432. Korg, Jacob. Dylan Thomas. New York: Twayne, 1965, pp. 29, 40, 69, 73, 74, 83, 130-31, 137, 141, 146.

Includes several references to The Poetry of Dylan Thomas. The bulk of the passages dealing with Olson summarize or reproduce readings of particular lines or poems, usually juxtaposed to accounts of the same lines or poems by Tindall or Kleinman, and special attention is given to decriptions of how these critics have diversely untangled the perplexities of the "Altarwise by owl-light" sonnets and the "Ballad of the Long-legged Bait." While admitting that the "zodiacal parallels" on which Olson's interpretation of the "Altarwise" sequence is based "account for much," Korg says that Olson's failure to "explain many obscurities" is "not reassuring."

433. Krieger, Murray. The Play and Place of Criticism. Baltimore: The Johns Hopkins Press, 1967, pp. 168n, 169-70.

Summarizes the argument of Olson's "Rhetoric and the Appreciation of Pope" as a preliminary to his own analysis of the "Epistle to Dr. Arbuthnot," which depends upon the notion that Pope intended to "give the game away"; he did not expect (as Olson would have us believe) the effectiveness of his work to be contingent upon "the illusion that we are overhearing an actual dialogue."

Miscellaneous

434. ______________. "Literary Analysis and Evaluation--And the Ambidextrous Critic." In *Criticism: Speculative and Analytical Essays*. Ed. L.S. Dembo. Madison, Milwaukee, and London: University of Wisconsin Press, 1968, pp. 16-36.

Asserts that in their efforts to avoid the *a priori* the Neo-Aristotelian critics fall prey to their own *a priori* generic categories; they see only what their previously established generic categories enable them to see.

435. Kropf, C. R. "Unity and the Study of Eighteenth-Century Literature." *ECent*, 21 (Winter, 1980), 25-40.

Cites with approval Olson's observation in "Rhetoric and the Appreciation of Pope" that a convention functions as both a limitation on and a source of structure.

436. Lawler, Justus George. *Celestial Pantomime: Poetic Structures of Transcendence*. New Haven: Yale University Press, 1979, p. 169.

Peremptorily asserts that Olson "could not have been more wrong" when he argued (in *Tragedy and the Theory of Drama*) that Shakespeare's language is profound, not as "meaningful verbal expression," but as action generating implications revelatory of "character and situation."

437. Leech, Clifford. *Tragedy*. London: Methuen, 1969, pp. 69, 82-83.

Briefly describes Olson's *Aristotle's Poetics and English Literature*.

438. Lemon, Lee T. _The Partial Critics_. New York: Oxford University Press, 1965, pp. 150-55.

Focuses on R.S. Crane's "formalistic approach" to poetry but says that his judgments are relevant to all the "Neo-Aristotelians." Suggests that Crane, Olson, and the others, in their efforts to develop a definition of form, argue themselves into a double-bind: if "its nature"--in the formulation that the excellence of any work involves the "maximum actualization, within the necessary limits of the artistic matter, of what _its nature_ is capable of"--refers to the _"species,"_ then "external critieria" are imposed on particular works; if, on the other hand, the phrase refers to the nature of particular poems, then each work is its own standard, and evaluation is superfluous.

439. ______________. _Approaches to Literature: A Guide to Thinking and Writing_. New York: Oxford University Press, 1969, p. 235-36.

Describes the "neo-Aristotelians" as critics who emphasized "internal structure or, in their terminology, 'the intention of the work.'" Cites Olson in his discursive bibliography and notes that _Critics and Criticism_ is the "most complete statement" of the "Chicago" position.

440. Lipking, Lawrence. _The Ordering of the Arts in Eighteenth-Century England_. Princeton: Princeton University Press, 1970, pp. 89, 182.

Quotes from Olson's discussions of "Hermes" Harris and Sir Joshua Reynolds in the introductions to, respectively, _Aristotle's Poetics and English Literature_ and *Longinus' On the Sublime and Reynolds' Discourses*.

441. Lodge, David, ed. *Twentieth-Century Literary Criticisim: A Reader*. London: Longman, 1972, pp. 147, 592.

Briefly comments on the "Neo-Aristotelian" alternative to "New" criticism, stressing its endorsement of a "more pluralistic and inductive approach to literary criticism" and its use of the *Poetics* as a model for critical analysis. Also, cites Olson's essay on Empson in his introduction to the criticism of Empson.

442. Marsh, Robert. "Historical Interpretation and the History of Criticism." In *Literary Criticism and Historical Understanding* (English Institute Essays). Ed. Phillip Damon. New York and London: Columbia University Press, 1967, pp. 1-24.

Refers the reader to Olson's "*Hamlet* and the Hermeneutics of Drama" for a demonstration of the rich "practical consequences" to be derived from observing the distinction between "language as action and language as saying."

443. ____________. *Four Dialectical Theories of Poetry: An Aspect of English Neoclassical Criticism*. Chicago and London: University of Chicago Press, 1965, pp. 6n, 183n.

Says that Olson and Crane are "prominent" among the modern critics who have conducted "problematic criticism" on a "systematic basis" and appeals to essays by McKeon and Olson in support of his interpretation of Aristotle's "problematic" theory, i.e., one concerned with the problems confronting poets in the construction of artistic wholes.

444. Marucci, Franco. Il Senso Interrotto: Autonomia e Codificazione nella Poesia di Dylan Thomas. Ravenna: Longo, 1976, pp. 63, 66, 73n.

Makes use of Olson's and Ralph Maud's classifications of Thomas's "verbal tricks" (trucchi verbali) in his discussion of such devices as "reversal," "enjambement, and "dislocation." Also cites Olson's interpretation of two lines from Thomas's "When, Like a Running Grave" ("Love...is ...hauled to the dome") and disagrees with Olson's conclusion that these lines refer to love as it is "intellectualized" in old age.

445. Maud, Ralph. Entrances to Dylan Thomas' Poetry. Pittsburgh: University of Pittsburgh Press, 1963, pp. 167-69.

Objects to Olson's astronomical reading of Thomas's "Altarwise by owl-light" sonnets. Olson's interpretation can derive its warrant only from "internal indications" of a preeminent concern with the symbolic significance of the Hercules constellation (since we have no external evidence of Thomas's interest in "star maps"), but the details of the poem--for example, the specific reference to the crucifixion and the many echoes of the Bible--seem to "demand a Christian, rather than Herculean interpretation."

446. Merchant, W. Moelwyn. Comedy. London: Methuen, 1972, pp. 69-70, 83.

In chapter eight, "The Aristophanic and Shakespearean Traditions," Merchant initiates his discussion of the argumentative or "Aristophanic" mode of comedy by referring to Olson's judgment (in The Theory of Comedy) that all but one of the surviving plays is organized to develop a proof "of a single main statement." Also quotes a passage in which Olson describes the artistic devices employed by Aristophanes in the construction of his "dramatic cartoons."

447. Miller, J. Hillis. Poets of Reality: Six Twentieth-Century Writers. New York: Atheneum, 1969, p. 193.

Notes that Olson is correct in pointing out that the term "atlas-eater," in Thomas's "Altarwise by owl-light in the half-way house," does not literally mean "world-devouring," as Thomas had said, since an atlas is not literally the world, but a representation of it.

448. Moore, Arthur K. Contestable Concepts of Literary Theory. Baton Rouge, La.: Louisiana State University Press, 1973, p. 74.

On the issue of poetic obscurity, asks the reader to consider the opposing views of Delmore Schwartz (in "The Isolation of Modern Poetry") and Elder Olson (in The Poetry of Dylan Thomas). Also notes that in his book on Thomas Olson presents an argument that is less than comforting to those who are willing to believe that modern poetry is complex because we live in complex times.

449. Mottran, Eric and Malcolm Bradbury. The Penguin Companion to Literature. London: Penguin Press, 1971, pp. 56-57.

Lists two of Olson's works (The Poetry of Dylan Thomas and Tragedy and the Theory of Drama) at the end of an entry describing the "Chicago Aristotelians" as a "major force in modern American criticism" and as critics who derive their "pragmatic approach" to poetry from Aristotle and achieve importance in large part as a result of their "close philosophical analysis of criticism itself." (This entry is by Malcolm Bradbury.)

450. Moynihan, William T. The Craft and Art of Dylan Thomas. Ithaca: Cornell University Press, 1966, pp. 72, 85, 154, 161, 229, 249.

Refers to The Poetry of Dylan Thomas at several points, generally agreeing with Olson's readings of Thomas's poems but arguing that the "geographical landmark" underlying "In the White Giant's Thigh" can be understood from the syntax of the poem without having recourse to special, local information, which Olson thinks Thomas should have supplied in a note.

451. Murray, Michael. Modern Critical Theory: A Phenomenological Introduction. The Hague: Martinus Nighoff, 1975, pp. 6, 35-36, 43-46, 56, 137, 216.

Notes at various points in his description and assessment of modern critical theories from a phenomenological point of view that the "new critics" and the "Chicago critics" shared many presuppositions and the same subject, the work "in itself." Treats Olson as the "most representative spokesman" of "Chicago" criticism, relying on "An Outline of Poetic Theory" and the essay on Empson as his chief texts of reference in his delineation of "neo-Aristotelian" poetics.

Accuses Olson of having "an extraordinarily shallow idea of Empson's work."

452. Nowottny, Winifred. The Language Poets Use. New York: Oxford University Press, 1962, pp. 195, 197n.

Observes that Olson clearly identifies the difficulty involved in taking literally what Thomas said should be taken literally (Thomas's "literalness" depends upon conceptual substitution, i.e., symbolism) and cites Monroe Beardsley's resistance to the "method of explication" adopted by Olson in his analysis of the "Altarwise by owl-light" sonnets. (See 186)

453. Piper, William Bowman. "Samuel Johnson as Exemplary Critic." TSLL, 20 (1978), 457-73.

Directs the reader to Olson's "lucid discussion of 'probability' in critical judgment" (in "On Value Judgments in the Arts"). Notes, in addition, that Olson shows that a poem "is actually an experience, that is, a system of mental events," his comments on the insufficiency of the senses to the full apprehension of a literary work notwithstanding.

454. Potter, E.J. "Molière's Amphitryon: Myth in a Comic Perspective." Orbis Litterarum, 32 (1977), 41-49.

Mistakenly identifies his view that "intellectual and emotional distance from the work is the essential comic response" with Olson's conception of katastasis (a relaxation of concern) as the end of comedy (in The Theory of Comedy).

455. Pratt, Annis. Dylan Thomas's Early Prose: A Study in Creative Mythology. Pittsburgh: University of Pittsburgh Press, 1965, pp. 184-87.

Calls Olson's book on Dylan Thomas a "careful study," one especially noteworthy for its delineation of the types of symbolism found in Thomas's poetry, but questions the validity of his reading of the "Altarwise by owl-light" sonnets, which is based on an "astrological" hypothesis. There can be no doubt that the pagans associated certain constellations with gods, demigods, and heroes, but the "question left dangling is, did Thomas?"

456. Press, John. The Chequer'd Shade: Reflections on Obscurity in Poetry. London: Oxford University Press, 1958, p. 61n.

Adverts to the justice and appropriateness of Olson's analysis of Thomas's "Altarwise by owl-light" sonnets in terms of "Christian and astronomical symbolism."

457. Pritchard, John Paul. Criticism in America: An Account of the Development of Critical Techniques From the Early Period of the Republic to the Middle Years of the Twentieth Century. Norman, Oklahoma: University of Oklahoma Press, 1956, pp. 280-82.

Devotes three pages to "The Chicago Critics," "one of the most interesting groups at present occupying the attention of literary men," in the last chapter, "Recent Practicing Critics." Presents a brief account of "Chicago criticism," the burden of the exposition falling heavily on paraphrases of sections of essays in Critics and Criticism, especially Olson's "An

Outline of Poetic Theory." Notes, among other things, that as pluralists they "stand opposed" to the assumption that one critical method is correct and that they work "inductively and concentrate upon the structure of the object under consideration." In short, identifies a few salient doctrines but neglects the coherent system of principles and assumptions only in relation to which the doctrines have meaning and value.

458. Rader, Ralph W. "The Concept of Genre and Eighteenth-Century Studies." In _New Approaches to Eighteenth-Century Literature: Selected Papers from the English Institute_. Ed. Philip Harth. New York: Columbia University Press, 1974, pp. 79-115.

Notes that Olson's developed discrimination between _lexis_ and _praxis_ (between speech as meaningful and speech as action) expresses the "basic semantic facts" subsequently and independently described by speech-act theorists and acknowledges that his own "principle of interpretation according to inferred intention," while more radical than anything postulated by Olson and Crane, has been influenced by their views.

459. _______________. "The Dramatic Monologue and Related Lyric Forms." _Critical Inquiry_, 3 (Autumn, 1976), 131-51.

Contrasts the views of Robert Langbaum and Olson on the dramatic lyric and dramatic monologue. Langbaum sees the matter of both kinds of poems as "essentially...free of the constructive control of the poet," whereas Olson considers both kinds as "artistic constructs" that are controlled by the poet and determinate in effect. Notes his indebtedness to both critics and finds a partial anticipation of his own reading of Browning's "My Last Duchess" in certain parts of The Poetry of Dylan Thomas.

460. Ransom, John Crowe. "Criticism, Inc." In The World's Body. New York: Charles Scribner's Sons, 1938, pp. 327-350.

Refers to R.S. Crane as "the first of the great professors to have advocated" the serious study of criticism "as a major policy for departments of English." Says that he, along with others at the University of Chicago, is revolutionizing the teaching of literature, though from a "limited programme" involving "the application of Aristotle's critical views" to the study of literature generally.

461. Reiss, Timothy J. Tragedy and Truth: Studies in the Development of a Renaissance and Neo-Classical Discourse. New Haven: Yale University Press, 1980, pp. 185-88, 192, 305n26.

Acknowledges that Tragedy and the Theory of Drama is "one of the most useful modern discussions of tragedy" but takes issue with Olson's reading of King Lear, especially with his treatment of Lear as a man caught between the conflicting demands of feudality and family; by so reading Lear, Olson projects something "anachronistic" "from outside the play into it," the nuclear family, and, as a consequence, construes the play in relation to a "particular social development." It is fair to say that Reiss misses the point of Olson's discussion (which is designed to define the moral character of Lear in such a way as to make intelligible the nature of his subsequent actions and the effect of his death upon us, not to elucidate the play in relation to any particular social development) and adjusts Olson's remarks to his own concern with a clash of discourses in the play.

462. Ridgeway, Jaqueline. "The Necessity of Form to the Poetry of Louise Bogan." _Women's Studies_, 5 (1977), 137-49.

Directs the reader to Olson's discussion (in "Louise Bogan and Léonie Adams") of the character of the woman who appears constantly in Bogan's poetry (i.e., of the poetic character of the speaker of Bogan's poems).

463. Rousseau, G.S. "On Reading Pope." In _Writers and Their Background: Alexander Pope_. Ed. Peter Dixon. London: G. Bell and Sons, 1972, pp. 1-59.

Refers to Olson's "Rhetoric and the Appreciation of Pope" as one of the most eloquent discussions of Pope's poetic innovations.

464. Sacks, Sheldon. _Fiction and the Shape of Belief: A Study of Henry Fielding with Glances at Swift, Johnson, and Richardson_. Berkeley and Los Angeles: University of California Press, 1964, pp. 65n, 241, 241-42n.

Borrows the phrase "devices of disclosure" from Olson's "An Outline of Poetic Theory" and seeks to show that in the novels of Fielding and Richardson the moral intention may be, not a "further consequence of the powers of art," as Olson claims, but the "_primary_ consequence intended by both Richardson and Fielding." Admits, however, that his "slight disagreement" with Olson may be "illusory."

465. Sanesi, Roberto. <u>Dylan Thomas</u>. Milan: Lerici, 1960, pp. 48n, 49, 57, 68, 69, 71, 73-90.

Cites and agrees with Olson's remarks that Thomas's poetry deals with "processes," not "moments," and that it often contains "pseudo-dramatic" elements, as when a supposed character utters the thoughts of a person thinking of him. Sanesi also depends heavily on Olson's reading of Thomas's sonnets (often incorporating, word for word and without acknowledgment, Olson's astrological information into his "own" commentary). Nevertheless, Sanesi remains skeptical about what he calls "the Olson experiment" with astrology in these sonnets, calling it "suggestive but unproven."

466. Schorer, Mark. "Introduction." In <u>A Symposium on Formalist Criticism</u>. Ed. William J. Handy. Austin: University of Texas Press, 1965, pp. 10-13.

Notes that Olson has long been "prominently associated" with the "Chicago critics," who have extended the "categories of Aristotle" and emphasized "plot, composition, and genre" in their discussions of literature. Appends to his remarks a brief biographical sketch of Olson, a leading critic and "a distinguished poet."

467. Shapiro, Karl. <u>A Bibliography of Modern Prosody</u>. Baltimore: Johns Hopkins Press, 1948, p. 20.

Cites and provides annotation for Olson's General Prosody, "an inquiry into the nature of prosody along Aristotelian lines."

468. Springer, Mary Doyle. Forms of the Modern Novella. Chicago: University of Chicago Press, 1975, pp. 10, 18, 90.

Acknowledges her indebtedness to critical principles articulated by Olson (as well as by Wayne Booth, Sheldon Sacks, and Ralph Rader). Takes the epigraphs for two chapters from Olson's discussions of plot forms; recognizes the utility of Olson's distinction between totals and wholes and, finally, adopts as she modifies his broad differentiation of didactic from mimetic productions.

469. Stacy, R.H. Defamiliarization in Language and Literature. Syracuse: Syracuse University Press, 1977, p. 2.

Interprets Olson's remarks on Dylan Thomas's use of "an odd form of periphrasis" to make a "familiar thing unfamiliar" as compatible with at least one of the meanings subsumed by his general term "defamiliarization."

470. States, Bert O. Irony and Drama: A Poetics. Ithaca: Cornell University Press, 1971, pp. 115-16, 182-83.

Extends as he adopts Olson's definitions of the "pattern plot" and the "descriptive plot" (in Tragedy and the Theory of Drama), but rejects the idea that the "didactic plot" is a distinctive plot form. The didactic is not a plot form but "an attitude toward the plot, any plot in fact."

471. Stovel, Bruce. "Traditional Comedy and the Comic Mask in Kingsley Amis's Lucky Jim." English Studies in Canada, 4 (1978), 69-80.

In an essay influenced by Northrop Frye and founded on the assumption that the end of comedy is the "achievement of...a morality of desire," Stovel notes that Olson explores the implications of "Aristotle's definition of the ludicrous" and finds the essence of comedy in a "relaxation of seriousness" (here slightly misreading Olson's discussion of katastasis in The Theory of Comedy).

472. Tate, Allen. "Longinus and the 'New Criticism.'" In The Forlorn Demon: Didactic and Critical Essays. Chicago: Regnery, 1953, pp. 131, 145. Reprinted in Collected Essays. Denver: Alan Shallow, 1959, pp. 507, 521.

Calls Olson's article on Longinus an "excellent recent study" and quotes Olson's distinction between the sources of the sublime in Burke and Longinus.

473. Taylor, Jerome. "Prophetic 'Play' and Symbolist 'Plot' in Beauvais' Daniel." Comparative Drama, 11 (1977), 191-208.

Cites Olson's "The Poetic Method of Aristotle" in support of his view that the Poetics supplies a set of "tools for philosophic analysis applicable to disparate forms of drama," not "a set of normative criteria," as Hardin Craig assumes.

474. Tellier, A-R. La Poésie de Dylan Thomas (Thèmes et Formes). Paris: Presses Universitaires de France, 1963, pp. 18-19, 28, 95, 103, 193-94, 245.

Miscellaneous

Cites and approves of Olson's analysis of Thomas's "When once the twilight locks no longer" and uses two entries from Olson's "Glossary" of difficult terms (those for "straw" and "sea") as the bases of several of his own readings. Praises Olson's book highly but says that his "astrological" interpretation of the "Altarwise by owl-light" sonnets is somewhat exaggerated and often unclear. States in his annotated bibliography that Olson's book is an "_etude approfondie que nous avons constamment utilisee_."

475. Tillotson, Geoffrey. _Pope and Human Nature_. London: Oxford University Press, 1958, p. 199.

Suggests that the arrangement of materials in "An Epistle to Dr. Arbuthnot" may have come later than Olson allows (in "Rhetoric and the Appreciation of Pope"), inasmuch as the 1734 poem was put together from "fragments written much earlier."

476. Vivas, Eliseo. _Creation and Discovery: Essays in Criticism and Aesthetics_. New York: Noonday Press, 1955, p. 91.

Asserts, somewhat cryptically, that because such "neo-Aristotelians" as Crane and Olson do not do "justice to the creative act," they fail to understand the relation between the "language of the poem" and "what it is about."

477. Wasiolek, Edward. "The Future of Psychoanalytic Criticism." In _The Frontiers of Literary Criticism_., Ed. David H. Malone. Los Angeles: Hennessey and Ingalls, 1974, pp. 149-68.

Remarks that the proponents of "New Criticism" argued energetically with, among others, the "Chicago neo-Aristotelians" and that what the "Chicago" critics can tell us about the artistic causes of emotional effects is not necessarily "in conflict with psychoanalytic criticism."

478. Watson, George. The Literary Critics: A Study of English Descriptive Criticism. Baltimore: Penguin Books, 1962, pp. 222-23.

Describes the "Chicago critics" as a heretical branch of the "New Criticism," deviating from orthodoxy in their more "tolerant attitude to historical data" and in their attacks against the hierophants' emphasis on, for example, irony, tension, and paradox. Directs the reader to Olson's article on Empson and Crane's essays on I.A. Richards and Cleanth Brooks.

479. Weiman, Robert. "New Criticism" und Die Entwicklung Burgerlicher Literaturwissenschaft: Geschichte und Kritik Neuer Interpretationsmethoden. Halle: Max Niemeyer, 1962, pp. 80, 89, 112, 339.

Refers to Olson's criticism of Empson, especially to his judgment that Empson does not seem to know himself what he means by "ambiguity." Also calls attention to attacks against Olson by John Holloway and Eliseo Vivas.

480. Weinsheimer, Joel. "Impedance as Value: Roderick Random and Pride and Prejudice." PTL--A Journal of Descriptive Poetics and Theory of Literature, 3 (1978), 139-66.

Before going on to develop his own general theory of value, Weinsheimer says that Olson (in "On Value Judgments in the Arts"), Hirsch, Frye, and Murray Krieger have defined the issues that divide theorists of value today, namely, whether evaluation and interpretation are distinct activities and whether value "inheres in the text or is conferred from without."

481. Wellek, René. Concepts of Criticism. Ed. and Introd. Stephen G. Nichols, Jr. New Haven and London: Yale University Press, 1963, pp. 9, 320-22, 360.

In a survey of recent criticism, devotes a few pages to the "Neo-Aristotelians" of Chicago, who extol the virtues of "multiple working hypotheses" with one end of their pens, while dogmatically propounding the superiority of their method to all other methods with the other end. Accuses them, generally, of being direct descendants, not of Aristotle, but of the Renaissance Aristotelians, the affiliation being clearly discernible in their treatment of language as mere matter and in their rigidly schematic approach to genres. Accuses Olson, specifically, of exhibiting the faults of his colleagues in strikingly vivid fashion by asserting, for example, that the greater part of playwriting "has nothing to do with words" and that The Divine Comedy is "not mimetic, but didactic, not symbolical, but only allegorical." Further, Olson out-Empsons Empson in the uncontrolled ingenuity line in his book on Dylan Thomas. Acknowledges that these critics are scholars, but concludes that their "arid classifications of hero types, plot structures, and genres" display the show of scholarship without the power. To Wellek, such criticism "seems an ultra-academic exercise destined to wither on the vine."

482. ______________. Discriminations: Further Concepts of Criticism. New Haven: Yale University Press, 1970, pp. 211, 234, 269, 347.

In remarks scattered throughout the book, refers to the "Chicago critics" as proponents of views unknown to or neglected by Spitzer and Hamburger (with both of whom they have much in common) and attacked by John Crowe Ransom and John Holloway.

483. Willard, Abbie F. Wallace Stevens: The Poet and His Critics. Chicago: American Library Association, 1978, p. 149.

Briefly comments on Olson's article on Wallace Stevens, judging it to be "diffuse" when it explicates and "less than exact" when it seeks to isolate "the parameters of Stevens's philosophical poetry." A superficial and arrogantly disdainful look at Olson's essay.

484. Wimsatt, W.K., Jr. "Comment on 'Two Essays in Practical Criticism.'" University Review, 9 (Winter, 1942), 141-42.

Accuses Olson, in his analysis of Yeats's "Sailing to Byzantium," of coming to the verge of making "the intention of the author equal to the intent or total design of the poem itself." (Olson approaches this serious fallacy by insisting that words take "their significance from their context.") Since to Wimsatt the poem is a total order or words, Olson's subordination of words to their functions is, at best, wrongheaded.

485. ______________ and Cleanth Brooks. Literary Criticism: A Short History. New York: Alfred Knopf, 1964, pp. 692, 694.

Refers to Olson as one who has shown, in his attempt to define the species of lyric to which Yeats's "Sailing to Byzantium" belongs, how the terms borrowed from "an imitative theory of art" can be used arbitrarily by his adjusting the six necessary parts of tragedy specified by Aristotle to four: choice, character, thought, and diction. The writers ask why "plot" should not be a fifth part, since Yeats's poem" actually has a plot," or why the number of parts could not be reduced to three by omitting "thought," since neither "choice" nor "character" is possible without "thought." From this weighty argument, the writers conclude that Olson's terms seem to be matters of "convenience" rather than "inevitable or necessary elements of the poem," and that his efforts to define Yeats's poem would lead, if extended with ruthless consistency, to the recognition of "a special genre for each art work."

486. ______________. "'Jam Nunc Debentia Dici': Answers to a Questionnaire." Arion: A Journal of Humanities and the Classics, 9 (Summer/Autumn, 1970). Reprinted in Day of the Leopards: Essays in Defense of Poems. New Haven and London: Yale University Press, 1976, pp. 224-33.

Asserts, in a commentary on Horace's Ars Poetica, that the "Neo-Aristotelians" of the Chicago school "would have said that the American 'new critics,'" who tended "to think of all poems primarily...as poems" and not as kinds of poems, "could be summed up in the first 72 lines of Horace's Ars. [pun intended?] After that, they were entirely in contempt of court." (Genres are first mentioned in line seventy three. This passing reference to Wimsatt's steady antagonists is not without its pinch of contumely.)

487. ______________. "Battering the Object." In Contemporary Criticism. Ed. Malcolm Bradbury and David Palmer. London: Edward Arnold, 1970. Reprinted in Day of the Leopards: Essays in Defense of Poems. New Haven and London: Yale University Press, 1976, pp. 183-204.

In a discussion of the "most correct object of literary study," inserts a slight and slighting reference, not to the original members of the "Chicago School of Neo-Aristotelians," but to those recent critics, especially Sheldon Sacks and E. D. Hirsch, who are attempting to revive "genre" studies. The programmes of such critics "spring up like chestnut saplings round the venerable blighted grey trunk of" "Chicago" criticism.

488. Winters, Yvor. "Problems for the Modern Critic of Literature." In The Function of Criticism: Problems and Exercises. Denver: Alan Swallow, 1957, pp. 9-78.

Discusses the origins and development of "criticism" as a subject of inquiry and controversy in the first half of the twentieth century, giving some prominence to the "Chicago critics," especially to R.S. Crane, who is obliged to assume the role of faithful opponent throughout the text. Specifically chastises Olson for writing a book in praise of one of the "most naive romantics of our time," Dylan Thomas, such unregulated exuberance on Olson's part qualifying, in Winter's judgment, as an act of "sowing a belated crop of wild oats." Referring to Crane persistently and to Olson sometimes directly and sometimes indirectly, Winters says that these critics 1) seem reluctant to define any "final cause of literature" to which we could appeal in the evaluation of "different forms" and content to consider a work according to "the perfection of its own form"; 2) appear to believe that "imitation is the highest form of art"; and 3) seem ready to distinguish forms only to keep them "distinct from one another," thus refusing to compare works in one genre with works in another.

489. Yates, W.E. "Der Schwierige: The Comedy of Discretion." *Modern Austrian Literature*, 10 (1977), 11-17.

Quotes Olson's explanation of how the "extreme comic" is produced and calls *The Theory of Comedy* the "most distinguished of modern treatises on the subject."

INDEX OF WORKS BY ELDER OLSON

(Numbers refer to items, not pages)

Index

Index

Index

Index

AUTHOR INDEX

(Numbers refer to items, not pages)

Index

SUBJECT INDEX

(Numbers refer to items, not pages)

Index